Communication Skills, Executive Leadership, and Career Growth for Physicians

Neil Baum, MD

American Association for
PHYSICIAN
LEADERSHIP

978-1-960762-37-5 print
978-1-960762-38-2 eBook

Published by **American Association for Physician Leadership, Inc.**
PO Box 96503 | BMB 97493 | Washington, DC 20090-6503

Website: www.physicianleaders.org

13 8 7 6 5 4 3 2 1

Copyedited, typeset, indexed, and printed in the United States of America

PUBLISHER
Nancy Collins

PRODUCTION MANAGER
Jennifer Weiss

DESIGN & LAYOUT
Carter Publishing Studio

COPYEDITORS
Karen Doyle
Patricia George

TABLE OF CONTENTS

ABOUT THE AUTHOR

Neil Baum, MD, is professor of Clinical Urology at Tulane Medical School in New Orleans, Louisiana.

Baum is the author of *Marketing Your Clinical Practice — Ethically, Effectively, and Economically*, which is in its 4th edition, has sold over 175,000 copies, and has been translated into Spanish. He has written ten books on practice management and the business of medicine.

Baum was the columnist for *American Medical News* for more than 25 years. He wrote the popular column, The Bottom Line, for *Urology Times* for more than 20 years. He has authored or co-authored over 350 articles that have appeared in peer-reviewed medical publications on various urologic topics, as well as articles on practice management.

He recently published a book, *Medicine is a Practice: The Rules for Healthcare Marketing* (AAPL 2024), which emphasizes marketing strategies for the healthcare practice.

Baum offers practical ideas and suggestions that have been tested in his practice or used by other physicians to significantly improve their careers and productivity of their medical practices.

Neil Baum, MD
Professor of Clinical Urology
Tulane Medical School
New Orleans, Louisiana
doctorwhiz@gmail.com

CHAPTER 1

Let Your Communication Skills Equal Your Clinical Skills

ANN DEMARAIS AND NEIL BAUM, MD

Doctors, hospitals, insurance companies, and malpractice carriers have known for years that there is a direct correlation between patient satisfaction/patient complaints and lawsuits.[1] Physicians have always prided themselves on being good communicators, but surveys show that they often overestimate their ability to communicate effectively with their patients. A well-publicized study reports that the average doctor interrupts a patient after 16 seconds during the interview process.[2] So what can physicians do to improve their communication skills and lower their risk of lawsuits? Following are some ideas:

1. Prepare for your visit with the patient. Before entering the room, look at the chart or the electronic medical record, and know one or two facts about a new patient. This can be the patient's referring physician or employment, or where the patient lives. The same applies to an existing patient. Don't initiate the conversation by talking about the patient's medical problem. Regardless of your patient volume and how far behind in the schedule you are, start the conversation with some topic that is not associated with the patient's health issues. This clearly sends a message that you care more about the patient than simply his or her blood pressure, shortness of breath, or dysuria.
2. Sit down — don't stand — while speaking to a patient. Make every effort to be eyeball-to-eyeball with the patient. Never have a meaningful discussion when you are standing and the patient is sitting — or even worse, when the patient is lying down on the exam table.
3. If possible, don't have any barriers — psychological or physical — between you and the patient. Be on the same side of the desk or exam table as your patient if you can.

4. Lean slightly forward when you speak to the patient. The patient will notice your body language before you even open your mouth. Leaning forward in your chair demonstrates a sincere interest in the patient.
5. Lock eyes with the patient. People normally make eye contact 70% to 80% of the time. If you fall below this average, you come across as shifty or lacking confidence. People who make less eye contact often aren't aware of it, so ask a colleague to critique your eye contact.
6. Smile. Keeping a neutral face may feel natural, but the other person might perceive your expression as negative. People are looking for signs of approval, and the lack of a smile may even seem threatening and can make a patient defensive.
7. Don't spend all of your time looking at the chart or the computer. Doctors will often walk into the room with their head buried in the chart or walk over to the computer and scan the notes from the previous visit to get up to speed on the patient and his or her medical problems. This telegraphs the impression that the doctor is not prepared for the visit. We suggest that you review the chart before you open the door, and then look directly at the patient, call the patient by name, and perhaps shake the patient's hand. This humanizes the visit and makes the patient feel important and that you are focused on him or her and not on the chart.
8. Don't turn your back on the patient. This is disrespectful and a barrier to good communication. Avoid placing wall-mounted computers in the corner of the exam room in such a way that your back is toward the patient. This is certainly one advantage of mobile tablet PCs over fixed machines in the exam room.
9. Minimize interruptions. Nothing can derail your communication with your patient faster than being interrupted during the visit. It is very hard to get the train of thought moving in the right direction when you take a phone call, leave the room, or allow the staff to open the door to have you sign a prescription or an order. Set guidelines for interruptions. Examples include the emergency department, the intensive care unit, or the operating room. If another physician calls, instruct your staff to say, "The doctor is with a patient; and if it is an emergency, I can interrupt him/her. If not, I can arrange for him/her to call you when he/she is between patients, which will be in 10 to 15 minutes." Most physicians calling another physician will respect this policy and allow you to call back.

Neil Baum, M.D.
UROLOGY

What three questions would you like answered today?

1. ____

2. ____

3. ____

Please complete the back of this card.

FIGURE 1. Sample of a card for patients to use to record questions.

10. Always ask the patient if his or her questions have been answered and if there is anything else that can be done to make his or her visit complete. This should be said while sitting down and not with your hand on the doorknob. The latter situation sends the message that you are finished with the visit and that you have mentally left the encounter with the patient. Asking the patient if there is anything left to discuss indicates that you are caring and you want to be sure that nothing unanswered is left on the patient's mind.

    One technique is to use a 3 x 5 card (Figure 1) given to the patients when they check in that asks, "What three questions would you like to have answered on your visit today?" When patients are in the reception area or the exam room, they can be filling out the card. This is a nice way to occupy time spent waiting to be seen by the nurse or the doctor, and ensures that a patient's most pressing questions are answered during the visit. This also avoids the patient stopping the doctor in the hallway after the visit or calling back to have a question answered that the patient thought of after the doctor and patient have exited the exam room.
11. If possible, walk the patient yourself or have a nurse accompany the patient from the exam room to the checkout counter. Not only is this

a nice courtesy and a sign of respect but this also ensures that the patient will take care of the bill and make his or her next appointment.

It is estimated that 50% to 65% physicians are sued at least once during their career.[3] Although few lawsuits result in a damage award, the toll that a lawsuit takes on a doctor, his or her practice, and his or her family can be daunting. You can do damage control and stave off a lawsuit if you polish your communication skills and follow a few of the recommendations mentioned in this chapter.

Bottom Line: Improving communication with your patients means making the patient feel that he or she is the most important thing for that physician that day. Doing this will not only make you feel good and be a source of gratification, but will also reduce your liability and risk of lawsuits.

REFERENCES

1. Stelfox HT, Ghandi TK, Orav EJ, Gustafson ML. The relation of patient satisfaction with complaints against physicians and malpractice lawsuits. *Am J Med.* 2005;118:1126-1133.
2. Groopman J. *How Doctors Think.* New York: Houghton Mifflin; 2007.
3. Williams AG. *Physician, Protect Thyself: 7 Simple Ways Not to Get Sued for Medical Malpractice.* Pensacola, FL: Margol Publishing; 2007.

CHAPTER 2

Nonverbal Communication May Speak Louder Than Words

NEIL BAUM, MD

Body language — or, more technically, the study of body language — also is known as *kinesics,* which is derived from the Greek word *kinesis,* meaning "motion." Body language also is referred to as *nonverbal communication,* and, less commonly, *nonvocal communications.* Many body language experts and sources seem to agree that that between 50% and 80% of all human communications are nonverbal.[1]

In this age of telemedicine and online video communication with our patients, we must be ever-vigilant of the message we are transmitting to our patients. Your body language reveals your feelings and meanings to others. Certainly, it is much easier when we are eyeball to eyeball with our patients. However, now we are going to be challenged to make healthcare decisions with our patients when they are at a great distance from our offices and ourselves. Our bodies have a language of their own, and their message is not always in the best interest of effective communication with your patients. The doctors who have the best communication, the best patient satisfaction scores, and the best patient compliance and outcomes, are the ones who understand the power of unspoken signals in communication and carefully monitor themselves and their nonverbal communications, such as:

1. Turning your back on the patient to look at the computer is perhaps one of the most frequent faux pas committed by physicians who are transitioning from paper charts to an electronic medical record (EMR). The message you are sending to your patients is that the computer is more important than the patient. My advice is to configure your exam rooms so that the computer can be accessed without looking away from

the patient. This is also easily solved using an iPad or other handheld device rather than a desktop computer.

2. You shouldn't be looking at your cell phone or take a call while you are in the exam room with the patient.
3. Slouching is a sign of disrespect. It communicates that you're bored and not paying attention. You want to convey to a patient that he or she is important and has your undivided attention. The solution is to stand up straight with your shoulders back. This gives a strong impression that the patient is important and that you are present in the moment and are listening. Maintaining good posture commands respect and promotes engagement between you and your patient.
4. Exaggerated gestures can imply that you're stretching the truth. Aim for small, controlled gestures to inspire confidence and reflect complete command of the situation. Open gestures — like spreading your arms apart (but no wider than your body) or showing the palms of your hands to your patient — communicate that you have nothing to hide. They are another signal of transparency, which often is lacking in the healthcare profession.
5. Looking at your watch while talking to someone is a clear sign of boredom, disrespect, impatience, and inflated ego. It sends the message that you have better things to do than talk to the patient, and that you're anxious to leave them. If you must know the time, then peak at the time at the top of your EMR screen.
6. Leaning away from your patient, or not leaning into your conversation, portrays that you are unengaged, uninterested, uncomfortable, and perhaps even bored and ready to terminate the patient encounter. I suggest leaning toward the patient and tilt your head slightly as you listen to them speak. This shows the patient that they have your undivided attention.
7. Crossed arms are a classic defensive position and act as a physical barrier that suggests you're not open to what the patient is saying. Be certain to avoid crossed arms and even crossed legs — appearing defensive will interfere with communication between you and your patients.
8. Exaggerated nodding may be perceived as an attempt to show you agree with or understand something that you actually don't.
9. Fidgeting with or fixing your hair signals that you're anxious, over-energized, self-conscious, and distracted. Patients will perceive you as

overly concerned with your physical appearance and not concerned enough with them and the encounter.

10. Avoiding eye contact makes it look like you have something to hide, and that arouses suspicion. On average, Americans hold eye contact for 7 to 10, longer when we're listening than when we're talking. Lack of eye contact also can indicate a lack of confidence and interest, which you never want to communicate in a doctor–patient relationship. Looking down as you talk to a patient makes it seem like you lack confidence or are self-conscious, causing your words to lose their effect. It's especially important to keep your eyes at the same level as the patient if you're discussing a new or difficult diagnosis, an intended surgery or procedure, or a complication.
11. Rolling your eyes conveys a sense of lack of respect and not believing what the patient is saying. No matter what the patient says or how outlandish or preposterous the remark may be, don't transmit your disbelief by rolling your eyes. For example, if a patient says something disparaging about a fellow physician or colleague, don't register your disbelief with a negative comment or rolling your eyes. Just listen and don't respond.
12. Scowling or having a generally unhappy expression sends the message that you're upset by those around you, even if they have nothing to do with your mood. Scowls turn patients off. Smiling, however, suggests that you're open, trustworthy, confident, and friendly. The human brain responds favorably to a person who's smiling, and this leaves a lasting positive impression. It may be difficult if you are distracted by something happening in your personal life, a sick or dying patient, or a problem within the office, but it is necessary to mentally shift gears and put this in the back of your mind and give your full attention to the patient and turn the scowl to a smile.
13. Offering a weak or wet fish–like handshake signals that you lack confidence and may be intimidated by your patient. Your best strategy is to enter the room, use hand sanitizer before touching the patient to demonstrate you are practicing good hygiene, and then offer the patient a firm handshake and also smile and make eye contact.
14. Clenched fists, much like crossed arms and legs, can signal that you're not open to other people's points of view. It can also make you look argumentative and defensive, which will make people nervous about interacting with you.

15. Playing with anything in your hands during the patient encounter, like spinning a pen, can be very distracting to patients and indicates you are not giving the patient your undivided time. Rapidly tapping fingers or fidgeting can be a sign that you are bored, impatient, or frustrated.
16. Getting too close will interfere with patient communication. Standing too close to someone (nearer than one and a half feet) signals that you have no respect for or understanding of personal space. This will make people very uncomfortable when they're around you. There are certain cultural exceptions to the 1.5-foot rule. However, for most U.S. patients, this will be a safe distance.
17. A hand on the doorknob indicates eagerness to terminate the encounter with the patient. Be certain to ask the patient if all of his or her questions have been answered before you touch the doorknob. Better yet, when patients check-in, offer them a card that allows them to write down the questions they would like to have answered during their visit. Then you can look at the card and make sure you have answered all the questions that are important to the patient.

Bottom Line: Avoiding these body language blunders will help you form stronger relationships, both professionally and personally, with your patients.

REFERENCE

1. Pease A, Pease B. *The Definitive Book of Body Language*. Orion Publishing Group; 2017.

CHAPTER 3

Reputation Management: Your Most Precious Intangible Asset

Ron Romano, and Neil Baum, MD

The Internet has become our first choice to get any kind of information regarding just about everything including products, people, and services. We are totally aware of the fact that we can access all kinds of information simply for the asking. And ask we (i.e., our patients) do!

Nowadays when someone is looking for information regarding a medical condition, they Google it. And if your Web site comes up on the first page of search results, that prospective patient may actually click through to your site. That Web site visitor may even like what he or she reads and consider scheduling an appointment.

However, that Web site surfer will probably visit three or four other doctors' Web sites and will have to make a decision on which doctor to contact. In all likelihood, the potential patient will now try to find more information on each doctor and determine what other patients have to say about the doctors. It's no different than looking at the reviews for hotels or a product you are thinking of purchasing. Patients do research! And there are plenty of sites that will tell them about you and your practice.

What this means to physicians is that what we do and who we are is an open book — or an open Internet opportunity for patients to actually read what others are saying about us. A few short years ago, a physician's reputation was primarily known to his or her peers and patients by word of mouth. That's about as far as information went, and for the most part it was favorable. In this Internet era, there is no privacy. A physician's exposure is much greater, and negative comments can go viral and be viewed by thousands of potential patients.

The Internet has given existing patients an open forum to the world to say whatever they want about their experiences, good or bad. Unfortunately, the favorable experiences do not find their way online nearly as often as the bad!

In today's Internet-savvy world, you have to pay attention to how patients can easily affect your online reputation. So what do we mean when we talk about online reputation management (or ORM)? The definition is quite simple: online reputation management is the art of making your name and your practice look their best and exceed any negative comments that are sure to appear on the Internet.

There are many online physician review Web sites were your patients can express their experience with you and your practice, such as RateMDs.com, Vitals, ZocDoc, Healthgrades, and UcompareHealth.com, to name a few. And then there are the more general review sites like Google Plus reviews, CitySearch, Yelp, and a host of others.

Here is the reality of what you are dealing with when it comes to patients posting comments on the Internet. You will be rated by your patients on:

- How your staff treated them;
- Their wait time;
- Your diagnosis;
- Your attitude;
- Their level of trust in your decisions; and
- Their medical treatment and results.

And that's just your patients. There are unscrupulous doctors who will post negative comments about their fellow doctors to put their competition in an unfavorable light. Fortunately, this doesn't happen very often.

On average, most physicians have a very favorable rating score of 9.3 out of 10 with their patients, and 70% have perfect scores.[1] But if no one knows, the online surfer who is looking for a reputable doctor will believe what he or she finds on the online review sites.

Here's what we all know: people who are unhappy with their treatment will go out of their way to find every online review site possible, and tell the world, using the Internet as their forum, what a lousy doctor you are — regardless of whether their facts are accurate or not. The reality is that patients who are pleased and satisfied rarely, and in most cases never, bother to post a positive online review.

HOW YOU CAN CONTROL YOUR ONLINE REPUTATION

So what can you do? First, it is incumbent on you to monitor your online reputation at all times. If someone has posted a negative review, respond to those comments directly at the review site. Doing this does not violate privacy laws as long as you do not mention the patient's name or details about the patient that might identify him or her. Explain your office policy and how you respond to issues and concerns that a patient may have without confirming or denying that the reviewer is or was a patient. Do not talk about the specifics of any patient's condition. If you believe the online review is totally unjustified, dispute it with the review site. You do have that option, and many review sites will take into consideration that a patient is ranting and will remove the unfavorable comment.

Next, set up alerts with Google Alerts at www.Google.com/alerts. Google Alerts is a notification system that will alert you whenever your name appears on the Internet. Google Alerts provides vigilance to monitoring your name and the name of your practice, but you should still use Google to see exactly what surfaces when existing or potential patients insert your name in the search window. Google your name or the name of your practice at least once a month, visit all the reviews sites that come up, and read the comments. However, these are reactive solutions, and you must have a proactive plan in place.

DON'T WAIT FOR A BAD REVIEW TO START SOLICITING POSITIVE REVIEWS

You have a lot of control with respect to getting feedback from your patients and what you do with it once you get it. This does require you and/or your staff to set up a system to continually request feedback and testimonials from your patients.

This is where most medical practices fail. They have no system in place to solicit positive reviews. It can be as simple as having a quick meeting between the doctor and his or her staff mentioning that the practice will now have a system in place to get testimonials from patients. Usually there is a flurry of activity and solicitation from patients for a couple of weeks, and then it's forgotten. To prevent this from happening, make a checklist and decide who on your staff is responsible for each step in the process. Go over the results in your staff meetings on a regular basis (i.e., at least monthly).

There are two places you want to have patient reviews, or testimonials as they are commonly called, posted. The first is on your Web site, and the second is, of course, on review sites.

PATIENT TESTIMONIALS ON YOUR WEB SITE

Your Web site is the place prospective patients visit when they are looking for information on how to solve their problems. Placing patient testimonials on your Web site is an excellent process to provide impressions of you and your practice to online visitors.

The best time to get a patient's feedback is immediately after the follow-up appointment, once the patient's needs have been addressed and he or she has had a least two experiences with the practice. Everything is still fresh in the patient's mind, and he or she is probably happy with the outcome and more receptive to providing a testimonial. Follow this system used by one of us (NHB) when putting testimonials on your Web site:

1. Testimonials should be on the front page of your Web site and on every subsequent page. They should be visible to Web site visitors when they first view the page without having to scroll down the page to find them. Testimonials are worthless if site visitors don't see them or take the time to find them.
2. Testimonials should be in italics with quotation marks around them. This makes a testimonial look like someone posted a comment, and not like just another part of your Web page.
3. Each testimonial should have a headline in bold. The headline should be the key words in the testimonials that will resonate with readers. For example; if, within the body of the testimonial the patient says, *"I can now function in a normal manner"* or *"I had been to several doctors, but you were the only one that cured me,"* this becomes the headline above the testimonial. Here's an example:

   You Turned My Life Around
   "I had a surgical procedure, and it was a game changer. You turned my life around, Dr. Baum! Thank you!"
4. Have a main testimonials page on your site, and pick out different headlines from each testimonial so as to appeal to a diverse group of

prospective patients. This can be done by having a button directing the viewer of the Web site to the testimonials page, or a link to the testimonials can be placed on the home page on the left side of page (Figure 1). Web site visitors may not read the entire testimonial, but they will at least read and scroll through the headlines.

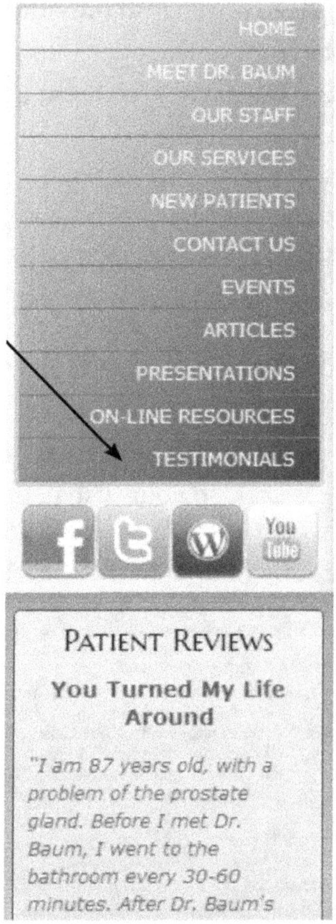

FIGURE 1. Home page of NHB's Web site with access to testimonials *(arrow)*.

PUT PATIENT FEEDBACK SURVEYS ON YOUR WEB SITE

Another way to get your patients to give you their feedback/testimonial is to have a "patient feedback survey" on your Web site. This is a convenient way for the physician to ask for patients' feedback. The doctor or staff member simply asks patients if they would go to the page on the practice's Web site and complete the survey. Many patients will agree to this suggestion, but few will actually complete the survey.

A far more effective way to get patients to complete the survey while they are still in your office is to have your receptionist hand them an iPad after their appointment, and ask them if they will take a couple of minutes to complete the patient feedback form on your Web site.

You can then have the information transcribed and put on your Web site. If you want to get really automated, you can provide a service that automatically posts the positive patient feedback to online review Web sites.

ASK PATIENTS TO POST THEIR TESTIMONIALS ON REVIEW WEB SITES

This is more difficult to accomplish, as most patients will not take the time to do it. So you have to make it as quick and easy as possible. This means you have to provide your patients with a blueprint of what to do and how to do it.

The first step is to provide your patients with a patient feedback form that has four or five questions for them to answer. (See a sample form in Figure 2.) The answers to these questions will provide a great testimonial for the doctor and the practice. Providing your patients with the proper questions will elicit an emotional response that helps them describe their experience with you and your practice. If you let the patient create a testimonial on his or her own, you'll probably receive a comment such as: *"I'm very happy with my results"* or *"He/She is a great doctor,"* and that's it.

Next, you will have to provide your patients with step-by-step instructions for which Web sites to visit and how to navigate the sites in order to get to the proper page to enter their feedback. This is often a daunting task for patients, so your instructions should be clear and simple.

Patient Follow-Up Satisfaction Survey

It is our intention to provide our patients with the absolute best medical care that is available so as to produce optimum results. Your feedback on your procedure and patient care is important and a measurement of our performance. Please take the time to let us know how you feel about your results.

1. What are the reasons you chose to have your procedure done?
2. How did your condition affect you physically and emotionally before your procedure?
3. Are you happy with the results and the patient care you received?
4. Can you compare how you felt before the procedure to how you feel now?
5. If a friend or business colleague asked you what you thought of the results of your procedure and if you would recommend my practice, what exactly would you say to them?

Your Name: ______________________________ Date: ______________

Thank you for letting us know the results of your procedure. How you felt about your experience helps us better understand both the physical and emotional needs of our patients. We would like to share your experience with others who might be struggling with the same issues as you so we can help them. By signing this form, you agree to let us share this information on our website and informational material to help other patients understand the benefits of having these types of procedures performed.

FIGURE 2. Patient satisfaction survey on NHB's Web site.

CONCLUSION

A well-respected physician, who is one of the best in his field, was complaining that the number of new patients coming to his practice had fallen off drastically in the past year and he didn't know why. The first thing I did was Google "Reviews for Dr. <his name>." I checked his online reputation with the review sites that came up, and found that his reputation had plummeted because there were four negative and zero positive reviews.

The good news is that your online reputation can be fixed. It takes time, so our recommendation is to start as soon as possible so you don't get caught with one or two unhappy patients ruining your well-deserved good reputation.

Bottom Line: The most precious asset a doctor has is his or her reputation. We spend our entire medical lives protecting that asset. A patient using the Internet and his or her right of free speech can ruin a doctor's reputation in a nanosecond. We can protect our reputation by practicing good medicine and taking good care of our patients. We can protect our online reputation by using the techniques that are described in this chapter.

REFERENCE

1. Tehrani AB, Feldman SR, Camacho FR, Balkrishnan R. Patient satisfaction with outpatient medical care in the United States. *Health Outcomes Res Med.* 2011:2(4):e197-e202.

CHAPTER 4

Taking the Pain Out of Time Management

NEIL BAUM, MD

The following suggestions will help you manage your time more efficiently.

1. **Never allow telephone interruptions while you are seeing patients.** Leaving a patient in the exam room while you answer a phone call does not make the patient feel important or that he or she has your undivided attention. However, my staff has a system of using certain numbers on my cell phone as a text message, such as 911 if there is a call from the emergency room, 411 if another physician is calling, and 000 if my wife or family must speak to me. Another option is to have the cell phone on vibrate mode, so the doctor can respond to the call as soon as he or she exits the exam room, and the patient does not see the doctor answering the call. In addition, make it a policy to return all routine calls at a specific time, such as 11:45 AM or after 3:45 PM. If your patients and colleagues know your telephone policy, they will respect it and interrupt you for emergencies only. This also alerts the patient when the call is going to be returned so he or she is not waiting for hours to hear from the doctor.
2. **Touch all paperwork and mail one time.** Read your mail and reports at a time of day when you can take action and delegate tasks to your employees. Make use of Post-it notes to alert you to special details that need attention from you or your staff.
3. **Dictate in real-time.** Do not wait until the end of the day or week to dictate letters or discharge summaries. Dictate in front of the patient when the facts are fresh in your mind. This adds to the accuracy of your history and allows your patients to make corrections or additions during your dictation. Dictating in real-time reassures your patient that you are communicating with his or her referring physician. Dictate discharge summaries when the history and hospital course are easily

remembered. The same rule of real-time applies to completing the electronic medical record encounter while you are with the patient.

4. **Learn effective scheduling.** Leave a half hour open during morning or afternoon office hours to accommodate add-ons and emergencies. Do not fill that half hour until the office opens in the morning when the phone is transferred from the answering service to the office phone. Do not worry about this open time. That half hour almost always gets used — if not with seeing patients then with catching up on your dictation and paperwork. We refer to this 20- to 30-minute slot each morning around 10:30 and each afternoon at 2:30 as "sacred time." It is reserved for urgencies and emergencies.
5. **Estimate the length of a patient visit, and schedule accordingly.** A new patient with a chronic problem may take 25 minutes of your time, whereas a returning patient with a recurrent urinary tract infection, for instance, may require only 5 minutes. However, a patient with a newly diagnosed cancer may require 35 to 40 minutes and should be scheduled at the end of the day when you have time to answer all of his or her questions. A patient to whom you are disclosing a diagnosis of cancer or revealing a significant life-threatening diagnosis such as diabetes, lupus, or renal failure deserves your undivided attention.
6. **Create a to-do list for each day and week.** There are a number of paper and electronic systems on the market to aid you in keeping track of your schedule. You may want to use your mobile phone or one of the personal data assistants especially for physicians. Prioritize your to-do list with 1s, 2s, 3s, and 4s: 1s are must-dos, 2s are important but not imperative, and 3s and 4s are "sliders" — you can move these to another list. Check off completed tasks. It gives you a feeling of accomplishment to see a list with check marks beside the 1s and 2s. In addition, the Little Blue Book is now available for your cell phone. This is a program designed for use on a handheld device running either the iPhone or Android. Now you can have physician email addresses and pharmacy fax numbers on your handheld device along with other physician and pharmacy information, including direct dial to pharmacist phone numbers and fax numbers. The program also provides your area's hospital information and useful HMO numbers and can be downloaded from your computer to your iPhone. For information, go to http://www.thelittlebluebook.com/products.aspx

7. **Use office videos for patient education.** By using office videos to explain common procedures, I have been able to enhance my office efficiency by 20% to 30%. This translates to one additional patient per hour, which computes to $125,000 additional income per year with no added staff or expenses.
8. **Learn to delegate to and empower your staff.** Allow your staff to make nonmedical decisions about office procedures and equipment. Give them the responsibility to solve problems on their own. Hire and train employees who are self-starters and can take the initiative to solve problems effectively and efficiently. Just remind them to do whatever is in the best interest of the patient. Then if they make a mistake or incur more costs, you will not have any problems if you think of the patient first.
9. **Do not spend time between surgical cases drinking coffee and reading the paper.** Make phone calls, review lab and imaging reports, write a blog, or review emails in your inbox.
10. **Do not see pharmaceutical reps or vendors during patient hours.** You cannot be an on-time physician if you are being interrupted throughout the day by pharmaceutical representatives. Nothing is more discouraging to your patients than to see a drug rep walk into the office and be seen before they are seen, especially for patients who have been waiting for some time to see the doctor. I suggest that your office tell the rep that you do not see reps when patients are in the office and that you will schedule an appointment to see them at a time that is convenient for both of you. Most reps and vendors appreciate being seen on time and will accept this alternative. Another effective technique is to have an hourglass on your desk, and invert the hourglass when the vendor or the pharmaceutical representative sits down. This is a subtle reminder that the visitor is "on the clock"! I promise you that this very simple procedure keeps the visitor focused and suggests to them that your time is valuable and that the vendor or drug rep must be focused.
11. **Start on time.** If you start half an hour late, you can be sure that by the end of the day you will be 30 to 60 minutes behind schedule in seeing your last patient. You cannot expect your staff and patients to be on time if you are not on time. Be realistic when you make up your schedule: you must make allowances for rounds, coffee, and looking at

mail. If you are diligent about being on time, your patients and your staff will be on time too.

12. **Answer every patient's questions at the time of the encounter in the exam room.** Give patients a small card and encourage them to write down any questions that they would like answered during the encounter. If you look at the card and see their concerns or questions, then you can quickly and efficiently answer the questions while the patient is in the exam room. I suggest concluding every visit or encounter with, "Have all of your questions or concerns been addressed today?" I can assure you that offering this single question will enhance your patient satisfaction scores and your online reputation.
13. **Avoid phone tag.** If patients call with questions or concerns, have the staff inform the patient when to expect a returned call from the doctor. In my practice, I return calls at 11:45 AM and 3:45 PM, and patients are encouraged to be at the number that they leave for the call to be returned and to keep the phone line open to avoid receiving a busy signal or having to leave a message. Remember tag is for tots — not for doctors and their patients!

Bottom Line: In many ways, effective time management boils down to plain good manners and practice of the Golden Rule: if you treat patients the way you would like to be treated, the chances are good that they will continue to be loyal to you and your practice.

CHAPTER 5

Thinking Like Leonardo da Vinci and Its Implications for the Modern Doctor

NEIL BAUM, MD

Physicians have a reputation as being in a profession that is associated with innovation, creativity, and, now, entrepreneurship. However, most physicians pale in these regards when compared with one of the greatest thinkers and innovators of all time: Leonardo da Vinci.

For this chapter, I interviewed Michael Gelb (www.michaelgelb.com), the author of *How to Think Like Leonardo da Vinci* (Dell, 2000). This chapter explores the seven da Vincian principles that are drawn from an intense study of his notebooks, which are considered some of the most prized manuscripts ever written and may even rival the Dead Sea Scrolls in importance! After reading this chapter and this interview, you will learn how to incorporate these principles into your practice and personal life.

Da Vinci, according to Gelb, has a message that applies to contemporary physicians who are trying to improve their services to their patients. Da Vinci encouraged his students to continually develop professionally. He served as a role model for life-long learning. Not only does da Vinci inspire us to learn, but he provides us with seven principles that healthcare professionals can use to enhance their skills. Gelb states that most biographies on da Vinci focus on his art, accomplishments, and inventions. Gelb takes da Vinci to the next level, and teaches the reader how to develop a strategy for life-long growth and continual improvement.

CURIOSITA

The first principle is *curiosita,* or having an insatiably curious approach to life and an unrelenting quest for improvement. Probably no professional asks the question, "What if" more than a physician does. What if we could treat stomach ulcers with antibiotics instead of antacids or surgery? What if we could crush a kidney stone using shock waves instead of scalpels? These were questions that were asked and answered; and, as a result, changed the course of medicine.

Gelb quotes Carol Dweck, a professor of psychology at Stanford, who pioneered the idea that people can be classified into one of two mindsets: those with a fixed mindset or those with a growth mindset. She notes that less successful people have a fixed mindset. They may be very talented people, but they don't optimize their gifts. They are afraid of making mistakes and afraid of failure. These are physicians that practice defensive medicine and order expensive tests even when they are certain of the diagnosis.

On the other hand, most successful people have a growth mindset, which is the result of curiosity. Curiosity means always looking for feedback, even if it is negative. These physicians are always looking for ways to improve their service. They are the ones that survey their patients and ask their opinion of their care and how the service can be improved. Those with a growth mindset are always seeking knowledge. Yes, those with a growth mindset make mistakes, but they treat mistakes as learning experiences.

DIMOSTRAZIONE

The second principle is *dimostrazione,* a commitment to test knowledge through experience, persistence, and a willingness to learn from mistakes. Those students of da Vinci that practice this principle have the ability to look at a problem from multiple perspectives. They aren't part of the *status quo*; they are independent thinkers.

Doctors often have a difficult or challenging case, and they may initially feel uncertain about their opinion. After all, when you are involved in the care of another human being, there's a lot at stake. When patients feel that there is an element of equivocation on the part of the treating physician, they may obtain another opinion, which may differ from the original opinion. Da Vinci also encountered problems in his work, and he had a network of other artisans or colleagues and mentors with whom he could cross-reference his thinking. Do you have such a network of colleagues and teachers with whom you can consult in these situations? Da Vinci would suggest that you be open to alternative ideas sooner rather than later. He would remind you that your primary purpose is to be of service to your patient by serving your patient. This is far more important than being right. This is one of the most important lessons of da Vinci. Helping others and service to others is what the practice of medicine is all about. We should strive to be the best caregiver to each patient who is dependent on us for judgment and clarity of thinking.

SENAZIONE

Senazione is the continual refinement of the senses, especially sight and hearing, as the means to enliven experience. The best physicians pay attention to their patients and what the patients say and do. These physicians are looking at and listening to their patients during their interaction. These outstanding physicians gave their full, undivided attention the patient. They practice mindfulness, which, among other things, is an attentive awareness of the moment.

Doctors who are in the present moment are not distracted. Even if the doctor spends only five minutes with the patient, he or she spends 100% of his or her time meaningfully engaged with the patient and focused on the patient. If da Vinci were a doctor, he would really look at the patient and actively listen to what the patient says. Da Vinci would not be looking at the computer or the iPad, but at the patient. He would not be standing if the patient was sitting down. He would be asking open-ended questions and then listening attentively to the patient's responses. It is probably true that patients will use your focused attention as part of their decision-making to select and maintain a relationship with a physician.

SFUMATO

Sfumato is a willingness to embrace ambiguity, paradox, and uncertainty. As a physician, we can't always be certain of the right thing to do. There seems to be pressure on physicians to always have the right answer. For the most part, there are neither rewards nor much motivation for sleeping on a problem, but there are occasions when it is beneficial and in the patient's best interest to do just that. It is not possible to always know the answer immediately with each interaction with a patient.

According Gelb, da Vinci would advise you to think about a problem as hard as you can, and then think of the problem from multiple perspectives. Then da Vinci would recommend that you walk away and take a deep breath, have a little relaxation, then sleep on it. Gelb points out that neuroscience now validates what da Vinci suggested. When you sleep on a problem, you consolidate new patterns of connection in your brain. By sleeping on the problem, you integrate new learning and new thinking. Da Vinci would often take a nap and then note improvement in his problem-solving ability as well as his creativity. Research shows that pilots who take 20-minute naps increase their performance, reaction time, and fine motor movements significantly. It is a good idea to get plenty of rest; and if you are confronted with a challenge, sleep on the problem. Certainly doctors, especially surgeons, may be required to make split-second decisions. However, if you have time, take time to sleep on it.

ARTE/SCIENZA

Arte/Scienza is the development of the balance between science and art, logic and imagination (i.e., whole-brain thinking). The best physicians combine logic and imagination, and rationality and intuition. The best diagnosticians often have a gut feeling what the diagnosis is, although the doctor may still need to order tests to validate his or her intuition. As you continue to study the science of medicine, you will find that you will be listening more with your gut. The more you learn, the more patients you see, and the more curious you are, the more you will nurture your ability to process information quickly.

Malcolm Gladwell in his book *Blink* (Back Bay Books, 2007) describes a story in which a museum curator was asked whether an Egyptian statue was authentic or a fake. Immediately, the expert said it was a fake because he could tell that a machine crafted the fingernails on the statue. The curator knew from his experience of seeing thousands of statutes that the art piece was not authentic. Physicians who see patients day after day get better at making gut decisions. Da Vinci would advise you to analyze all the data first and then trust your gut.

CORPORALITA

Corporalita is the cultivation of grace, ambidexterity, fitness, and poise. This step requires the balance of both the body and the mind. Da Vinci was way ahead of his time in understanding the mind-body connection. He might advise the contemporary physician, "Doctor, heal thyself," meaning that physicians should learn to preserve their own health. Da Vinci was an advocate of the importance of a healthy lifestyle, recommending nearly 500 years ago to "avoid grievous moods and keep your mind cheerful."

The Vitruvian Man (Figure 1) is da Vinci's image of divine proportions, and it remains a symbol for holistic health. Da Vinci believed that the human body was a microcosm of the harmony of the whole universe. He suggested that you treat the part of the patient or organ system that you studied during the many years spent in training; however, you should pay attention to the whole person. I can remember a staff member referring to the "prolapse patient in Room 1," and this is emblematic of the health-care profession often using anatomic parts to discuss patients rather than referring to patients by at least their first names since using last names in the hallways can be a violation of the HIPAA guidelines.

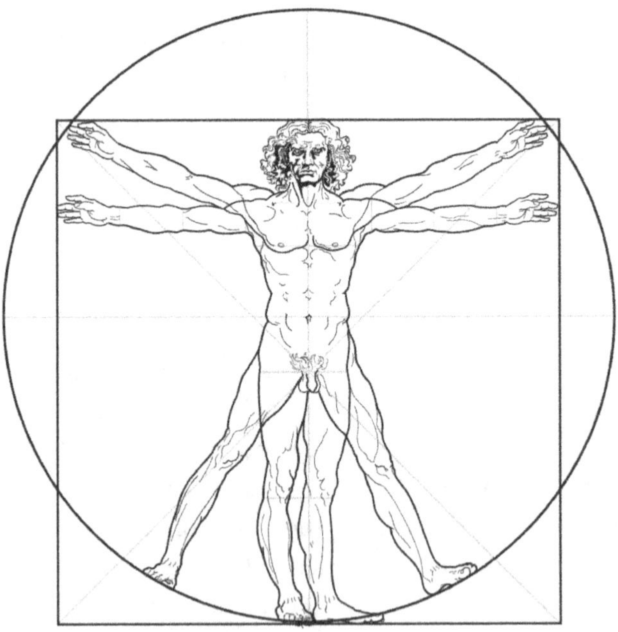

FIGURE 1. The Vitruvian Man.

CONNESSIONE

Connessione is a recognition of and appreciation for the interconnectedness of all things and phenomena — systems thinking. Da Vinci understood that everything connects to everything else. Da Vinci was one of the first systems thinkers. He suggested that we look at the person in the context of how everything is connected to everything else in the universe and related to everyone on the planet.

If da Vinci was a physician, he would ask, "What are the factors that are impacting this patient's illness?" He would make connections that others wouldn't see; remember that da Vinci tried to invent the parachute long before anyone could fly! He would consider that if he prescribed a drug, it might solve the patient's problem, but what other problems would it create? I know there have been times when I prescribed a medication, and the adverse effects of the drug were more problematic than the problem I was trying to solve by prescribing the medication. I think it is imperative that as physicians we think through these issues and discuss with our patients the risks and benefits of the treatments that we often offer them.

Bottom Line: No one knows for sure what the future will bring. We do know that there are going to be events that take place that may discourage us. However, we can still feel cheerful and bring joy to our patients. Da Vinci and his seven principles offer a way to enhance our relationship with our patients and to improve our level of care and compassion as we try to guide patients on a path to good health and well-being.

CHAPTER 6

Looking at Alternative Medical Careers: Finding the Hidden Opportunities in Healthcare Part I

Joseph E. Swartz and Neil Baum, MD

When Michelangelo was commissioned to create a sculpture of a hero who represented the virtues of the young Florentine Republic — strength, fortitude, and vigilance — he decided to use the David of the Bible. Many famous artists had sculpted hundreds of Davids in bronze or stone before, but all had created a small, weak, and effeminate David dressed as a prince.

Michelangelo's sponsors surely did not want one of those Davids standing at the entrance to the great city of Florence. Michelangelo had read Bible passages and envisioned a different David. He asked himself, "Could those Davids have protected Florence from her enemies?" He thought about David's reply to King Saul when Saul warned him against fighting the giant, Goliath: "I used to feed my father's flock; and if a lion or bear came and carried off one of my rams, I would go in pursuit, and snatch the prey from their jaws. Lion or bear, if they threatened me, I'd catch them by the throat and slay them." Michelangelo knew that none of the Davids created by the artists before him could have strangled a lion or a bear. He envisioned a unique David — one that was strong and powerful.[1]

Michelangelo further asked himself, "Is that the measure of a man — to portray him after his successes?" as the other artists before him had done? "Or is the measure of a man's greatness his courage to step up and face his giants?" He was not interested in creating a David who was confidently showing off after severing Goliath's head. He wanted a David who was tense and taut as a spring about to be released, yet also calm and determined just before facing the murderous giant. Michelangelo did not want to portray a prince who reigned in a palace, but a rugged shepherd who vigilantly defended his sheep from lions and bears. Michelangelo envisioned producing something with a unique value to the world.[1]

HOW TO DIFFERENTIATE YOUR PRACTICE FROM OTHERS

To differentiate your medical practice from all other practices in the community, you must first see, just as Michelangelo did in his piece of marble, a unique vision that can be carved into the stone of your practice. Differentiating yourself and your practice takes into account the "look and feel" of your office, your staff, and your materials. Every detail gives your patients clues as to who you are and what you value. The strategies that go into promoting your uniqueness must be envisioned, so your existing patients, as well as prospective patients, are attracted to and stay loyal to you and your practice.

The business side of healthcare is swiftly changing. Both physicians and office managers are looking for new ways to connect with patients. In the past, a physician would place an announcement in the paper and a listing in the Yellow Pages of the local phone book and then consider him- or herself ready to practice the art of medicine. Physicians would promote themselves by meeting colleagues, going to emergency departments, and waiting for patients to arrive. Today, with managed care plans, healthcare reform, the Internet, social media, and the Affordable Care Act, it is much more difficult to build a practice using these antiquated techniques. Now it is necessary to build a brand for your practice.

Is your medical practice unique and special? Everyone believes that he or she is a member of a truly unique practice or organization, but how do we convey that to our existing patients and to potential new patients? The objective is to create a name, a term, a symbol, or design that identifies and defines your practice and will differentiate your practice from other practices. A well-differentiated practice results in patients who will want to use you and your practice to solve their medical problem.

Marie Curie, who discovered two radioactive elements — plutonium and radium — was intent on obtaining a PhD, but in Europe prior to 1903 no woman had ever received that degree. Madame Curie differentiated herself by selecting physics, a discipline in which she was superior to others in the field. She and her collaborator and husband, Pierre, were awarded the Nobel Prize for Physics in 1903, and Madame Curie received a second Nobel Prize, for Chemistry, in 1911. Madame Curie knew how to identify an area of expertise in which she would differentiate herself from all other women, as well as men.[1]

Another example is Abbott Laboratories, which was in competition with Merck, the leading manufacturer in the world at creating new drugs. Abbott knew it couldn't compete with Merck in developing new drugs, so Abbott decided to compete by developing products that were less expensive, making Abbott's medications attractive to patients, physicians, and insurers. Abbott focused on postoperative drugs and medications used for diagnosis of various medical conditions. Abbott became successful because of its ability to differentiate itself from a world leader in the pharmaceutical industry.[1]

Nearly every physician is trained to diagnose and treat diseases. These two skills make up a basic level of proficiency for all physicians. But merely being able to identify medical diseases and recommend treatment will not differentiate your practice from others in the community. Only a handful of doctors who can claim to be the best surgeon or the best diagnostician in the community. However, everyone can find a niche where they can excel. One example of differentiation could be offering early morning, evening, or weekend hours to provide services when other offices are closed. Another area of differentiation might be to provide the opportunity for a patient to make an appointment, see the doctor, obtain imaging studies and lab work, and also obtain their medications on the same visit. This would make the practice user-friendly and certainly would differentiate itself from most other practices in the area.

What area can you can find that will make you unique and special in the eyes of your patients? Every practice has this opportunity and potential. We, like Michelangelo, need to see the David in the stone and remove the excesses. Differentiation is about finding and seizing great opportunities. In today's healthcare environment, we've seen doctors and practices rise out of simple ideas executed well. Don't ever forget that opportunities are all around us; it's just a matter of us finding and seizing them.

REKINDLE YOUR PASSION TO LEARN

Always be a student. If you want to differentiate yourself from others, it is imperative to be a lifelong student. Medicine is a lifelong commitment to learning. Doctors can't be on top of their game if they are still using only the knowledge and skills that they received when they completed their education or training. Balance is achieved if you continue to follow a lifelong pursuit of knowledge. A medical career is a journey and not a destination. You should always make time to be a student for your entire career.

The great artist Pablo Picasso while walking on a street in Paris was recognized by a woman who asked him to draw her portrait. In a matter of minutes Picasso gave her a portrait drawing, as she had requested. The woman asked how much she owed the great painter and he said 5000 francs. The woman was aghast and said, "But you did that in thirty seconds." Picasso responded, "No, it took me forty years!"[1]

The take-home message is that we are valued by our knowledge and skills. The skills that you learned as a medical student and resident probably were on the cutting edge when you transitioned from your training program to practice. However, if that's the extent of your knowledge and skills 10 or more years after you became a practicing physician, you will probably find yourself behind, or even antiquated. You must continue to learn and update your knowledge and skills to be an effective physician.

CARPE DIEM (SEIZE THE DAY) OR CARPE POTESTATEM (SEIZE THE OPPORTUNITY)

There are multiple opportunities available to all doctors and all practices. All we need to do is find unmet needs in the marketplace, become an expert in those areas, and fill those unmet needs.

Michelangelo applied for a position in a commercial studio and was told that he must carve only what the patron requested. Michelangelo asked, "What if the sculptor thinks of something new or an idea that has not be carved before?" The owner of the studio told Michelangelo, "We carve here what others have carved before us." The art world is a better place because Michelangelo didn't take that job. How many times do we practice just the way it has been done by others or in a way that does not deviate from what has been told to us or what is written in the textbooks? We need to think the seemingly impossible and seize the opportunity.[1]

TWO EXAMPLES OF MEDICAL OPPORTUNITIES

Before the Salk vaccine became available, nearly 50,000 people had been paralyzed with polio. The party line in the 1950s was that a person had to *experience* a live virus to become immune. Jonas Salk was skeptical of that theory. He deactivated a live virus and injected it into human subjects. It worked, and a vaccine was developed that dramatically decreased the risk of paralytic polio to fewer than 10 cases per year! Salk saw an opportunity where others saw the only the way it has been done before.[1]

In an even more recent example, Dr. Barry Marshall, a primary care doctor in Australia, noted that gastric ulcers contained bacteria in pathology specimens. Marshall proposed that it was not hyperacidity that causes gastric ulcers but that a bacterial infection, *Helicobacter pylori,* was the culprit. The elite scientists and doctors, who did not believe that any bacteria could live in the acidic environment of the stomach, ridiculed his theory. In 1984, Marshall decided to experiment on himself. He had a baseline gastroscopy performed on himself, and shortly thereafter drank a solution containing *H. pylori.* Three days after drinking the *H. pylori* solution, he developed nausea, vomiting, and abdominal pain. A repeat endoscopy eight days later showed massive inflammation, and *H. pylori* was cultured in the gastric juice. On the 14th day after ingesting the *H. pylori,* a third endoscopy was done that showed the typical gastric ulcer. Marshall's illness and recovery, based on a culture of organisms extracted from a patient, fulfilled Koch's postulates for *H. pylori* and gastritis. In 2005, the Karolinska Institute in Stockholm awarded the Nobel Prize in Physiology or Medicine to Marshall and Robin Warren, his long-time collaborator, "for their discovery of the bacterium *H. pylori* and its role in gastritis and peptic ulcer disease." It took several years from his identification of the bacterial culprit until the medical establishment accepted that ulcers were caused by an infection, not increased acid, spicy food, or alcohol. Today, gastric ulcers are treated with antibiotics, not surgery.

FINDING OPPORTUNITIES

You are surrounded by opportunities every day and everywhere. Look for ideas and trends that match your interests and your expertise. Develop a habit of looking at everything to see how you might improve it — how you'll make it more fun, faster, more user-friendly, less expensive, and more helpful to patients. Choose the opportunities that benefit not only your patients, but also your staff, and they will support you.

Ask yourself a few questions to identify opportunities:

- What could I do to reduce waiting time for patients to obtain an appointment?
- What could I do to prevent patients from spending excessive time in the reception area or in the exam rooms?
- How could I respond to emails in a timely fashion?
- How could my staff spend less time on the phone obtaining prior authorizations?
- How could I encourage patients with certain conditions and diagnoses to become patients in my practice?
- How could I increase the number of procedures I do each month?
- How could I add more value to my practice?
- How could I interact with patients over secure Internet operating systems (i.e., telemedicine)?

Finding opportunities starts with curiosity, the desire to try something new, something that will make a difference in some meaningful way. Acting on new opportunities takes courage and the steadfastness to know that failure is part and parcel of finding and then implementing opportunities. Begin by finding opportunities; then use your creative juices to solve the problems you have identified that get in the way of the opportunities.

Practices that get to the next level have learned to successfully differentiate themselves and find opportunities that make a difference to their patients. These exceptional practices learn to leverage their expertise and become the very best at providing the special services that maintain existing patients and attract new patients to the practice. Finally, these outstanding practices have identified opportunities that result in a good return on the investment of their time, energies, and resources required to make the opportunities a reality.

Bottom Line: It is vital for the success of a hospital or medical practice to leave the pack or take the road less traveled and find that unique, special activity or behavior that separates your practice from all the other practices or hospitals in the community. Every doctor who graduates from a reputable medical school is able to diagnose and treat diseases — that's a given. The vital questions that you must answer are: What makes you different and special? What can you offer your patients that will be in awe of you and your practice? How can you, like Michelangelo, cut away the unnecessary marble leaving you with a world class service and product that you will be so very proud? It all begins with finding great opportunities.

REFERENCE

1. Swartz JB, Swartz JE. *Seeing David in the Stone: Find and Seize Great Opportunities.* Carmel, IN: Leading Books Press; 2006.

Looking at Alternative Medical Careers: Finding the Hidden Opportunities in Healthcare Part II

Are you one of the many providers or office managers who are frustrated with the imperfect U.S. healthcare system? Do you feel like you are beating your head against a stone each day? Did you know that Michelangelo was given an imperfect stone to carve his David? The stone had been badly damaged by several artists before him and had a gaping hole through its lower half. In fact, the great Leonardo da Vinci had rejected that stone. For years the "spoiled" block of marble lay rejected in Florence, Italy. However, Michelangelo saw possibilities in that unwanted stone. He pictured in his mind exactly where David, who had the courage to stand and face his giants, could exist in that stone. He then created one of the world's greatest works of art from a stone that was so imperfect as to have been considered unworkable and unusable by most artists of his time. Giorgio Vasari, a contemporary of Michelangelo, in his book *The Lives of the Artists,* said, "truly it was a miracle on the part of Michelangelo to restore to life a thing that was dead."[1,2]

What made Michelangelo so remarkable is that he had not only the extraordinary ability to picture in his mind a unique David, but also the ability to visualize that image in a block of imperfect, rejected marble.

The Michelangelos of the world are able to imagine the highest potential for themselves and others, and they are able to help others carve away the excess and release that potential within imperfect organizations.

There are so many marvels inside the "stone" of each physician. How do we release those rough ideas or projects? How do we identify those opportunities that are available?

Physicians are seeing reimbursements steadily decreasing, and every year CMS threatens to slash reimbursements further and then chip away a smaller percentage of their payments, which eventually may result in physicians refusing to care for Medicare patients. For example, cardiologists have seen a 35% to 40% cut in Medicare reimbursements for key cardiovascular services, such as stress tests and echocardiograms.[3] In addition to lowered reimbursement, there are rising overhead costs. This translates to a loss of income to levels that may send doctors rushing to become employed by hospitals, where their incomes are assured and they don't have to concern themselves with overhead and the hiring and firing of staff.

SUPPLEMENTAL INCOME FOR PHYSICIANS

It's a common story, and primary care physicians and even specialists are keeping their ears to the ground looking and listening for other ways to boost their bottom line. Luckily, physicians have some fairly lucrative options that can help them maintain their income — and perhaps even increase it.

There are several ways to generate additional income that do not require a tremendous amount of additional time. Participating in just one or two activities can put enough money in the bank to make breathing easier when the bills come in. Let's look at a few options that can release the "marvel in the stone" for many physicians.

Work with Attorneys

Yes, that's right. Lawyers who handle personal injury and medical malpractice cases have come to rely on the expert opinion of practicing physicians to bolster their clients' claims. Physicians are hired for everything from examining the relevant medical records in a case and rendering an opinion, to testifying in court on behalf of a plaintiff or a physician-defendant. To do this job, it is useful to also have strong people skills. If called to the witness stand, it is especially important that physicians be able to communicate complex subjects clearly and simply to laypeople who are on the jury.

Pros: Reviewing records could pay $200 to $300 per hour or more, depending on the complexity of the case, your expertise, your previous experience as an expert witness, and a number of other factors. This work usually can be done at night or on weekends, and it generally does not take time away from one's practice. Depending on a physician's medical specialty, credentials, and experience, you can earn $2000 to $5000 per day, plus expenses, to testify at a deposition or at a trial.

Cons: Expert witnesses who are physicians, especially those who testify against fellow physicians, run the risk of being labeled "hired guns," which does not always endear them to their colleagues. This is a particularly slippery slope if you testify against a physician located in the same practicing community. To avoid this, physicians can choose to be expert witnesses on causation rather than damages.

How to find out more: National Medical Consultants, based in Bayside, New York, is a physician-owned company that has about 1800 medical experts available to law firms throughout the country (www.nationalmedicalconsultants.com). A more direct approach to finding this sort of work would be to offer your services to local law firms that specialize in medical malpractice cases.

See Nursing Home Patients

Rounding at nursing homes was more lucrative in years past. Like medicine in general, the threat of reduced reimbursement and increased liability risks have made it less appealing to many physicians. However, some MDs and DOs still see patients regularly in long-term-care facilities and believe that it is worth the effort. It is not uncommon for physicians to earn $15,000 to $30,000 a year for this extra work.

Pros: The pros include very low overhead, flexible hours, and the gratitude of patients who are often forgotten or neglected by their families and caregivers.

Cons: The cons include malpractice risks and unreasonable demands from family members, who may visit sporadically and who may not communicate well with each other. The watchful eyes of insurance companies, as well as state and federal regulators, make this less attractive because of the added paperwork. Malpractice insurance is generally *not* an issue because you are covered under your regular policy. However, some malpractice insurance companies may make a distinction and charge more for seeing nursing home patients.

How to find out more: Talk with colleagues who work in nursing homes or call the medical directors at facilities in your area. A good resource for basic information is the website for the American Board of Family Medicine (https://www.theabfm.org).

Become a Medical Director

In most states, the law insists that all long-term-care facilities must have a medical director who can oversee the quality of care, preside over monthly staff meetings, and be available to help create policies and procedures for the facility. This is probably not a full-time job. Serving as a medical director is a good opportunity for a board-certified family physician, geriatrician, or internist who has an interest in geriatric medicine, with compensation averaging about $1000 to $2500 a month for 5 to 10 hours of work per month.

Pros: Overall, there are fewer difficult reimbursement issues with long-term-care work because physicians are paid directly by the facility on a contract basis. However, not all of the perks are monetary: Medical directorship offers a welcome change of pace from regular practice.

Cons: Medical directors often are undervalued, despite how much patients may love them. They often are underutilized in establishing policies and procedures, in helping to ensure patients' rights, and in averting ethical issues before they happen. Of note, it is important to make sure that the facility has business liability coverage, which covers the administrative functions of a medical director. Some facilities have dropped this coverage, so it is important to ask about it. Alternatively, it is important to explore whether a rider can be added to a physician's existing coverage to include medical directorship.

How to find out more: The website of the American Medical Directors Association (www.amda.com) has a link to career opportunities on its homepage. The site also details the steps required to become a Certified Medical Director in Long-Term Care, and is an excellent source of education and management tools for directors.

Participate with Pharma

Drug and device companies spend billions of dollars each year to discover and promote new medicines and treatments, and they rely heavily on physicians to participate in these endeavors, whether through clinical trials or serving as a speaker or consultant. It is not uncommon for physicians to earn a five-figure honorarium per year by either speaking or conducting clinical studies within their medical practice. Some physicians make in excess of $100,000 annually, on top of their income from seeing patients.

Pros: With typical payments running about $1500 to $2500 for a talk, there is substantial opportunity for supplemental income. With regard to clinical trials, the amount of compensation for participating in clinical trials depends on one's specialty and how one's medical group divides income. Some clinical trials will actually pay more to physicians who are active in negotiating contracts with pharmaceutical companies, than to those taking part in the actual research. Beside the revenue from this work, one can become an occasional author or coauthor of articles in high-profile publications. The arrangement also may allow patients to gain earlier access to new medications.

Cons: These arrangements are coming under increasing scrutiny from hospitals, legislators, regulators, and the media. Chief among the concerns is that generous payments to MDs and DOs are further inflating the costs of healthcare. Moreover, physicians have been accused of not informing their patients of their ties to the very products that they may be prescribing or using in medical treatments or surgical procedures.

How to find out more: Talk to colleagues who are already working with pharmaceutical companies. Ask them how they got into it, and what they find satisfying (and frustrating) about their assignments. Most companies are always looking for talented, well-credentialed researchers and speakers. Another resource is the website of the Pharmaceutical Research and Manufacturers of America (www.phrma.org). Contact information for member companies is listed on the homepage under "About PhRMA."

Become a Media Mogul

Media outlets want physicians who can explain technical subjects in easy-to-understand terms. As an expert, physicians can help journalists do their job better by providing a local angle on a national medical topic — in the form of a quote, a column or opinion piece, or an on-air appearance.

Pros: A physician can get exposure for his or her practice and attract new patients. If, for example, 50 or more potential patients come to a practicing physician over the course of a year, that could mean thousands of dollars in additional income. Also, here's a bonus: a physician just might become the next Dr. Sanjay Gupta, the talented medical correspondent on CNN.

Cons: It is unlikely that you will become the next Dr. Sanjay Gupta or Dr. Oz. Those opportunities are few and far between. Nor is there much compensation when working with media outlets in rural areas of the country. Some newspapers may pay as little as $50 to $100 for a column, whereas TV or radio stations are apt not to compensate at all. Again, the larger financial benefits are likely to be indirect, in the form of new patients who see physicians on TV or read a quote or column in the newspaper.

How to find out more: One may start by offering their services locally, as a resource for reporters working on stories. If interactions are enjoyable and feedback is positive, calling a public relations firm with extensive healthcare contacts would be the next move. Not all firms have solid healthcare relationships, and some physicians have been burned by companies making promises that they later could not keep. To narrow the search, start with the respected Public Relations Society of America (www.prsa.org). Click on the "Find a Firm" link on the homepage. A recent search of the United States yielded 11 matches using "health/medical" and "media relations/training" in the drop-down menus.

Consultant for Wall Street

How do mutual fund managers and other financial professionals who analyze healthcare companies decide in what to invest? Besides perusing balance sheets and working their contacts at the companies themselves, they talk to physicians. Their opinions on how well a drug or a device works, as well as a description of some of the common problems that they're currently experiencing, can go a long way toward helping financial professionals decide whether to increase or decrease their stake in a company.

Pros: The pay is generous — about $250 per hour to do everything from filling out surveys to participating in phone calls and panel discussions.

Cons: One will have to be very careful about the type of information that is revealed, lest there be a violation of any of your nondisclosure or confidentiality agreements. For instance, if a physician participates in ongoing drug trials, critical details cannot be discussed that might be used by a brokerage firm in deciding whether to buy or sell a stock. (Can anyone say "insider trading"?) Sometimes even a hint of impropriety or a conflict of interest might be enough to cause legal troubles.

How to find out more: Contact a "matchmaker" firm that connects physicians and professionals in other fields with professionals on Wall Street. One of the industry leaders is Gerson Lehrman Group (www.glgroup.com), which has established relationships with mutual funds, global banks, and private equity firms. To get started, go to "Contact Us" on their homepage.

Other Opportunities

Several years ago, locum tenens was the primary purview of retired doctors. This is no longer the case. Now, recent medical graduates can work as locum tenens to gain more experience and explore different work environments and different geographic locations. Working as a locum tenens does not always mean being on the go and being uprooted to travel to distant practice locations. Depending on where one lives, work opportunities may be available near one's home. This option may be ideal for mid-career physicians who want more time with their families or for late-career physicians who want to ease into retirement.

Providing medical consultation over a secure video connection is growing in popularity because of its convenience and cost-containing nature. Medical jobs in telemedicine are now more available, as the field is growing. According to research conducted by the American Telemedicine Association, the telemedicine market is expected to grow more than 14% each year through 2020.[4]

Other possible opportunities include educating patients or medical students. In addition, off-shore medical tourism is growing, and can be worked short- or long-term. Finally, medical missions to underserved areas may not offer strong supplemental income, but some medical mission organizations have been known to help pay off student loans. They also have helped many physicians rediscover the reason why they went into medicine — to help people. Two websites to find out more about medical missions are: *Timmyglobalhealth.org* and *MedSend.org*.

Bottom Line: Physicians are not relegated to only taking care of patients. Although that is what they are trained to do, they are not locked into a clinical practice of medicine. There are other Davids hiding in imperfect stones waiting to be released. These hidden Davids can be revealed by careful visioning and sculpting of their own marble.

REFERENCES

1. Vasari G. *The Lives of the Artists*. New York: Oxford University Press; 1991:427.
2. Swartz JB, Swartz JE. *Seeing David in the Stone: Find and Seize Great Opportunities*. Carmel, IN: Leading Books Press; 2006.
3. Farmer SA, Darling ML, George M *et al.* Existing and emerging payment and delivery reforms in cardiology. *JAMA Cardiol.* 2017 2:210-217.
4. Lacktman NM. Five telemedicine trends transforming health care in 2016. November 16, 2015. www.foley.com/en/insights/publications/2015/11/five-telemedicine-trends-transforming-health-care.

CHAPTER 7

Physician-Hospital Alignment: "Employment Lite"

Craig Hunter, and Neil Baum, MD

TRENDS IN PHYSICIAN EMPLOYMENT

Physician employment has become widespread as healthcare reform evolves. Physicians are opting for employment by hospitals/health systems or by other private practices for a variety of reasons. These typically include:

- Improvement in quality of life;
- Need for financial and job security;
- Response to reimbursement reduction;
- High cost of practice overhead;
- Consideration of compensation options;
- Responsibilities for call coverage; and
- Unknown factors of healthcare reform.

While other reasons exist, the trend cannot be ignored. This message rings true for both established physicians and those recently completing their training.

CONSIDERING THE OPTIONS

The good news is that while the environment continues to change, multiple options are available to a practicing clinician who is considering transitioning to a different structure. While the factors that influence one's decision may be deeply personal, or the result of previous interactions, there are still alternatives that allow a physician to maintain a measure of autonomy and that provide additional security. These options include:

- Merging with another group;
- Full hospital employment; and
- "Employment lite."

Many aspects must be considered as part of the equation for physicians considering joining another private practice. This may include the decision to join a single-specialty group or a multispecialty group with like-minded vision, goals, and objectives. Autonomy and economic considerations must also be taken into account.

Because much has been published on mergers and hospital employment, we have chosen to focus on the relatively new concept of employment lite in this chapter.

WHAT IS EMPLOYMENT LITE?

"Employment lite" is a term indicating a high level of physician-hospital integration that falls just short of full employment. It is formalized by a professional services agreement (PSA) that is specific to the arrangement. Under the employment lite arrangement, the hospital engages the physician to provide certain services without being a W-2 employee. Following is an overview of PSAs currently in place between physicians and hospitals.

PROFESSIONAL SERVICES AGREEMENT

A PSA between a hospital and a physician practice can fall into one of four basic scenarios. Although the details in the deviations are unlimited within each arrangement, following are four recognized and most commonly used variations on the PSA model:

1. **Global Payment PSA.** The hospital contracts with the practice for services in exchange for a global payment rate, which includes all physician compensation and benefits as well as all practice overhead expenses. Further, the practice retains all management responsibilities.
2. **Practice Management Arrangement.** The hospital employs the physicians; the practice entity is retained and contracts with the hospital for management services; and administrative management staff is not employed by the hospital, as the practice provides these services via a management contract (another agreement) and receives a corresponding fee.
3. **Traditional PSA.** The hospital contracts with the physicians (via their historical practice entity) for professional services. The hospital employs staff and "owns" the administrative structure.

4. **Hybrid Arrangements.** The hospital employs/contracts with the physicians, the practice entity is spun-off into a jointly-owned MSO/ ISO, and various scenarios exist involving "mixing/matching" of both professional and administrative services.

Global Payment Model PSA

With the physicians still employed by the practice, under the global payment PSA model the practice acts as an independent contractor for the hospital. Under the self-employed status, the physicians receive no employee benefits (e.g., health insurance, malpractice coverage) from the hospital. The practice invoices the hospital for actual services rendered, usually defined by work RVU (wRVU) production. The wRVUs are then converted to dollars to determine the payment back to the practice.

Thus in essence, the hospital becomes the source of most of the revenue for the practice (excluding income such as research fees, medical director fees, etc.). The hospital pays the practice directly without making any withholdings. The hospital files an IRS Form 1099, subject to regulatory requirements, issued to the practice — not the individual physicians; the responsibility for withholding taxes, therefore, belongs to the practice.

The global payment model as a comprehensive alignment strategy is similar to employment in many ways, but stops significantly short of it. The hospital engages the practice, which continues to employ the physicians, to provide comprehensive services through a PSA. The hospital compensates the practice on a global ("top line") basis, allowing the physicians to maintain their practice independently. (*Note: A caveat to this top-line payment is that in some global payment PSAs, the payment is in two components: one to cover the practice's overhead, usually a combination of mostly fixed dollar amounts and some variable expenses, and the other component for the physician/provider compensation and benefits, typically paid on a rate per wRVU basis.*)

Other notable facets of the global payment PSA model are that post-alignment, the hospital:

- Owns the accounts receivable;
- Establishes the fee structure; and
- Contracts with payers.

Often, the practice continues to perform the billing services for the hospital at fair market value (FMV) rates. Practices generally tend to do a better job of billing for their services than a secondary party. Nevertheless, the function as to who does the billing is a negotiable matter; regardless, all services performed by the physicians are billed under the hospital's tax identification number (as opposed to the practice).

Practices continue to be responsible for paying their overhead expenses. They are able to do so by the hospital providing a base fee that is intended to cover all expenses, including physicians' compensation. This fee is determined by wRVU conversion factor rates, tiered for higher production levels, separately calculated by specialty. Or the payment could be separated to entail a payment to cover the practice's overhead, then a second payment for the physician/provider compensation/benefit component.

Under a PSA, the hospital normally acquires the practice's ancillary services equipment and furnishes these services through the hospital, typically on an outpatient basis. Often, in connection with this sale, the group practice will agree to a restrictive covenant, pursuant to which the practice is prohibited from providing the ancillary services in competition with the hospital. The practice, as a result, no longer can rely on ancillary services revenue to support physician compensation. Accordingly, the physician compensation structure and levels contemplated must be acceptable to the physicians while meeting various compliance guidelines relative to FMV and commercial reasonableness requirements. Typically, the parties attempt to negotiate the per-wRVU rate so as to accomplish this objective and to stay within the corridor of FMV and commercial reasonableness.

The global payment rate may be applied in one of two ways:

- Option One: Include physician compensation/benefit expenses and overhead expenses in a single rate/wRVU, truly, a "global payment"; or
- Option Two: Include separate payments for each component.

Practice Management Arrangement

The practice management arrangement model is structured wherein the physicians (and possibly midlevel providers) are employed by the hospital, but the infrastructure of the former practice entity remains independent and under the control of the physicians. This structure is most viable when the practice has an especially adept management infrastructure and overall administrative skill. It also applies when the practice and the physicians may have some question as to whether their employment with the hospital is to be a long-term commitment. By retaining their practice infrastructure, it would be much easier to revert to a private practice setting or perhaps to align with another health system, assuming the restrictive covenant and/or noncompete terms allow for this action.

Under the practice management arrangement, the physicians operate as managers of the practice, providing all administrative services, space, equipment, and support staff. The hospital contracts with the practice entity for these services and pays a FMV management fee. The negotiations relative to this management fee can be sensitive given the fact that the physicians are now negotiating with their employer. The compensation structure for the employed physicians is often a productivity-based system. In essence, the employment of the physicians is no different than any other employment structure between hospitals/health systems and physician groups.

The advantage of the practice management arrangement is that it can be more easily dissolved than the other PSA models (and certainly more than a traditional practice acquisition and employment model), as the practice entity stays outside the hospital's administrative and management control. This may be perceived as too great a negative factor for the hospital, but could easily be an effective tool for ultimately transitioning to complete control and ownership, even of the administrative infrastructure, by the hospital.

Another possible variation of the practice management arrangement is for the hospital and the practice to develop a jointly owned management company where the hospital buys an equity position in that entity (i.e., the formal management structure of the practice), and the practice and the hospital jointly manage, subject to a management contract and FMV management fee.

Traditional PSA

Under the traditional model PSA, the hospital contracts with the physicians for professional services. Specifically, the physicians remain employees of the practice, keeping the practice entity intact, and the hospital contracts with the practice for the professional services rendered by the physicians. While the physicians remain in their existing practice structure, their support staff members become employees of the hospital. Typically, this includes all employees, from clerical to clinical to practice administrators and management staff. Under this model, many of the operational and administrative duties become the responsibility of the hospital, as opposed to the practice. The ultimate result is a structure that looks and feels like employment in that the practice gives up its "ownership" of all management and operations. The practice is relieved of all day-to-day operational oversight, including the risk of operating from a financial/economic standpoint. The "practice" stays intact, but only from the view of the physicians (and perhaps the nonphysician providers).

The ownership of the practice from a professional standpoint is at the hospital/health system level. By this we mean that the hospital controls the payer contracts, including the negotiation thereof, and bills for all professional charges going forward, and thus owns the accounts receivable. While the practice stays intact from the standpoint of the physician ownership of that professional entity, all other areas of the practice transition to the ownership/control of the hospital. The only remaining component of what was previously the practice is its professional members (i.e., the physicians and perhaps some or all of the nonphysician providers).

Hybrid Arrangements

In hybrid arrangements, the hospital employs/contracts with physicians; the practice entity is spun-off into a jointly owned MSO/ISO; and various scenarios involving "mixing/matching" of services (both professional and administrative) exist.

OVERALL BENEFITS OF EMPLOYMENT LITE MODELS

The benefits to each of the four models include the following:

- Physicians maintain their independence from the hospital by remaining either employees of the practice or controlling their management infrastructure, which would enable them to go back into private practice easily.
- While these models are more complex than straight employment, their structures offer great flexibility, which physicians often initially prefer upon entering such an alignment arrangement.
- The structures are similar to employment, yet there are very specific differences that often are prevailing in preferences for the physicians.

- The PSA structures can be viable segues to full employment; many physicians need time to make certain that the hospital partner is the right long-term affiliate.
- While perhaps slightly less stable than employment, the PSA models offer a high level of stability relative to the hospital and physician relationship going forward.
- The PSA models present opportunities for physicians and hospitals to expand services together without being totally fully aligned (i.e., employment).
- Wraparound agreements are easily structured within the PSA models and are usually a viable complement to them.
- The ability to unwind and effectively disengage from the relationship is greater under the PSA models than straight employment, particularly if there is no post-termination noncompete.
- From the hospital system, often the PSA models are actually more attractive because they reduce the typical economic and financial risk of owning and managing a medical practice (especially applicable with the global payment and practice management arrangement PSA models).
- A management committee should be structured to jointly develop strategies and other day-to-day operative initiatives, such as budgets and areas of opportunity for growth and expansion. Thus, the management committee within the PSA contract provides many of the governance and decision-making processes that should exist, regardless of the alignment model.
- While the three PSA models are the primary structures, hybrid variations can be shaped to accommodate the specific needs of both the hospital and the practice.

IS EMPLOYMENT LITE FOR YOU?

The checklist in Figure 1 will help you evaluate whether a PSA is the appropriate alignment model for your unique situation.

CONCLUSION

The paradigm has shifted from solo practices to hospital-owned practices where the doctors are employed by the hospitals. The employment contract and process can be daunting but employment lite may be the course to take to brace for the waves of change.

Question	Answer
1. What does this agreement encompass? Does the hospital provide all clinical support services or just those within the service line?	
2. Are the staff employed or are they independent contractors? If so, which staff are included (provider vs. non-provider)?	
3. How are ancillary sources of revenue (e.g., diagnostic services, physical therapy, etc.) to be handled within this structure?	
4. How is leadership and governance addressed? What are the voting rights and reserved powers the health system may require? What will be the effect of ethical and religious directives (ERDs), if applicable?	
5. What about criteria for quality and clinical outcomes? Will a portion of the compensation plan include consideration of such non-productivity based criteria?	
6. Is the compensation reasonable? At fair market value (FMV)/commercially reasonable rates? Has an independent valuation expert provided an opinion?	
7. Are there adequate compensation incentives to motivate productivity? Would it appear that these incentives are consistent with FMV/commercial reasonableness? Are there compensation incentives to incent other desired behaviors, such as patient satisfaction or cost control?	
8. What about the term of the agreement and associated termination rights? Is there a thoroughly documented unwind provision?	
9. Overall, are the duties and obligations of the practice and the hospital thoroughly defined?	
10. What strategic, relational, economic, and functional advantages or disadvantages would result from such a working relationship between the hospital and the medical group? Does the "employment lite" structure give effect to "full" alignment?	
11. Are there "wraparound" services that in and of themselves would entail limited or moderate forms of alignment but are added to the employ- ment lite structure to add more overall integration to the relationship?	

FIGURE 1. Professional services agreement checklist.

CHAPTER 8

Taking the Stand: Marketing Your Expertise as an Expert Witness

GILBERT MEADOWS, MD, AND NEIL BAUM, MD

In the past, doctors were able to generate nice incomes from their practice when the reimbursements were fair and reasonable and overhead costs were under control. Today, that situation is markedly different: reimbursements are decreasing and overhead costs are continuing to rise. As a result, doctors' incomes are decreasing. One prospect that has not been fully explored is the expert witness opportunity that generates a nice profit margin and has minimal overhead expenses for the doctor.

If you are comfortable speaking in public, have honed your public speaking skills so that you can communicate complicated medical terms in direct and simple lay language, and enjoy the arena of a courtroom, this may be an activity that can be both lucrative and enjoyable.

This chapter gives you an overview of the expert witness process, the expectations, and the pitfalls, and prepares you to choose whether or not to embark on this process.

WHY BECOME AN EXPERT WITNESS?

Why would physicians knowingly subject themselves to a process where they can guarantee that they will be grilled, cross-examined, and criticized, and have their reputation publically called to question?

Serving as an expert witness is both professionally and personally rewarding, and it should be economically beneficial as well. Physicians don't work by the hour, but the hourly production rate for a doctor is anywhere from $100 to $400. For those doctors who wish to serve as an expert witness, the hourly rate is approximately $500, and the overhead required is negligible.

WHAT IS INVOLVED?

Generally, an expert will have several roles. Traditionally, in a malpractice case, you will be asked to provide a comprehensive review of records and various documents to familiarize yourself with the case. Experts must review all the facts so they have a complete picture of the case. This is a time-consuming process, and most doctors opt to do this outside of the office in the evenings and on weekends. Of course, this means you may well have to review voluminous medical records, copies of deposition transcripts, and other reports generated by consultants. And you will want to remember that it is the standard of care and modes of treatment at the time the treatment was rendered that are in question. At the time of trial, many years have often passed since the incident, and treatment protocols are continuously evolving. Once you have a thorough understanding of the facts, you must compare them to the standard of care at the time in question.

YOUR REPORT, PLEASE

In many jurisdictions, a report setting forth your opinions and the basis for your opinions will be required. The attorney who has retained you should provide the requirements for the jurisdiction in which you will be testifying. These can vary significantly from state to state, so make sure the attorney supplies you with specifics.

Attorneys usually first contact the physician via telephone and ask if the physician will review the records. The attorney will request a phone conference after the physician has reviewed the records to be sure that the physician's opinion is favorable to the case. If the opinion is not favorable, the attorney does not want any written record in his or her file, and will request that you submit a bill for the review of the records.

If the opinion is favorable to the attorney's case, then the attorney will most likely want to proceed to the next step, which is to have the physician produce a written report. The report the physician generates is an important document, and testimony and cross-examination hinge on its wording. In many courts, the physician will be limited to what he or she has stated in the report. Opinions that are not set forth within the report are often excluded at the time of trial.

Attorneys advise physicians to state the diagnosis in a definitive and clear manner. Many medical reports are ruined and become great liabilities when the physician writes negative statements such as "unknown etiology." Many physicians throw in such terms because they do not know if the history that was provided was accurate. The physicians will spend hours on the stand regretting they mentioned such terms in their report. For example, if the only explanation of the symptoms is trauma, then clearly state that the medical condition is a result of that trauma. There is no need to provide an opportunity for mental reservations and verbal gymnastics when the history is clear.

It is important to remember that physicians are scientists and require scientific accuracy (p value of .05 or confidence interval of ≤ 1) to make a medical judgment regarding diagnosis or treatment. However, in the civil litigation arena, the benchmark is "more likely than not," indicating that a criterion only has to have a 50.1% chance of being true. Physicians who are not skilled in legal matters often revert to their scientific training and forget the basis for judgment in civil litigation matters.

At the appropriate time, your report will be shared with opposing counsel and often with the court, and can become an essential piece of evidence upon which even decisions about settlement may be made.

An updated *curriculum vitae* (CV) should also be provided with your report to set forth your expertise and experience. Including your CV lends legitimacy to your report and validates why, in fact, your opinion should be given the appropriate amount of weight. Many attorneys will ask that you submit information on previous cases in which you have testified as an expert witness. Your credibility is much greater if you have testified for both plaintiffs and defendants rather than only one side of the legal equation. The federal court system *requires* a list of cases in which you have testified either in deposition or trial for the last four years in order for you to be a recognized as an expert witness.

TIPS ON DIAGNOSIS

You may be asked to make an appointment for the plaintiff or defendant and take his or her history and perform a physical examination. At the time of this examination, you have an opportunity to review his or her medical records. In taking a history, always give the patient an opportunity to share his or her complete story and then ask relevant questions.

OTHER STEPS

In some jurisdictions, even though you have completed a report, you may be deposed under oath to tell only the truth by the opposing party for discovery purposes. The attorney who has retained you will want to prepare you carefully for the deposition. The attorneys taking the deposition want to see your demeanor, understand your opinions, and try to draw information from you that can be used later during cross-examination at trial. If your trial testimony veers away from what you gave previously at a deposition, you can count on your credibility being impeached. At all these junctures, consistency — in your report and during deposition and trial testimony — is the name of the game. Depositions can be given for discovery purposes (to evaluate you, your presentation, credibility and opinions) or for perpetuation (to actually take testimony that will be used at trial either by being read or shown on video to the jury). These two types of depositions are very different, and you should discuss with the attorney who retains you what type of deposition is being taken and what role you will play.

In addition to reviewing records, preparing a report, and participating in a deposition, you may be asked by the attorneys to help them understand certain medical facts about the case or even prepare cross-examinations for opposing attorney's experts. This can be an important part of the process, so you can play a critical role in this regard.

WALK THE WALK AND TALK THE TALK

Obviously, the most difficult job you will be given as an expert is at the actual trial. Many attorneys will ask you at the time you are retained whether or not you will be willing to come to the trial and participate as a live witness. Most attorneys prefer that the expert testifies in person, but with new technology, including large screens that can project this testimony, a videotaped deposition, done correctly, can be very effective and obviates the need for you to travel and miss a day or days away from your practice. Either way, preparation time will be necessary for you to connect with the attorney who will be asking questions during direct examination and be adequately prepared for cross-examination.

DO YOUR HOMEWORK

It is essential that you make time to meet with the lawyer before you get on the witness stand. At this trial preparation meeting, the lawyer should apprise you of his or her medical theory about the case and what other physicians have diagnosed and concluded. Before the conference, the attorney should provide you with copies of all pertinent medical records. The attorney should let you know about his or her theory of the case. You and the attorney should come to a conclusion ahead of time about where the "holes" are in the opposing theory and why your side is medically correct and accurate. This information is vital for the expert to understand before taking the witness stand.

Of course, you and the lawyer should go over the questions that are going to be asked, the order in which they will be asked, and the anticipated answers. You should construct in the examination the use of visual aids and reasons to move from the witness stand into the teaching position addressing the jury. Jurors have learned from childhood that teachers are right, and they should believe teachers. If the physician even unconsciously becomes a good teacher in the jury's eyes, he or she is more likely to be believed.

The expert must be prepared to defend his or her opinion from attack. If you have written articles on the subject matter, the opposing lawyer will have read those articles and will bring them to court. Nothing is as embarrassing to a physician and destroys credibility as much as being unfamiliar or unable to defend articles he or she has published in medical journals. You should also review pertinent medical textbooks and literature that might be used to attack your position.

DO NOT LET CROSS-EXAMINATION CROSS YOU UP

Medical experts usually feel that cross-examination is one of the most grueling and exhausting parts of the job. The importance of the case weighs heavily on their minds. They want to do a good job, while being fair with the facts and the medicine. It is quite a balancing act, and it takes a lot of skill, perseverance, and preparation to do the job right.

Cross-examination opens you up to a wide array of questions. You can expect questions about your own credentials and experience and even your malpractice history. You can also expect questions about financial arrangements you have made with the attorney and financial arrangements you make generally when doing this type of testifying. You may be asked about prior testimony you have given, and count on a thorough search of your credentials, background, training, and previously recorded testimony. Attorneys will always obtain the previous testimony of opposing experts to determine whether they might have given contradictory testimony in other cases.

FEE ARRANGEMENTS

Throughout all this, the expert should be appropriately compensated for his or her time. In this regard, it is important to set an amount that is consistent with what your peers are charging and that fairly compensates you for your time. It is almost impossible to give a set amount, but checking with your peers in the geographical area of the trial is usually helpful. If a doctor charges too much, this will come out during cross-examination, and he or she will look like a highly paid hired gun. This detracts from the testimony and can hurt the case in which he or she has been retained to help. When asked about your fee, state it confidently; and if the opposing attorney attempts to imply how high your fee is, then merely state that you have spent hours preparing for the testimony, you have had to leave your practice for hours and days, and you have also had meetings with the attorney prior to the court date. This puts the fee in the proper perspective and won't appear so unreasonable to the jury.

On the other hand, being an expert witness is hard work, and the fee arrangement is an important consideration when deciding whether to take the case. Fee arrangements should be in writing, completely discussed, and disclosed from the start so there are no questions once the matter is completed.

There is no uniform fee. Experts charge one hourly rate for reviewing the records and consultations, which is usually less than the hourly rate for the deposition. The deposition hourly rate is usually less than the hourly rate for testifying in court. For example, some specialists charge $300 to $350 for review of records; $1000 to $2500 for the deposition, usually dependent upon the time required for the deposition; and a flat rate for the trial testimony, usually quoted in half-day increments. The rates vary according to the specialty and the area of the country; in New York, California, and Florida, the fees are much higher.

It is appropriate to have language in the fee agreement that addresses the issue of cancellation. There is some compensation, usually 20% to 25% of the fee, if the case is canceled within one or two days of the expected appearance. Also the physician needs to be certain that all travel expenses are *in addition to* the fee for the testimony.

WHERE THE OPPORTUNITIES LIE

Becoming a successful expert witness often depends on locale. Because many local physicians are reluctant to testify against a colleague within the community, plaintiffs' lawyers often have to look outside of the local area to recruit an expert witness. Thus, the opportunities to be plaintiffs' witnesses are more national in scope, while openings for defense expert witnesses are more likely to be local.

What do trial attorneys look for? Academic qualifications, such as being a professor at a medical school or the head of a department at a major hospital, are highly regarded. However, many academic institutions prohibit their faculty from becoming expert witnesses or require them to turn over all fees to the faculty practice plan, even though the physician does this work on his or her own time. Second, an attorney would consider how well a doctor can articulate his or her position and how good a witness he or she is likely to be. The essence of any trial is the ability to communicate medical opinions to the jury in clear, simple, and concise fashion.

There is a fine line between using layman's language and talking down to the jury. Attorneys are looking for physicians who are articulate and who can simplify complex medical topics and issues. The doctor needs to explain the situation and educate the jury in layman's language. There is a fine line between using layman's language and talking down to the jury, which must be avoided at all costs. Both the jury and the judge must understand the doctor. Attorneys look for physicians who have an aura of confidence and can look an opposing attorney and the jury in the eye.

Attorneys suggest that the doctor make every effort to be memorable. Attorneys don't want a dry, boring presentation. They want you to ask the judge if you can approach the jury for a detailed explanation and get close to the jury members. The attorneys want you to get off the witness chair and to move to an anatomical drawing to point out the medical issues and situation involved with the plaintiff or defendant. It is always helpful to use models and props that provide a visual explanation of the medical situation for the plaintiff or defendant. These are far more effective than a mere verbal description or using a complex artist drawing.

Another thing to remember for doctors wanting to be expert witnesses is to talk slowly. If you talk too fast, you run the risk of the jury not being able to understand your testimony.

Attorneys also look for promptness in making a report after the records have been reviewed or the patient has been examined. The other attorney may be contacting your office to take your deposition. If you don't make yourself available, the other attorney may make a "motion to compel," which can actually force you to be deposed, or alternatively to prohibit your attorney from using you as his or her expert witness. If this happens too often, word will get out that you can't be counted on, and you will receive fewer calls to serve as an expert witness.

Bottom Line: Becoming an expert witness is serious business. It requires commitment, attention to detail, and the ability to communicate in public. Those who choose to follow this route can add to their professional and personal rewards, as well as their economic ones.

ADDITIONAL RESOURCES

- Technical Advisory Service for Attorneys (TASA), 800-523-2319, www.tasanet.com. TASA is a nationwide organization that accumulates expert information and provides it to attorneys for a fee. Physicians can contact them, fill out forms, supply a CV, and get listed with this organization. When a physician or expert is retained through TASA, the organization gets a fee for the referral.
- The American Association for Justice publishes an award-winning magazine called *TRIAL*. The association can be reached at 800-424-2725 or www.justice.org/. Advertising in this journal is the best way to reach large numbers of attorneys. Additional journals in which to advertise are *National Law Journal*, 800-274-2893, www.nlj.com/contact; and *American Lawyer*, 800-888-8300, www.americanlawyer.com.

- American Medical Forensic Specialists, 800-275-8903, www.amfs.com/become_expert.html. This organization is for both plaintiff and defense counsels who are looking for medical experts to address contested medical issues.
- MedWitness, 847-673-4422, www.medwitness.com. This firm provides medical experts in any field of medicine and surgery who will evaluate the case for merit and testify if merit exists.
- SEAK, 508-457-1111, http://seak.com/default.htm. This educational company provides customized training, seminars, publications, and professional directories for expert witnesses, physicians, attorneys, independent medical examiners, and workers' compensation professionals.

CHAPTER 9

Public Speaking for the Healthcare Professional: Part I — Preparing for the Program

Neil Baum, MD

"People's number one fear is public speaking. Number two is death. This means to the average person, if you go to a funeral, you're better off in the casket than doing the eulogy."

— Jerry Seinfeld

Most doctors and healthcare professionals pride themselves on being good communicators. After all, that is how we take a history, discuss our findings with our patients, and then provide them with advice for restoring or maintaining their health. Except for bedside presentations to faculty or a presentation at grand rounds, we have received little training on public speaking. Except for those doctors who have had formal media training, few of us are polished or comfortable in front of the TV camera.

For the most part, public speaking is a learned skill, and with just a little practice and preparation all of us can become good or even excellent public speakers. As a result, we can learn how to make a presentation in front of peers and lay audiences and not panic when we are in front of the TV camera. This chapter is intended to provide tips and techniques to enhance your public speaking skills.

SPEAKING BEFORE YOUR PEERS

Many of you will have attended a speaker training program sponsored by a pharmaceutical or a medical device manufacturing company. The company will make available a deck of PowerPoint slides and review with you the salient points that the company would like you to cover during your presentation to a group of your peers. Because of pharma guidelines, you will be asked not to deviate from the slides you were given. This usually means that you will not be allowed to delete slides or add your own slides if you are speaking at a program that is sponsored or supported by the company. But these restrictions need not limit your creativity and ability to make a compelling presentation that will educate your peers and make you a requested speaker on behalf of the sponsoring company.

The evening or dinner program with 10 to 15 of your peers is one of the most common examples of public speaking. This is one public speaking program that nearly all of us will have an opportunity to participate in. This will usually be industry sponsored, and you will use the slide deck provided to you by the pharmaceutical company or the medical device manufacturer whose product you are discussing.

There are three areas that are important to discuss: (1) preparing for the program; (2) the program; and (3) after the program is over.

BEFORE THE PROGRAM

You need to know and review your slide material thoroughly. It is important that you understand every slide in the deck and that you are comfortable with the material on the slides. I have found that the best speakers are so comfortable with the slides that they can discuss a slide without having to look at it. You want to avoid reading from the slides. Reading from the slides results in boredom and loss of interest on the part of the audience. If you are looking at the slides, you are not looking at the audience, and you will lose your ability to connect with them. The best speakers practice and rehearse their presentations. Your audience will be able to tell immediately if you took the slide deck directly from the CD and loaded it into a computer, and are giving the talk for the first time.

I suggest that you rehearse your talk several times out loud with all the props and audiovisual equipment you plan to use. This kind of preprogram practice will help to control the filler words such as "a" and "um." It is helpful to practice your slide transitions, your pauses, and even your breathing. You also need to know how long the program is going to last and how long you are to speak. I suggest that you practice with a timer and be absolutely certain that you do not exceed the allotted time. I have also found that most dinner meetings don't start on time as doctors are often delayed by unexpected events that occur in the practice. As a result, you may have to shorten your program, so you need to allow time for the unexpected.

AUDIOVISUAL REQUIREMENTS

Before the program, find out if the sponsoring company will provide the computer, projector, and screen. If not, let the planner know what you will bring and what kind of a computer you have, and make sure it is compatible with the projector. I found this out when I brought a MAC computer that didn't have a cable to connect to the LCD projector that was PC compatible. Also, although you probably won't need a microphone for a small group, it can be helpful if you are speaking in a loud restaurant.

It is highly recommended that you be the first to arrive at the program. This way you can be sure that the computer, projector, screen placement, and seating are all in order before the program. Nothing can sidetrack even the best-seasoned speaker like a problem with the computer or the equipment — that your flash drive with a USB port does not load into the pharmaceutical representative's computer or that your MAC-created program does not work on the representative's PC.

When you are one of the first to on the scene, you can greet some of the physician audience members as they arrive. I have found it is far easier to speak to a group of friends than to strangers. Also, if you can remember their names, you can call on them and ask their opinion or how they might manage a patient in their practice with the condition you are discussing. You might suggest that the meeting planner provide name tags for the attendees to place on their clothing when they enter the venue.

It is a good idea to find out the agenda from the pharmaceutical representative before the program. Are you speaking before the meal, which I believe is the least favorable idea as you are almost holding the doctors hostage to hear the program before they can eat; during the meal; or after the meal? My preference is to speak after the appetizer is served and the orders have been taken by the wait staff. This way the doctors have some food as well as some alcohol, and they are not starving. You can tell the waiters that they won't be disturbing you, and they should, if possible, avoid walking in front of the projector. Ideally, you should end before the desert arrives and use this time to conduct the questions and answer session. I also ask the company representative what the goals and objectives are for the program and make certain that I can deliver on his or her requests.

I usually like to prepare a handout for the program. I suggest that you don't distribute the handout before the program as you want your audience to focus on you and your slides and not on the handout. Further, tell the audience that you will be providing a handout of your presentation so that they will not waste time taking notes.

PREPARE AN INTRODUCTION

You need to prepare an introduction. I suggest you write your own introduction and send a copy by email to the person who will be introducing you. Tell the introducer that you are providing him or her with the introduction as a "suggestion" and that he or she is welcome to modify it. I have found that the majority of introducers or meeting planners are delighted to have the introduction and will use it just as you have written it. It is a good idea to bring a hard copy with you, as you can be sure that many of the introducers will not have downloaded a copy and remembered to bring it with them. Figure 1 is an example of the introduction that I use, and you are welcome to modify it.

> Dr. Neil Baum is a urologist in private practice in New Orleans, Louisiana. He is on the clinical faculty of both Tulane and LSU. For 10 years, he wrote the popular column "Marketing Dynamics" in *American Medical News*. For 15 years, he has written the marketing column, "Bottom Line," for *Urology Times*. He is the author of *Marketing Your Clinical Practice — Ethically, Effectively, and Economically*. This book has sold over 175,000 copies and has been translated into Spanish. His presentations are famous for providing practical ideas that each member of the audience can easily and inexpensively implement into their practices to increase the services that you offer your patients.
>
> Dr. Baum is also an amateur magician and usually includes at least one special effect in his presentations.
>
> His talk today is also the title of his new book, *Improving the Profitability and Productivity of Your Practice*. Please help me welcome Dr. Neil Baum.

FIGURE 1. Neil Baum bio and introduction.

SUMMARY

Public speaking is one of the best ways to market and promote your skills as a physician. It is an ethical way of communicating with your peers and an opportunity to showcase your speaking skills and your areas of interest or expertise. It all begins with conscientious preparation.

Public Speaking for the Healthcare Professional: Part II — The Program

THE OPENING

In Part I of this chapter, I mentioned the importance of the introduction. You have given a copy of a "suggested" introduction to the introducer, and he or she reads from your introduction and invites you to the front of the group. What you do and say in the next 30 to 60 seconds will set the stage for your program. It is at this moment that you will have the audience's undivided attention. You will use this time to establish your expertise as a spokesperson on the disease state, topic, or drug that you will be discussing.

You can begin by thanking the meeting planner, the pharmaceutical representative, or the group for the opportunity to speak. If you are from out of town, you can connect with the city you are visiting by mentioning some unique aspects of the city or region you previously researched on the Internet.

You can also begin with a statistic to capture the attention of the audience. For example, a talk on prostate cancer might begin with, "There are 26,000 deaths each year from prostate cancer. To give you an idea of how many people that is, can you imagine one-third of the capacity of the Superdome dying each year from a disease that can be detected and cured with an annual rectal exam and a PSA blood test?"

I suggest that you avoid clichés such as, "I'm delighted to be here." One exception would be if you can make that cliché humorous. For example, if I am in the northern part of the country in the summer months, I might begin by saying, “Most speakers will often start with how delighted they are to be here, and you often question their sincerity. However, if like me you are from New Orleans and the temperature is approaching 105 degrees with 95% humidity, you know when I say ‘I’m delighted to be here,’ I really mean it!”

Another example is the use of a story as an opener. A story about a patient or, better yet, a personal experience that unites with your topic is a great way of connecting with your audience members and capturing their attention. For example, if I am giving a talk on practice management and efficiency, I might tell the story of when I was called from a room three times to answer “emergency” phone calls from a patient who only requested his medical records. I talk about how devastated I was and how I subsequently put in place a system, which I describe to the audience, that ensured this would never happen again.

Another technique to gain the attention of the audience is promising the attendees you will tell them how they can get something they want. (This is often referred to as“WIIFY,” or What’s in It for You). A talk on practice productivity might begin by telling the audience members how they can increase their collections by $250,000. I promise to show them how they can increase the number of patients seen by just one patient an hour, and how this results in an increase in revenue of nearly one-quarter of a million dollars a year. The promise type of opener is sure to capture the attention of the attendees as it goes straight to their self-interest. I refer to this opening as “tuning into Station WIIFM, or What’s in It for Me!”

I highly recommend that you avoid beginning your program with an apology. Don’t mention to the audience the problems with the audiovisual equipment or the reason that you are late for the program. Members of the audience don’t care about these issues, and you will immediately lose their attention. They want to be educated, informed, and entertained. There’s no better way to do this than by having a compelling and captivating opening that begins immediately after the introducer welcomes you to the front of the audience.

Another caveat to avoid is the “royal I.” You should avoid the comment, “I’m here to talk about XYZ.” This places you in a superior position above the audience. This is a turn-off to audiences. Instead, I suggest you begin by saying, “The reason you are here is to learn about XYZ.” This places the audience on equal footing with the speaker, and attendees know that there is something in the presentation for them.

HOUSEKEEPING NOTES

I think it is helpful to tell the audience how long you plan to speak and that you will take questions during or at the end of the program. If the group is small (i.e., fewer than 20), I will often encourage the audience to ask questions during the program and not wait until the end. I find this to be a more conversational method of speaking as it generates more questions from the audience. My preference is to speak while the audience is eating, and I usually start after the waiters have taken the orders and the attendees have had their appetizers. I state that I will finish the program by the time they are ready for their dessert. I also mention that a handout will be distributed after the program is over so that they don't have to worry about taking notes, trying to eat, following the handout, and watching the speaker.

THE BODY OF THE PROGRAM

I suggest that you follow the rules set out by Aristotle nearly 2300 years ago and tell the audience what you are going to discuss, make your points, and lastly summarize. So I begin with the goals and objectives that I want to discuss during the program. This is usually limited to three or four objectives. Even with a talk sponsored by a pharmaceutical company where the slide deck is fixed and the speaker is not permitted to add or subtract slides, I can still begin by telling the audience what I want to accomplish during the program. For example, a talk on the treatment of androgen deficiency in men with localized prostate cancer might mention: (1) the history of testosterone in men with prostate cancer; (2) which men qualify for androgen supplements; and (3) how to monitor the patient with prostate cancer who receives hormone replacement therapy.

I like to begin a clinical program with a case history. I tell about one of my patients who had the specific problem and how I used the drug, treatment, or device to manage the case. I try to select a patient very similar to patients who would be seen by members of the audience.

I then go through the slides exactly as they have been provided by the pharmaceutical company. Most company slides have far too many words as well as difficult diagrams that are often difficult for the audience to follow. I make an effort to find one salient point on each slide, and focus the audience's attention on that single word, phrase, or sentence. I can do this in a small audience by walking over to the screen and pointing it out, or I can use the laser pointer to focus attention.

Let's be honest: most medical talks are boring and dry. Therefore, try to inject some energy and enthusiasm in the middle of the program. Every few minutes, I will ask a question, tell a story, or ask the audience a question. For example, during a program on practice management, I will relate a story about an unhappy patient and then ask a doctor how he or she might handle the disgruntled patient. This is a nice break from the main content of your presentation and reengages the audience. This will make for a more fun, interactive, and engaging program that will involve your audience.

It has been my observation that few physician speakers make use of visual aids during their program. They tend to rely heavily upon their slides. I have learned that you can keep the audience's attention focused on you if you make use of visual aids. For example, if I am speaking about urinary incontinence, I will use a balloon to demonstrate the bladder and the urethra. (I haven't figured out how to avoid the sound of flatus when I allow the balloon to deflate!)

Studies have repeatedly shown that there are more nerve endings from the eye to the brain than from the ear to the auditory portion of the central nervous system. Science has demonstrated that we receive 25 times as much attention from visual cues than from auditory ones. The Japanese proverb is true that one seeing is better than 100 times telling about!

A few suggestions regarding the use of visual aids:

1. Keep the visual aid out of sight until you are ready to use it. You don't want the audience to be looking at your visual aid when they should be focused on you or your slide material. I usually keep my visual aid under the table that supports my computer and the projector.
2. Make certain that your visual aids are large enough to be seen by everyone in the audience.
3. Do not hand out the visual aid to the audience during your program as the aid will certainly take the attendees' attention off you and your material.
4. When you have finished using the visual aid, put it away.

I go through my objectives, and then I let the audience know I am coming to the end of the program. For a dinner program, I try to time my ending just as the plates are being cleared and just before dessert is served. I then restate the objectives and how they might pertain to the audience members' patients and practices. At this time, I take questions from the audience if they weren't asked during the program. When a question is asked, I repeat the question so that everyone can hear it. (This also gives me a few seconds to think about and frame my answer!) If there are many questions, I state that I want to finish on time and will stay around after the meeting is over to answer any additional questions.

Here are a few suggestions regarding taking questions from the audience. When responding to a question, direct your attention to the person who asked the question. Then spend 20% of your time focusing on that person and 80% on the rest of the audience. If you focus only on the questioner, you create an atmosphere of a one-on-one conversation. You want to end your response to the questioner with your eyes on the group and not on the questioner. This will bridge or segue to the next question. After answering the first question, you can look out at the audience and generate additional questions by saying "Next question" or "Any other questions?"

After hearing a question, I have often used the comment, "That's a great question," but I suggest avoiding this comment. If after you answer the "great" question, you then go to the next questioner and don't mention that he or she has a "great question," the next questioner may feel slighted.

Avoid "Is that clear?" which is often used by a speaker during a presentation to check whether the audience understood what the speaker has just said. Unfortunately, the expression has two negative implications: (1) Uncertainty on the part of the speaker about the accuracy or credibility of the content; and (2) Doubt about the ability of the audience to comprehend or appreciate the content. Instead of casting negativity on the content, all you have to say is, "Do you have any questions?" With this query, you can ascertain whether your audience comprehends your material.

USE OF HUMOR

Most physicians attempt to use humor during their program. Let's be honest: few of us are a medical version of Jay Leno. If we were, we wouldn't be practicing medicine! However, if humor is used judiciously, like French chefs use seasoning, humor can do great things for a program. It can break the ice, drive home a point, and make you more likeable.

However, it can also backfire. I recall giving a program to large pharmaceutical audience. I put up a slide from *The Economist* that showed two camels in the mating position. My closing line was that pharmaceutical reps need to "hump to it" and get involved with their physicians and be value-added when it comes to their details with physicians. The meeting planner spoke to me afterwards and told me that he would never hire me again because of that comment. He said I had a great program, great material, and a good connection with the audience but this was over the top. I learned my lesson and made a promise to never use material that could potentially offend anyone in the audience. If you want to use humor, use self-deprecating humor as it is always the safest.

I then wrap up with my summary statement. This is the take-home message that I want each member of the audience to have. Again, when you say, "I would like to conclude my program with . . . ," you can be assured that this is that magical time when you have the complete attention of the audience. It has been shown that the last words the audience hears from the speaker are the ones remembered the longest. For example, a talk on staff motivation might conclude, "Remember, your staff members are the first people that patients encounter and the last ones that patients see before they leave the office. You can make sure that every patient has a positive experience with you and your practice by ensuring that your staff members are highly motivated and that you make every effort to recognize their accomplishments." (Hold up your hands and spread out your arms as you say . . .) "Thank you." You are certainly likely to receive applause and, maybe if your speech is truly exceptional, that sought after standing ovation!

BE SEATED

Franklin Delano Roosevelt summarized the art of speaking when he said, "Be sincere, be brief, and be seated!" When your time is up, it is time to sit down and return the program to the head of the organization, the meeting planner, or the pharmaceutical representative.

Bottom Line: There's a lot we can do to add punch and pizzazz to our presentations. In Part III, I will discuss what to do after the program is over.

Public Speaking for the Healthcare Professional: Part III — After the Program

You aren't done even if you receive a standing ovation!

It is after the program is over that you have a chance to mingle with members of the audience and get to know them, and more importantly allow them to know you. I, as so many dinner speakers, used to start putting away the computer and disconnecting the audio-visual equipment, ignoring the audience. Leave your equipment alone, and use this time to walk around, sit at the tables, and chat with the doctors. Many of the physicians will use this time to ask you about some of their cases, which may be related to the product or device you are discussing. Often the doctors will want to ask you about another medical problem in your area of interest or expertise.

PERSONAL FOLLOW-UP

I suggest that you take the names of the doctors and make notes. Then follow-up with a personal letter and include an article that you or another credible source has written. For example, if I am giving a program on the medical management of benign prostatic hyperplasia and after the program a doctor asks me guidelines for prostate-specific antigen (PSA) testing in older men, I will send him or her a note and an article from the American Cancer Society on the topic.

Now I am fully aware that very few physicians will read the entire article, so I highlight the one or two sentences in the article that mention PSA testing in older men. I then place a Post It note on the front page of the article directing the doctor's attention to the page that has the answer to his or her question (Figure 1). This simple follow-up technique makes you a value-added resource long after you step down from the podium or complete your presentation.

If I am speaking out of town on behalf of a pharmaceutical representative, I will email the article to the representative and suggest that he or she take it to the doctor's office on his or her next call. Again, this gives added value

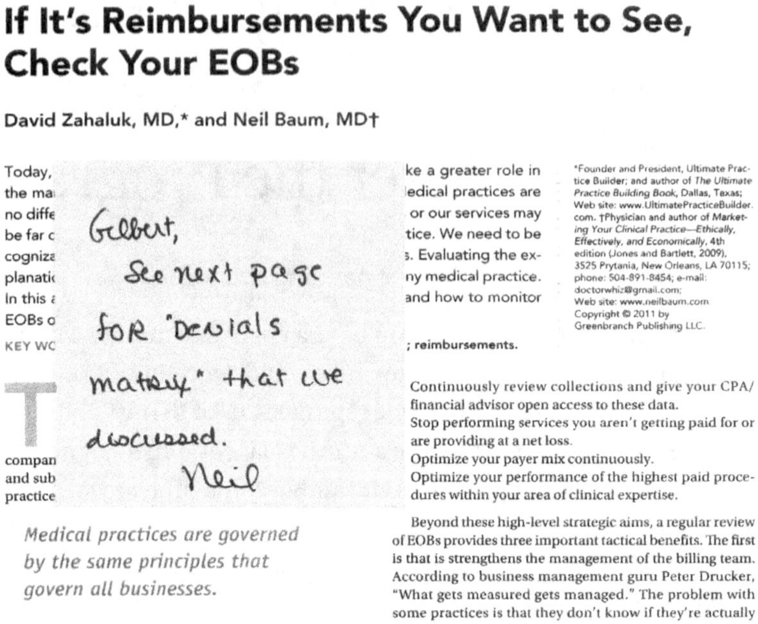
If It's Reimbursements You Want to See, Check Your EOBs

David Zahaluk, MD,* and Neil Baum, MD†

Today, ... ke a greater role in the ma... edical practices are no diffe... or our services may be far c... tice. We need to be cogniza... s. Evaluating the ex- planati... ny medical practice. In this ... and how to monitor EOBs o...

KEY WC... ; reimbursements.

*Founder and President, Ultimate Practice Builder; and author of *The Ultimate Practice Building Book*, Dallas, Texas; Web site: www.UltimatePracticeBuilder.com. †Physician and author of *Marketing Your Clinical Practice—Ethically, Effectively, and Economically*, 4th edition (Jones and Bartlett, 2009), 3525 Prytania, New Orleans, LA 70115; phone: 504-891-8454; e-mail: doctorwhiz@gmail.com; Web site: www.neilbaum.com. Copyright © 2011 by Greenbranch Publishing LLC.

Gilbert,
See next page for "Denials matrix" that we discussed.
Neil

T... compan... and sub... practice...

Continuously review collections and give your CPA/financial advisor open access to these data.
Stop performing services you aren't getting paid for or are providing at a net loss.
Optimize your payer mix continuously.
Optimize your performance of the highest paid procedures within your area of clinical expertise.

Medical practices are governed by the same principles that govern all businesses.

Beyond these high-level strategic aims, a regular review of EOBs provides three important tactical benefits. The first is that is strengthens the management of the billing team. According to business management guru Peter Drucker, "What gets measured gets managed." The problem with some practices is that they don't know if they're actually

FIGURE 1. Follow-up note to an audience member.

to the representative, and it is likely that he or she will tell others about your follow-through and invite you back.

BUSINESS CARDS AND HANDOUTS

After the program is the time to give out your business card. I suggest that you have an ample supply of business cards and give them out if someone asks for your contact information.

After the program is also the time to distribute your handout. This may consist of your PowerPoint slides but I think it is better to distribute a single page with the salient points that you would like the audience to take away from your program. Be certain that each piece of paper or your handout contains your name, address, phone numbers, and email and Web addresses.

Another suggestion is to collect the business cards of all the members of the audience and have a drawing. I will often give away a copy of one of my books but you can offer a small gift. This is a very unobtrusive way of getting the names of all those who attended your program.

GETTING FEEDBACK

I will always speak with the meeting planner or the pharmaceutical representative from the sponsoring company and ask what he or she thought of the program. I will ask for constructive criticism and how I might make the program better. I also ask if I was able to get across the most important points about the product or device.

Finally, I always send a thank you note to the meeting planner or the pharmaceutical representative thanking him or her for the invitation and offering to provide any additional information the rep might want for his or her doctors' practices.

EXPAND YOUR PLATFORM

If your talk is valuable to other venues, consider converting your presentation into an article. You usually have to include all of the medications and/or devices used to treat a certain condition if you want your article to be published in a credible medical journal.

If you do write an article, consider sharing it with your colleagues and your patients. You might also consider placing the article you write on your Web page. If you record your presentation, you can edit the video to less than 10 minutes and upload it to YouTube.[1]

Bottom Line: Public speaking before your peers can be a daunting process. However, it is an excellent method of communicating and educating your colleagues. You can make an impressive and compelling presentation by being prepared, practicing, and having a polished presentation. And remember, you aren't finished when your last slide is shown!

REFERENCE

1. Jackson R, Schneider A, Baum N. Social media networking: YouTube and search engine optimization. *J Med Pract Manage.* 2011;26:254-257.

CHAPTER 10

Public Speaking: Creating Presentations that Are Awe Inspiring Not Yawn Producing

MARSHEILA DEVAN AND NEIL BAUM, MD

Many physicians want to improve their public speaking skills. Here are some tips that can show you how to connect with your audience and make you a memorable presenter.

THE OPENING

We suggest that you open your presentation by listing the goals and objectives that you expect to accomplish during the program. This needs to be accomplished in the first 30 to 45 seconds of your program. If you want to attract the audience's attention, you have to use those few seconds in the beginning of the program to make that critical connection between you and the listeners. Find an engaging opener, or a "grabber," such as a question, a quote, a factoid, or an anecdote that will get the audience involved. For example, I (NB) have opened a program on prostate cancer with the statistic that 40,000 men, which is half the capacity of the Super Dome in New Orleans, die each year from prostate cancer.

Next, you want to bring the "value" to your audience in the very beginning of your program. An example of value is that you will provide information and examples to physicians on managing their patients with a certain problem in a noninvasive and cost-effective fashion. Think about the value that you bring to the program. If it is just a meeting and dinner but offers no value, you will not be able to engage your audience.

We recommend thinking about "Station WIIFM," or "What's in It for Me." You are asking the members of your audience to pay attention to your presentation, and they need to know from the very beginning of your program that there is a benefit to them for listening. Be sure to state your purpose as well during the opening few seconds. Adult learners want to know why they are there. It may be helpful to offer a case study or a patient scenario that the audience members may recognize as similar to patients in their practice.

After the opening, explain your agenda. Let's be honest; doctors are tortured by lots of meetings and pharma programs. Tell the audience exactly what's going to happen. For example, you might say, "We will have dinner, I will speak during [or after] your meal, and we will be done on time."

Also tell the audience how you will be managing the question and answer session. Will you take time at the end of the program for Q and A, will you take questions and interruptions during the program, or will you remain after the program is over to answer any questions? If you plan to distribute a handout, let the audience know. If the talk is accessible on the Internet, be sure to point that out.

Ultimately, your agenda is building a roadmap for your audience. You are letting the audience know where you are going to take them by giving them an overview.

It is important to also provide the housekeeping rules, perhaps suggesting that even doctors either turn off their cell phones or at least switch them to vibration mode.

PRESENTING YOUR PROGRAM

Your physical delivery skills such as eye contact, voice, gestures, posture, movement, and limiting vocal pauses can enhance and reinforce your message. These practical techniques can make the difference between a good or great presenter.

Eye contact is one of the best ways to keep people listening. What the face and eyes say is tremendously important for communication. This is a way for you to say to everyone in the audience, "You are important." Connect with one set of eyes, instead of scanning the entire audience. Make a verbal point while looking at one person, and then move on. Good eye contact is equated with openness and honesty. Be sure to avoid the tendency to ping-pong back and forth to the same people in the audience, as this gives the impression that they are the only ones that are important.

The use of vocal dynamics will engage the listener with animation and a varied pace. Raising the volume will provide natural animation to your voice, which engages the listeners' ears. Avoid a flat, noninflected voice that will put audience members to sleep or lose their attention.

"What do I do with my hands?" is a common concern of many presenters. Let your hands complement your language and vocal expressions naturally. Use open hand gestures that are natural to you and appropriate to your topic. When hands are not in use, they should fall naturally to your sides. Keep your hands apart as much as possible to keep your body posture open. Common gestures to avoid are the "clamp-on" to the podium and "frozen elbows" with the laser pointer, which is used to prevent a tremor at the end of the pointer.

A grounded stance with deliberate movement communicates professionalism and presence. Feet should be hip-width apart and firmly on the floor, with your weight evenly balanced. This provides a strong, grounded base.

Have you ever lost your train of thought? It's common to fill that space with vocalizing an "um" or "ah." To get rid of vocal pauses, replace them with silence. Practice pausing before speaking; this will help to limit vocal pauses. It may be appropriate to silently review your notes or your visual support materials in order to find your place.

Finally, your image should be appropriate for you and for the situation. Dress with professionalism and respect for your audience. Following these tips will enhance and support your message.

THE CLOSING

You want to end your program with a summary of the key learning points and a "call to action," or a power close. This is where you wind back to your opening remarks and restate what you said at the beginning. For example, you might say, "I hope you can see that this treatment will improve the quality of life of your patients, that the safety profile is very favorable, and that the treatment is covered by most insurance companies." Another way to close is by using a factoid or something memorable.

If you opened your program with a case study, you might finish your program with discussing how you resolved the medical problem. You might want to finish by offering something of value such as a handout, an article, or a patient education piece that will help embellish your message for patients in the doctors' practice.

Bottom Line: Whether you are speaking one-on-one, to a small group, or to a large audience, you want your peers and your audience to remember your message. You want the audience to remember your key points long after you have left the podium. By using a few of the techniques described in this chapter, you will be able to make that memorable presentation. So speak up!

CHAPTER 11

Public Speaking: Managing Challenging People and Situations

Neil Baum, MD, and Leonarda Boughton

As someone who has given several thousand presentations, I (N.B.) have on occasion encountered difficult audience members. For example, at one speaking engagement, which was at a dinner meeting accompanied by alcohol, two members of the audience were loudly carrying on a conversation, making it difficult for the rest of the audience to hear my presentation. I first asked them if they would lower their voices so others could hear, and then, when I could see that the audience was getting upset with them, I asked the meeting planner if she would ask them to leave the room to talk. The disrupters refused to leave and even raised their voices, making it impossible for the audience to hear the program. In exasperation, I asked the meeting planner if the presentation could be terminated, and she agreed. This was not handled as effectively as one would have liked.

The example above is an extreme one and hopefully not very common, but it does bring up a recurring question: *How do you deal with difficult people and situations?* Most presenters have a horror story about that one person who tried to derail their talk. They share their stories with great relish. However, at the time, the disruption was not as amusing and was most unwelcome. Knowing how to manage challenging dynamics is key to running a successful presentation. The reality is that you can choose your subject matter but you can't always choose your audience! The good news is that there are practical ways to work with the even the most challenging participants. Small disruptions are to be expected when you present, especially to medical audiences. It's crucial to defuse them before they become a problem. A difficult audience member is a person who is not paying attention, who is disengaged, or who is being disruptive. A heckler is someone who interrupts the speaker with awkward or hostile questions or comments. It is important to realize that people show up for presentations with their own agendas and concerns. Getting them on board with your presentation style is part of the challenge — to persuade them that listening to you is worth their time and attention.

NIP IT IN THE BUD! HOW TO AVOID DISRUPTIONS FROM THE START

Give yourself a winning advantage by doing the necessary preparation beforehand. We suggest that you arrive early to check the physical space where you will be speaking. Are the tables and chairs placed as planned? To lessen distraction, arrange the room so that latecomers enter and sit at the back of the room so as not disrupt those who are seated close to the front. How are the lighting and temperature of the room? Just like Goldilocks and the porridge, they should be just right! Are window shades closed to keep audience attention focused inside the room? Check audiovisual equipment and visual aids, and do sound checks with and without a microphone.

Ask someone to help you gauge the volume of your voice so that those in the back can clearly hear your presentation. On a scale from 1 to 10, how loud do you sound? Remember, you always sound louder to yourself. Your voice is one of the most powerful tools you have for grabbing and maintaining audience attention. Speaking with an animated and energetic voice leads to an interested and engaged audience. Enthusiasm is contagious, so make sure yours is worth catching! A full-volume voice gives the impression of confidence and conviction. On the other hand, a weak, monotone voice is the quickest way to lose the audience's attention and allow for the possibility of disengagement and boredom, which may lead to all sorts of other trouble. Starting out strong is key to a successful program and will help minimize disruptions.

Arriving early also gives you the opportunity to meet and greet audience members. The seemingly unimportant small talk at the beginning of a program often provides insights about your group and helps establish rapport. Finding commonalities to weave into the presentation can help personalize the message. Get a feeling for who they are and what they know. You will impress the audience if you can remember a few of their names and address them personally during the presentation.

SET EXPECTATIONS IN ADVANCE

It's not enough to simply know your material. You must manage the process:

- Start on time to avoid rewarding tardiness.
- Make time visible by posting start and end times and the times that breaks will take place.
- Assign someone to brief late arrivals.

Set expectations from the start:

- Request that cell phones be turned off prior to beginning your presentation.
- Let your audience know the length of the talk, what to expect, when to participate, and when to ask questions.
- Whenever possible, specifically adapt the program so that the audience becomes invested in your presentation. At the beginning of the program, ask the audience, especially if you are speaking to a lay audience, what they would like to take away from the presentation. Cater to their needs and interests within the boundaries of your topic. Creating a goals chart by jotting down their feedback is a way of ensuring relevance to the group and avoiding mistaken expectations. This simple step makes a big difference in connecting you to your audience and helping them feel more involved in your presentation.

Start with a bang! Make sure to engage the audience right from the start. Your only chance to make a strong first impression is at the beginning. Piquing their interest with an engaging opening will set the perfect tone. Climbing back from a dull beginning is very hard to do.

BE AN OBSERVER

Listen and watch for subtle, nonverbal cues. Be sensitive to what you observe your audience doing. Are they restless, or do they appear eager to listen? Are any slouching or looking at their phone? Are they smiling or frowning? Depending on their behavior, you should inject more or less energy into your delivery. Are there side conversations? Pay attention to any lull in their interest as a signal to shift gears. For example, if there appears to be a lack of attention from the audience, consider lowering your voice to an almost inaudible whisper, which generally results in audience members looking up from their cell phone, the handout, or a side conversation and paying attention to the speaker. These are all potent tools to gain attention. Use eye contact to connect with audience members. We suggest that you move from where you are standing to be closer to those who are less engaged. Raise the volume and animation of your voice if you see attention slipping. To shift audience dynamics, use change-ups, such as asking questions and involving the audience in the conversation. For long programs, create an exercise by breaking the audience into small groups, or offer a short reprieve by allowing the audience to stand up, move around, or go to the restroom. Your ultimate success may depend on how well you observe and adapt to the audience's reaction. Modifying your presentation when necessary will make all of the difference.

ADDRESS THE SITUATION

Sometimes, no matter how well prepared or attentive you are, you may still get unexpected and unwelcomed audience reactions. Correctly judging your response requires reading their body language and sensing their mood. For example, if you notice that an audience member is not paying attention, use eye contact to connect with them. It may be all that is needed to bring their attention back. If you and the audience are distracted by a side conversation, walk over to that part of the room. Your physical presence alone often will deter side conversations. Wherever you move, the eyes of the audience will follow. This spotlight on that part of the room will make them aware that they are acting separately from the group and drawing attention. Usually, words are unnecessary. Looking at a disruptive person directly is more aggressive and should be considered only if a stronger approach is needed. Another effective technique to shift the group dynamic is to have the audience break into small groups and work on an exercise. Prepare several exercises before your presentation so you have them ready when a change-up is needed. For example, in the case of the dinner meeting described above, nonverbal cues were not enough, and asking the disruptive parties to be quiet also was ineffective. In this scenario, breaking into groups with an exercise could have been a very helpful tactic in splitting up that disruptive duo. Placing them in different groups at different tables would be a sure-fire way to cut their conversation, while allowing them to save face. It's an old technique, but very effective!

DEAL DIRECTLY

When someone is being clearly disruptive, and all the more subtle attempts have failed, take a more direct approach. First and most importantly, be detached and don't take it personally. Remaining neutral and objective is to your best advantage. Ask questions to gain insight. Usually what a heckler wants more than anything is your attention. Ask him or her, "Is there something you'd like to comment on?" Simply voicing the concerns may take care of the situation and shed light on the problem, giving the presenter the opportunity to resolve it. If the question is relevant, answer it and move on. If the comment is off-topic, suggest talking about it after the program or encourage the person(s) to leave in order to take care of the matter outside of the room. If the question is hostile or combative, paraphrase the question to neutralize the language and remove the hostility from the tone.

Be deliberate with your eye contact, visually connect with the heckler briefly, and then make eye contact with another participant to end the one-on-one conversation. When finished answering, ask the group, "Does anyone else have an alternate perspective that they'd like to share?" If taking the reins from the heckler does not work, refer to the agenda by saying, "We have a lot of material to cover, I'd rather not get sidetracked. Let's continue this conversation at the break and move on to the next topic."

At the break, go directly to the complainer, and address the issue and look for ways to resolve it immediately. When dealing with a heckler, avoid saying anything critical, as this will only escalate the problem and reflect poorly on you. Be level-headed, positive, and in charge. Once you go toe-to-toe with someone who is bothered, you set up a competitive dynamic. You will lose credibility if your temper flares. Be detached and impersonal. As a speaker, you are fulfilling a role. Reduce the potency of a negative participant's anger by knowing the cause of the person's discontent and making him or her feel heard and respected.

As a final resort, if the disgruntled person continues to take attention away from you, invite him or her to leave in a decisive voice. One way of doing this is to suggest, "You don't really want to be here, do you? Let's make a deal, stay for another 10 minutes, and if after that time you would still like to go, please feel free." Then change the dynamic — break into groups for an exercise, ask questions, shift things up. Reenergize the room with a creative change-up. When people get bored, they begin to drift and may become disruptive.

In the case of what happened at the dinner meeting, all of these suggestions may have helped dissipate what became a completely distracting and disrespectful side conversation. Catching it early would have been the best bet. However, once in a while you may just get a couple of *bad* lemons!

TURN LEMONS INTO LEMONADE

Sometimes the most challenging participants end up being the most passionate and engaged audience members when they feel listened to and have their contributions valued. Remember that disruptive behavior is the result of an unmet need. The best strategy is a sense of humor and an understanding of what is propelling the behavior. The next time you encounter a difficult audience member, try following the above steps: Listen. Address. Deal. And smile!

Bottom Line: Public speaking is an art form. Like any art form, public speaking requires practice. Even practiced and seasoned speakers will encounter a disruptive audience member. You will be a hero to the rest of the audience if you can move the disruptive member of the audience from antagonism to affability. So speak up, and enjoy the podium.

CHAPTER 12

Controlling Public Speaking Jitters: Making the Butterflies Fly in Formation

Hannah Harvey, PhD, and Neil Baum, MD

THE STRESS CYCLE

To understand the impact that stress has on public speaking, we need to go back thousands of years to the time when humans lived in a cave and had to worry about the saber tooth tiger that might enter the cave and hurt them and their families. Primitive humans developed a fight-or-flight response, which prepared them to fight the tiger or to flee and run from the cave to protect their families. When this primitive response is elicited these days in a person who perceives a threat or danger — such as getting up to make a speech to a group he or she has never met before — several events take place. With the perception of imminent danger, the nerve cells release chemicals such as adrenaline, noradrenalin, and cortisol into the bloodstream.

The release of these chemicals triggers blood flow away from the digestive tract and pelvis into the muscles that control the limbs, making it possible to run away from the danger. Heart and respiratory rates also increase, providing the additional oxygen necessary to make those legs run faster than the tiger. Other changes include dilated pupils, improved eyesight, increased awareness, and the ability to be clearly focused on getting out of harm's way. The immune system is activated, and even the ability to perceive pain is diminished, making it possible to get out of danger even if you have been injured by a bite from the tiger.

This hardwired stress response is your body's way of protecting you from danger. If the stress response is working properly, it helps you stay focused, energetic, and alert, and ready to channel that negative stress into good stress (i.e., eustress) and give an outstanding presentation. In an emergency, this same stress response can save your life, giving you increased physical strength to protect yourself and loved ones.

When the fight-or-flight reaction is triggered, the human body is flooded with cortisol and adrenaline, making you strong and ready to take on the danger of that saber-toothed tiger at the opening of the cave. It is this very reaction that allows a soccer mom to pick up a car off a trapped child — something she would not normally be able to accomplish under nonstressed conditions. So the fight-or-flight response helps to preserve our species and protect us from outside dangers and stressors. When we face very real dangers to our physical survival, the fight-or-flight response is invaluable. It is this same fight-or-flight response that is elicited when we are introduced to make a presentation, and we move from the audience or from behind the curtain to the podium.

STRESS RELIEF

The first step in successful stress relief is the recognition that stress is part and parcel of the public speaking process. Public speaking is known to be the greatest fear, even greater than the fear of death,[1] experienced by nearly everyone before giving a speech in public, especially if the speaker does not know the people in the audience. The symptoms of excessive stress include a fast heartbeat, fast breathing, sweaty palms and sweating in general, back pain, a stiff neck or tight shoulders, and urinary symptoms such as frequency and urgency.

Controlling the Butterflies

To tame the butterflies associated with public speaking you must perform an "anxiety bypass." In essence, you are training your body not to overcome the anxiety, but to channel the powerful physical responses into a more energized speech or performance. Just as an athlete cannot expect to run a proper race without stretching and training, you cannot expect to speak clearly and effectively in public without a vocal–physical warm-up. A warm-up consists of rehearsal using cognitive behavioral training techniques, the first steps of which involve relaxing and limbering up your body.

Warming up your whole body involves limbering up your spine, shoulders, arms, and legs; warming up your voice involves relaxing and stretching the smaller facial and jaw muscles as well as your vocal chords, or the vocal folds, located in your trachea. We recommend warming up large muscles first (your full body), then moving to warm up the smaller vocal-oriented muscles. The following sections describe a few techniques that professional actors and storytellers use when preparing to speak in public.

Full-body Stretches

Begin the stretching exercises by standing up and placing your feet about shoulder width apart, microbending your knees so that they do not lock while you stand (this helps you avoid passing out as you stretch!). Roll your shoulders back a few times. Take your hands and clasp them behind your back, roll your shoulders back again, and stretch down to the floor with your clasped hands — you will feel a good stretch again in your shoulders and upper chest. Roll your head from one shoulder, down to your chest, then to the opposite shoulder, then reverse. Avoid rolling your head all the way back, though, because this can damage your voice.

Stretch your hands up toward the ceiling, keeping the microbend in your knees — stretch all the way to the tips of your fingers. Reach with your right hand toward the left wall, placing your left hand on your hip to stabilize your balance. Repeat with your left arm, stretching the left hand toward the right wall with your right hand on your hip. You should feel this stretch all along the sides of your torso.

Bring both hands back up, stretching with the tips of your fingers toward the ceiling. Drop your head, let your shoulders droop, and follow the weight of your head and dangling arms to let your upper body dangle toward the ground, *keeping your knees bent.* In her book *Freeing the Natural Voice,* professional vocal coach Kristin Linklater suggests fully relaxing your neck in this position by nodding your head while letting it droop.[2]

The tendency when you come back upright is to lead with your head — but this re-strains all the lovely neck muscles you have just relaxed! Instead, beginning with the base of your spine, roll yourself back up one vertebra at a time, saving your neck and head for last. Repeat this stretch a few times, fingers to the ceiling, then release your hands, arms, head, neck, and shoulders, and allow yourself to droop to the ground, then roll yourself back up. This is called "taking yourself to zero," a way not only to relax your muscles but also to get them ready to spring to action — you are now poised in a state of balance.

Vocal–Physical Stretches

Yawns can work wonders to stretch and relax your jaw muscles — and you can make yourself yawn at any time. The key in using yawns to relax your jaw is to not chomp or bite down on the yawn at its conclusion — this tenses your muscles back up and defeats the purpose of this relaxing stretch. Try yawning as wide as you can, adding that good yawning sound as you open your mouth, and then, as you begin to close your mouth, leave your lips about an inch apart (Linklater recommends placing two fingers into your mouth to stop yourself from fully closing your mouth).

Linklater also recommends a tongue stretch. Linklater suggests placing the tip of your tongue behind your bottom front teeth and pushing outward with the middle of your tongue. Your middle tongue will extend out of your mouth, while the tip of your tongue remains behind your bottom teeth. You should feel the stretch all the way to the base of the tongue, deep in your throat where the trachea resides. This is a lovely stretch, but be warned: you can sprain your tongue doing this stretch too much, so three or four stretches will do it!

Massaging your jaw muscles is also useful. Take both hands and place your fingers on either side of your jaw, and while relaxing your mouth (let your lips part and your jaw hang loose) gently massage your jaw with circular motions, moving from the jaw hinges down to your chin, around to your upper lip and cheeks, and back to your jaw hinges.

Humming is a safe and effective way to warm up your vocal folds, especially in the morning. Apart from humming your favorite tune, making the sound *mmm-wow, mmm-wow* helps to stretch both your facial and vocal muscles. Try to open your mouth to its fullest extent when articulating "wow" — you'll feel the stretch.

Another useful warm-up is to pair consonant sounds with vowel sounds: *buh buh buh ba, cuh cuh cuh ca, duh duh duh da . . .*

Getting Oxygen in All Parts of the Lungs

To get oxygen deep into your lungs, roll your shoulders back, opening the chest cavity. Many of us breathe from our chests throughout the day, giving our lungs only short, shallow breaths and not the deep breath needed to support your speech. Take a deep breath, allowing your belly to expand as you inhale — you will feel your diaphragm muscles (resting at the bottom of your lungs) stretch as you take air into your full lungs. Remembering to breathe from your diaphragm: take deep breaths but don't hold your breath. Try to make the exhalation as long as the inhalation.

Increasing Endorphins

The easiest way to increase endorphins is to jog in place. Endorphins are some of the most potent painkillers but they also help oxygenate your muscles and increase the oxygen in all areas of your lungs.

BE PREPARED: NOT JUST A BOY SCOUT MOTTO!

Even experienced surgeons get nervous before they touch a scalpel to a patient, and the most practiced actor or storyteller still feels his or her heart race before stepping out on the stage. However, with years of preparation, the surgeon becomes very comfortable providing care for his or her patient. The same applies to public speaking. If you are comfortable with your material, you have rehearsed, and you are warmed up, you will be in a much more relaxed state of mind and ready to give an outstanding program.

Visualization and Self-Talk

One way to help break away from your scripted speech and become more familiar with your talk is to "visualize" your speech or story. Visualization involves breaking your talk down into key movements or themes, and then concretely visualizing those themes so that you "see" each of the mini-stories you are telling in the overall "story" of your presentation.

Use the room itself to help you isolate and focus these themes. Begin your introduction addressing the full audience. For the first theme or topic, primarily address the left side of the room; for the second, address the middle of the room; for the third, address the right. At your conclusion, address the whole room once more. Rehearsing with this "blocking" (an acting term) will help you remember where you are in your speech as you move from point to point.

Jack Nicklaus, one of the most famous professional golfers of all time, used to prepare for big tournaments by closing his eyes and playing the 18-hole course in his mind, actually visualizing the club selection, the drive, the approach shot, and putting on each hole. You can do the same thing by closing your eyes and see the audience and see in your mind's eye their reaction to your presentation.

Visit the Venue

Test takers are often advised to study where they will be taking the examination. This is based on the positive relationship between knowledge learned in a place and knowledge remembered or recalled. We suggest that you do the same thing and become familiar with the venue where you will be speaking. You want to be familiar with the location of the podium, the kind of microphone you will be using, where the teleprompter will be if you are provided with one, and where you will enter after your introduction. If you just show up minutes before the presentation, you can expect to be more anxious and nervous because of the unfamiliarity of the venue. A few minutes to become familiar with the lighting, the stage, the microphone, and the audiovisual equipment will certainly help calm those butterflies.

Bottom Line: Public speaking is an art just like medicine. With preparation and proper warm-up, the butterflies can be coaxed to fly in formation. You can expect anxiety before a speaking engagement but with preparation and a few exercises, you will calm the jitters and just may get that standing ovation.

REFERENCES

1. Zimbardo P. *Shyness: What It Is, What To Do About It.* Berkeley, CA: Perseus Books, 1977.
2. Linklater K. *Freeing the Natural Voice: Imagery and Art in the Practice of Voice and Language.* Berkeley, CA: Drama Publishers, 2006.

CHAPTER 13

Why Doctors Should Seek Publicity: 15+ Reasons to Seek Media Attention

NEIL BAUM, MD

What are the obvious reasons to desire to attract publicity? It is a fact: doctors' reimbursements are going south, and overhead expenses are headed north. This translates into a decrease in the size of your bank account. The trend today is for doctors to become employed by hospitals, which essentially leaves them with a fixed salary. An acceptable solution is to find ancillary income, and one way to do that is to become famous and attract added income from your fame and public recognition.

Publicity allows you to become noticed and to ethically send your message to others who need your services and expertise. This results in people developing a relationship with you, liking you, and then believing in you. If they believe in you, then they believe you can solve their healthcare problems. Those who hear your message may become your patients.

Here are 15+ reasons doctors should seek publicity:

1. **Achieving fame is a challenge.** It is every bit as difficult as achieving admission into medical school. No one said publicity was easy. If it was easy, then everyone would be seeking publicity, and the rewards wouldn't be as great.
2. **Publicity is exciting.** There are few things as exciting as introducing yourself to the media of a television program and then appearing on a three- to five-minute segment on the evening news in your community. Contacting a local reporter from your hometown paper and having a story written about you and your practice is also a thrill that is hard to describe. And when you do this a few times and have samples to show the major television networks, you can achieve that rare status of being on the "Today Show" or "Good Morning America."

3. **Achieving publicity makes you feel important.** An appearance on TV or the radio or an article in a publication makes you visible. You can expect that after your appearance or the publication of your article, people will mention that they saw you on TV or heard you on the radio. Yes it is nice to be a healer and to feel a sense of satisfaction by providing medical care to our patients, but there is also a feeling of great satisfaction and an enhancement of self-esteem to being a darling of the media.
4. **Publicity builds confidence.** Everyone becomes anxious and nervous when they are in front of the camera and the lights are on. It's natural to feel that way. However, after a few appearances, you develop a sense of confidence that ultimately makes you comfortable when you are "on the air."
5. **Publicity helps you define your niche or area of expertise.** I'm a urologist. I can't do cancer surgery, robotic surgery, vas reversals, or kidney transplants. It's impossible to be an expert in everything. However, you can find one thing and do it very well, and others will recognize your expertise if you narrow your niche. That's why I have selected urinary incontinence as my niche. I enjoy taking care of women. I enjoy the surgery. I feel truly gratified when a woman who was wearing diapers becomes diaper-free! Publicity doesn't mean you can't do all the procedures you are comfortable doing and treat all the patients you have training to treat. However, if you want to become famous, select one area and become the expert in your community, your region, or in the nation. Remember you can have everything you want if you position yourself to be a real expert.
6. **Creating publicity helps you overcome obstacles.** Doctors are used to instant gratification. A woman has a urinary tract infection. She receives antibiotics and soon gets well. A patient fractures his or her hip, the doctor operates and pins the hip, the patient starts rehabilitation, and in a few weeks the patient is walking again. Publicity is not that easy. You contact the TV station or a reporter by phone, and leave a message regarding a possible story. The station or the reporter doesn't call you back. You send an email that goes unanswered. You send a FedEx package with your story or idea, and you don't get a response. Most of us, myself included, get discouraged. The publicity experts opine that it takes on average seven attempts to reach the media before you receive a response. Often, a busy doctor will decide

that it takes too much effort and the return on the investment is too low to continue to reach out to the media. Yes, there are obstacles, but learning the process gives you faith that you can overcome them.

7. **Achieving publicity encourages you to leave your comfort zone.** Let me be candid: doctors are creatures of their comfort zone. We don't like anything that deviates from the *status quo*. We often use the same medications, the same procedures, and the same treatment options that we learned during our training. Few of us are early adopters that implement the latest and greatest items promoted by pharma and vendors of new devices. There is nothing more anxiety provoking than public speaking or working with the media. And doing so initially will be outside the comfort zone of most doctors. However, when you do it often, you become more comfortable. Certainly you can expect to have butterflies in the gut before you sit in front of the camera, but with enough practice, you can get the butterflies to fly in formation!
8. **Publicity makes you prioritize your time and your to-do list.** The time commitment for interacting with the media can be daunting. Doctors are very busy professionals, and our first commitment is to our patients. However, with proper use of our time and with delegation of responsibilities, we can accomplish both media and medicine. Yes, you will have to return calls promptly, answer emails, write content for your Web site, create videos for YouTube, and write your book. However, if you prioritize and use your time wisely, you really can do it all.
9. **Publicity is an ethical way to promote yourself.** Doctors are not very good at self-promotion. For the most part, we are modest and reserved. However, achieving publicity is a way to showcase your skills, your expertise, and your personality.
10. **Publicity is ethical marketing.** Your peers can't fault you for appearing on TV. You don't violate the Hippocratic Oath by writing an article for a local publication. Publicity is to be differentiated from advertising. Advertising is what you pay for and often rankles with your colleagues. However, if a reporter comes to you for an interview about something that you offer your patients, that puts you in a different light. Instead of being a pariah, you may become admired by your fellow physicians.
11. **Publicity gives you permission to make money from your message.** I can't promise you that the phone will ring right after you give a talk to a service club or appear on a local radio station. But I can assure you that if you become a media darling, others will soon recognize

your areas of medical interest and expertise, and will be contacting you to help solve their medical problem(s).

12. **Publicity is a hedge against declining reimbursements.** The Affordable Care Act is sure to be implemented, and you can expect that reimbursements are going to go south. Doctors are searching for ancillary income. There are so many spinoffs from achieving publicity. If you become really good at it, you can have your own talk show, a newsletter that people will pay for, and/or a book you can sell on Amazon and in bookstores.
13. **Publicity teaches you to overcome your fear of public speaking.** It has been said that the greatest fear people have is public speaking. Most people would rather die than get up in front of an audience. As Jerry Seinfeld so poignantly said, "That means for most people they would rather be in the coffin than having to stand up and give the eulogy!" Public speaking is a tremendous way to start your quest for local fame. There are so many ways to get started. Service clubs, church groups, and schools are always looking for physicians to come and speak to their organizations. With practice, you will overcome your fear. And when you get good at public speaking, you will be ready to move on to larger venues like radio and TV.
14. **Publicity is a new direction in addition to your traditional medical practice.** Let's be honest. If you happen to be a urologist, seeing one more patient with a urinary tract infection, prostate infection, or overactive bladder gets a little boring after you have seen several thousand of these cases. But becoming famous and becoming a media darling or a top-selling author will move your medical career into a new and exciting direction.
15. **You can become a big fish in a bigger sea.** Many of us are big fish in our own community and in our own hospital. But publicity teaches us to swim in the ocean of Internet, social media, and national TV and print publications.

15+. **Publicity can be fun, and it can make your dreams come true.** Walt Disney said, "If you can dream it, you can do it." Many of us dream of being famous and just don't know how to go about it.

Bottom Line: Doctors are for the most part uncomfortable seeking publicity. However, there are reasons that doctors should seek publicity for their practices. While not easy to do, it is very exciting and rewarding when you get comfortable with the media and publicity. I suggest that you follow these suggestions, and you just might be the next Sanjay Gupta or Dr. Oz!

CHAPTER 14

How I Became a Medical Advisor for TV and Movies

Walter Dishell, MD, and Neil Baum, MD

GETTING STARTED

Dr. Walter Dishell was the chief resident in Head and Neck Surgery at UCLA. His wife worked with the wife of a TV producer who was working on a pilot called "Medical Center." Dishell and his wife ran into the producer, Frank Glicksman, in a restaurant, where he told them that he was working on a show about UCLA Medical Center and mentioned his frustration that every attempt to communicate with or obtain information from the medical center resulted in a dead end, and that his calls were never returned. When he learned that Dishell worked in the medical center, he asked him if he would have dinner with him and his partner. Shortly thereafter, Dishell's new career as a medical advisor was born.

The producers needed medical advice to help them with the pilot. They offered compensation of $75 per hour, which at the time (1969) was a considerable amount for a surgical resident. Dishell provided the medical advice for the pilot. The show was picked up by CBS and ran for seven years.

After completing his residency, Dishell was inducted into the Air Force. He was stationed in Dayton, Ohio, for two years, during which he received a TV script every day by special delivery. He would edit and revise the script and write all of the medical dialogue. Then at 8 PM Eastern Time every evening, he would call MGM studios for their 5 PM story meeting with the writers. Dishell was given dramatic story ideas for the show, and then it was his job to figure out medical situations and diseases to match the plot, using ideas from his own practice or from stories from his medical colleagues and friends. Dishell was involved in every show from the initial outline through the final draft of the script.

When "M*A*S*H" came to CBS in 1971, Dishell was asked to become the medical advisor for that show as well. "M*A*S*H" became one of the longest running and most popular shows in television history. Dishell was one of the few people who worked on the show for all 11 years, from the first episode to the last one. It was, and still is, the most watched show in the history of television.

When "Medical Center" went off the air, the producers were asked to create another show, "Trapper John," based on the character from "M*A*S*H." Because of his history with both of these shows, Dishell was asked to be the medical advisor for "Trapper John" and the short-lived show "Aftermash."

Dishell's numerous assignments as an advisor to the motion picture and television industries resulted in his becoming the first medical reporter for KNBC in Los Angeles on its first 4 PM news show, from 1983 to 1985. Dishell had his own camera crew, who would go with him and film all of his interviews at doctors' offices, hospitals, or wherever the story required. Once he had enough tape, Dishell would return to KNBC and sit with his tape editor and prepare his on-air segment for the news. He usually was on the air twice a week unless there was a breaking medical story, such as a celebrity illness. Then he would have to be available for the various newscasts that evening. He felt the visibility he achieved on the news enhanced his reputation and helped to build his practice.

Because he was also a full-time practicing physician, he performed his movie and TV responsibilities in the evenings and on the weekends. Because he was not able to be physically on the set during shooting of the episodes — which often occurred during his time in the operating room or during office hours — Dishell hired a registered nurse to go to the set on his behalf and make sure the medical details were accurate.

SKILL SET REQUIRED FOR BEING A MEDICAL ADVISOR

Dishell does not have a background in theater, drama, or creative writing. However, his advice is that you must have a dramatic sense. You must be able to revise the script, and you must understand script structure. You must be willing and able to work with the dramatic story idea that the writer wants to present by figuring out what illness or medical situation will fit the necessary story structure and time line. You also must be able to shift those timelines and events to match the storyline while keeping the content medically correct. It can be difficult to keep the writers in line, because they usually are much more interested in telling their story than in medical accuracy. Dishell admits that he is not a talented creative writer, but he does believe that he has the skills to be a good revisionist or editor of material that is already created.

Dishell provides an example of writing and revisions from his standpoint. The script in this case describes a runaway girl who has been involved in an auto accident. She suffers with blunt abdominal trauma and presents to the emergency department with abdominal pain. When the girl hears through the nurses that her parents are on their way to the hospital, she becomes frightened and leaves the emergency department against medical advice. In order for the script to have credibility, the girl has to have a problem akin to a "ticking time bomb" or something that is going to endanger her life if she leaves the hospital without treatment. Now the medical advisor has to come up with a disease or condition that fits the story and the script. Dishell knows from the writers' story line that they need to find her, get her back to the hospital, and save her life with an emergency surgery at the end of Act 3. That way they can resolve the family issues in Act 4. Dishell goes to his surgical textbooks and provides the diagnosis of a subcapsular injury to the spleen, also providing information on the current treatment for that injury. Now the team makes a decision on how to manage the storyline while keeping the medical details accurate.

An interesting case that was one of the most meaningful of Dishell's career as a medical advisor came from his own practice. In 1974, Dishell removed a parotid tumor that involved the seventh, or facial, nerve, from a young woman. As part of the procedure, Dishell performed a nerve graft to repair the severed facial nerve. The patient, a teacher in the Los Angeles School System, was discharged from her teaching position because at that time, no one with a history of cancer discovered or treated within a five-year period could work in or receive insurance from the school system. This provided a great storyline for the TV program, especially because the story was true, and nothing needed to added or subtracted from the script. Of course, because it was a TV program, the surgery could not involve the face, so they replaced the patient with an exercise instructor with breast cancer. A California state legislator saw the episode program and became involved in the real-life story by authoring a bill in the California state legislature that made it illegal to discriminate against any employee with a previous history of cancer. Dishell and the show's producer both went to the state capitol for the bill signing ceremony with the legislator and then-Governor Jerry Brown. Of course, TV programs and movies usually do not result in changing healthcare laws, but sometimes a program or story connects with a viewer, with amazing results.

Of course, not all plots or dialogue in the episodes Dishell consults on are related to his specialty — so how does he advise a writer or actor on those topics? That usually requires reading, research, and asking for advice from friends in other specialties.

Dishell says said that being a medical advisor for TV and movies is, for the most part, fun and stimulating, and provides a nice diversion from the rigors of a medical practice. He also admitted that it is nice to see his name roll by in the credits at the end of each episode. He also said, "Let's face it, who doesn't want to be on TV?"

Of course, there also are downsides to being a medical advisor. Dishell has always made his family a priority, and he found that serving as a medical advisor and reporter occupied all of his discretionary time outside of medicine. Also, because he rarely missed any of his children's events and attended almost all of their school functions, he had little or no time left for himself.

As far as financial remuneration, once he was finished residency, the role was not worth the time compared with what he could earn as a surgeon. The fee for most TV shows was $750 to $1000 per script. And for his twice-a-week TV segment, which often required five hours to produce each segment, he routinely received a grand total of $350. Therefore, his message is that although serving as a medical advisor is a fun and an exciting "gig," it certainly does not provide a significant financial return on the time invested. It's really something you do more for the creative and intellectual challenge — unless you want to give up your practice and do it full time.

Dishell cautions that large numbers of viewers of these TV programs get their medical advice from the shows, and, therefore, it is very important for the medical information to be accurate. For example, "M*A*S*H" was set in 1949 during the Korean War. When a script called for the use of cortisone, Dishell checked and discovered that cortisone was not available in 1949. That part of the episode, therefore, had to be revised, because it was important to make the medicine accurate for the time frame of the program. This was especially true for "Medical Center" and "Trapper John," both of which were set in real time. Dishell often received letters or phone calls from viewers asking for information on cutting-edge treatments for diseases that they or someone in their family were suffering from.

It was a constant to make the dramatic points yet keep the content medically accurate. Often it was necessary to write a script that required the TV patient to live with a condition or a disease that was incurable. Dishell needed to be careful to avoid giving false hope to viewers who had a disease or condition that was being showcased, but at the same time he had to be careful not to scare people with the medical material in the script.

Bottom Line: Becoming a medical advisor or consultant can be an arduous process. If you know someone in the business or if you happen to practice in the New York or Los Angeles area, it might be a little easier. According to Dishell, there are always going to be windows of opportunity available to all physicians in all areas of their lives. You just have to pay attention to what's going on around you and be receptive when one of those windows opens.

CHAPTER 15

Helping the Impaired Physician

TOM HARBIN, MD, MBA, AND NEIL BAUM, MD

DEFINITION OF "IMPAIRMENT"

In 1973, the American Medical Association defined the impaired physician as one who is unable to fulfill professional and personal responsibilities because of a psychiatric illness, alcoholism, or drug dependency.[1] The prevalence of substance abuse and chemical dependence among physicians is difficult to ascertain. Conservative estimates indicate that 8% to 12% of physicians will develop a substance abuse problem at some point in their careers.[2] Within the medical specialties, anesthesiologists and emergency medicine doctors appear to be at highest risk. It is unclear whether it is the particular specialty that increases the risk of abuse, or that the already at-risk physician is more likely to choose that specialty.[3]

In addition, other mental illnesses, such as dementia, bipolar disorder, and personality disorders, or physical injuries can lead to an inability to safely perform one's duties as a healthcare provider.

RECOGNIZING THE IMPAIRED PHYSICIAN

An early identifier of impairment is change in the behavior of a colleague. Physicians who are normally on-time for seeing patients or attending meetings become chronically late and make excuses that don't hold water. Physical appearance can change. Clothing now covers the arms to hide evidence of needle tracks, or a doctor becomes sloppy in attire and personal hygiene. Such doctors may have changes in personality with more evidence of temper problems or outright abusive treatment of staff. They become upset and confrontational over trivial matters. The impaired physician may raise his or her voice at fellow physicians, or more commonly at staff members, over minor problems. Other signs of impairment include signs of depression or being easily distracted, withdrawn, or disengaged. If the doctor's workplace provides access to drugs, he or she may work long hours to stay close to the source of the addiction.

Still other behaviors that signify a problem include unpredictable behavior to staff or patients, as well as lack of availability when on-call or making careless medical decisions. Some impaired physicians will isolate themselves — they close or lock their office door or make hospital rounds at odd hours.

Impaired physicians seeking employment may present with "red flags" on their resume, such as unexplained lapses between jobs, frequent job changes, multiple relocations, and vague letters of referral. Any letter of referral that is not glowing calls for a personal conversation with someone in the organization from which the letter came.

In some cases, substance abuse problems can remain undetected for years before coming to light. Impaired physicians can function at an adequate level until their problem becomes more advanced and their ability to care for patients deteriorates. In these cases, the family may recognize problems before colleagues. Marriages usually suffer, and impairment can lead to separation or divorce.

Healthcare providers and behavioral health professionals have made great efforts to characterize psychiatric illnesses such as addiction and depression as diseases rather than as moral failings. Nevertheless, physicians who suffer from such illnesses often have difficulty acknowledging that they are susceptible, while in fact addiction and depression are as common in healthcare providers as in the general population.[4]

For all these reasons, physicians in a group, and especially the group's leaders, should be vigilant and have a low threshold for investigating suspicious behavior for substance abuse. Moreover, leaders need to have some knowledge of the other mental illnesses that can lead to impairment: dementia in the older doctor, bipolar disorder, decompensating schizophrenia, and the like.

Leaders of groups need to be sensitive to the natural reluctance of staff or colleagues to report problems and should pay attention to any hints of problems that surface. Even better, an anonymous way to report problems within an organization can lead to earlier detection.

WHY ARE PHYSICIANS AT RISK FOR IMPAIRMENT?

Doctors have a lengthy training schedule, work long hours, and have significant stress. As a result, they are ripe for addiction to alcohol or drugs. In addition, doctors have easier access to addicting drugs, enhancing the potential abuse of these substances by susceptible doctors.

Alcohol is the most commonly abused substance among physicians. Next most common is prescription drug abuse, particularly benzodiazepines and opioids.[5] Although the drug of choice for anesthesia personnel entering treatment for substance abuse is usually an opioid, abuse of propofol, ketamine, sodium thiopental, lidocaine, nitrous oxide, and the potent volatile anesthetics has also been reported.[6] These drugs lend themselves to self-treatment and are easily accessible. Anesthesiologists in particular are at risk for controlled substance abuse. Despite strict controls and accounting measures, it remains relatively easy to divert controlled substances for personal use. Some have cited the high stress environment in which anesthesiologists work as a contributing factor, and others have suggested that exposure to trace quantities to these agents in the workplace sensitizes the reward pathways in the brain and promotes substance abuse. Still others have proposed that individuals with novelty-seeking behavior traits may be both more likely to choose a career in anesthesia and more prone to the development of addiction.[6]

MANAGING THE PROBLEM DOCTOR

An impaired physician has deleterious effects on his or her patients, colleagues, and staff of both the practice group and hospital. Members of a practice, group, or hospital staff that recognize or suspect an impaired physician are morally and ethically responsible to take steps so that the appropriate leadership can investigate and, when necessary, help the impaired doctor receive treatment and, just as importantly, protect patients from receiving poor care.

Staff and colleagues should take action sooner rather than later. Failure to take prompt action may put the offending doctor at risk of permanent damage to his or her reputation and can also put patients at risk for injury or improper treatments.

Practice leaders that hear a complaint about a fellow colleague by the staff or another member of the practice must take such complaints seriously.

Begin by getting all of the facts. Remember there are always two sides to every story. No matter how egregious or damning one side of the story is, you should keep an open mind until you've heard the other side and have all of the details. Get as many facts as you can from as many people as you can, and make certain that there really is a problem.

Some large practices and almost all hospitals have a committee specifically set up to manage the impaired physician. This is the avenue for reporting suspicions for practices that belong to such an organization. Many states have a legal requirement to report any physician that may be practicing while impaired. It may seem tempting to privately question or confront the physician about the possibility of a problem, but this often results in denial and can cause more harm than good. Once the physician becomes aware that others may know of the problem, there is the potential for self-harm.

Virtually all state medical societies and licensing boards have a Physician Health Program (PHP) for dealing with impaired physicians. Nine states have legislated impaired physician programs administered by state medical boards, independent agencies, or medical societies through contracts with medical boards. All other state programs are administered by medical societies.[7] The Federation of State Physician Health Programs is a nonprofit organization that serves as a forum for information exchange among these various state programs.

All shared information is treated confidentially and can be divulged without fear of retaliation. It may seem difficult to report a colleague, but failing to do so puts the patients of the impaired physician at risk. The PHP can serve as an advocate for the physician before the medical board. The potential consequences of licensure suspension and revocation for the physician are greater if the physician is reported to the board without involvement with the PHP.

After the initial contact is made with the PHP, it will arrange for a comprehensive assessment of the physician to help identify a substance abuse problem or psychiatric illness. If the PHP determines that an intervention is needed, a small group consisting of representatives for the PHP or local physician wellness committee and, sometimes, colleagues will meet with the physician and recommend a formal evaluation be done to determine if any treatment is necessary. The physician can voluntarily follow the recommendations of the committee. If the physician chooses not to, he or she could be reported to the state board and face serious consequences.

Treatment of physicians with substance abuse problems is different than that of the general public. Short-term outpatient therapy relapse rates are greater than 60%, which is unfavorable, considering physicians will be returning to a workplace where judgment must not be compromised. Extended treatment that lasts three to four months and takes place in a center with other impaired physicians has a better success rate.[8]

Treatment usually begins in a hospital setting in order to focus on the physical consequences of withdrawal and overcoming initial drug cravings. This may take a few days to a couple of weeks. During this time, psychological therapy, behavior modification, and education are initiated. The intermediate and late phases take place in a recovery setting where physicians can gain insight by interacting with others that are further along in their recovery.

A nine-year study of physicians in the New Jersey PHP reported a recovery rate of 83.8%, with no relapses at the end of two years. Including those who had one relapse (13.8%), the success rate was 97.6%. Most relapses occur during the first two years after treatment. A structured aftercare program can increase the success rate and help identify a relapse. Typical monitoring is usually done for the following five years, but longer periods may be chosen.[9]

Bottom Line: Most of us will encounter an impaired physician during our medical lifetime. It is imperative to help the impaired physician and not ignore the problem thinking that it will get better by itself. Disruptive behavior due to impairment seldom gets better without intervention. With compassionate hand-holding and effective treatment, the disruptive behavior goes away, the impaired physician keeps his or her job and often his or her family stays intact, and the practice is happier and avoids the problems associated with firing a colleague or taking away his or her medical privileges.

REFERENCES

1. The sick physician. Impairment by psychiatric disorders, including alcoholism and drug dependence. *JAMA*. 1973;223:684-687.

2. Brewster JM. Prevalence of alcohol and other drug problems among physicians. *JAMA*. 1986;255:1913-1920.
3. Boisaubin EV, Levine RE. Identifying and assisting the impaired physician. *Am J Med Sci*. 2001;322:31-36.
4. Yancey JR, McKinnon HD. Reaching out to an impaired physician. *Fam Pract Manag*. 2010; 17:27-31.
5. Karp D. Dealing with an impaired colleague. *Med Econ*. 2007;84:30.
6. Bryson EO, Hamza H. The drug seeking anesthesia care provider. *International Anesthesiology Clinics*. 2011;49:157-171.
7. Ikeda R, Pelton C. Diversion programs for impaired physicians. *West J Med*. 1990;152:617-621.
8. Bohigian GM, Croughan JL, Sanders K, Evans ML, Bondurant R, Platt C. Substance abuse and dependence in physicians: the Missouri Physicians' Health Program. *South Med J*. 1996;89:1078-1080.
9. Reading EG. Nine years experience with chemically dependent physicians: the New Jersey experience. *Md Med J*. 1992;41:325-329.

CHAPTER 16

Dealing with Difficult Patients

NEIL BAUM, MD

"Those who enter to buy support me. Those who come to flatter please me. Those who complain teach me how I may please others so that more will come. Only those hurt me who are displeased but do not complain. They refuse me permission to correct my errors so that I may improve my service."
— Marshall Field

All of us in the healthcare profession have had the experience of interacting with a difficult patient. It doesn't matter if you are a pathologist, pediatrician, or primary care physician, you will have had the experience of dealing with the difficult patient. Fortunately, difficult patients make up only a small percentage of the patients that we care for. Doctors report that about one in six patients are "difficult." That translates into three or four unpleasant visits with patients each day.[1]

Unfortunately; few of us have had any formal training on managing a difficult patient. It is something we have learned, or maybe not learned, by trial and error. Oftentimes, the errors associated with managing a difficult patient can lead to undesirable consequences. In this chapter, I will discuss how to identify the difficult patient and provide a three-step technique for managing a difficult patient.

WHY DO PATIENTS BECOME DIFFICULT?

First, most patients in the healthcare situation, such as in our offices or in the hospital, are out of their comfort zone. Even the most self-confident individual when placed in a situation of uncertainty may become uncomfortable, anxious, and even hostile when not knowing what to expect. This is an important reason to always explain what you plan to do to a patient. This relieves the patient's anxiety and can make the patient much more mentally comfortable when confronted with a medical test, procedure, or diagnosis with an unfavorable prognosis.

Second, patients are often in a stressful situation. Remember, what is commonplace to each of us is probably a first-time experience for our patients. Take, for example, the history and physical examination. Patients will be required to reveal personal secrets and issues that they wouldn't share with their partners, best friends, or clergyman or -woman. Then they will commonly get undressed and wear a gown that seldom covers the entire body, and then be probed in areas of the body that have never been touched or explored before. If we just imagine what our patients are experiencing, it is not difficult to understand why they are stressed when they come to the doctor's office. We even have a name for it, "white coat hypertension," as frequently these visits are associated with a mild elevation of the patient's blood pressure.

Finally, health issues and fear of the unknown lower a person's threshold for anger, potentially precipitating a conflict. When patients are placed in a stressful situation and when they are out of their comfort zone, their threshold for anger is lowered; and they will often say and do things that would not normally occur outside of the healthcare environment. Therefore, it is imperative that all of us in the healthcare profession, which includes receptionists, office managers, file clerks, and insurance and billing agents, be just as cognizant as the doctors, nurses, and physician assistants who spend more time eyeball to eyeball with the patients to the potential for patients to become anxious, uncomfortable, and psychologically disoriented in the medical environment.

WHY IS IT IMPORTANT TO SUCCESSFULLY MANAGE THE DIFFICULT PATIENT?

Studies have shown that happy customers/clients/ patients may tell one to three others about their positive experience with you and your practice.[2] This is exactly the positive word-of-mouth reaction that you desire to create for all of your patients. You want them to have a favorable experience from the time they make the phone call to make an appointment until they pay their bill and leave the practice. On the other hand, a dissatisfied patient will tell 10 to 20 family members, friends, existing patients, and potential new patients about his or her negative experience with your practice.[2] This is a situation that must be avoided. It is important to make sure that even the most difficult patient ends up with a positive experience; and that whatever the patient perceived that was unfavorable does not happen again. In addition, you must express that you are sorry that the patient had an untoward experience.[3]

It isn't hard to calculate or envision that patients with a bad result and a big mouth can impact hundreds of others with their negative experience. I am reminded of a lady that had a problem paying for durable medical goods and was upset that we asked her to pay for the goods since her insurance would not cover their cost. She probably told several hundred people about how mercenary and avaricious Dr. Baum is. I would have gladly given her catheters for a long time to avoid the damage and embarrassment that she caused!

A dissatisfied patient is more likely to have a poor outcome and make greater use of the healthcare system.[4] These patients are not likely to be compliant and follow directions, and thus their outcomes are less than optimal. Also, the dissatisfied patient is more likely to litigate against the physician for the unhappy experience or the patient's less-than optimal outcome from a procedure or test.[5]

If those aren't reasons enough to resolve the complaints of the difficult patient, it has been shown that those doctors who reported having more difficult patient encounters were 12 times more likely to report burnout than those reporting fewer difficult encounters.[6]

CLUES THAT YOU MAY BE CONFRONTED WITH A DIFFICULT PATIENT

What are the clues that you might be dealing with a difficult patient?

Just as there are signs and symptoms associated with various diseases and conditions, there are signs that you may have or may create a dissatisfied patient. First, listen carefully to the tone of voice. If the patient is speaking louder than expected or more rapidly than usual, then you must modulate and soften your voice and speak slower. Watch the body language. Look for signs for agitation such as wringing of the hands or tapping of the feet, which is a sign of impatience.

Look for fear or frustration. Clenched fists and clenched teeth are other signs that you are dealing with a dissatisfied patient. A furrowed brow or distended jugular vein indicates anxiety and tension. A patients who is in a defensive position, such as with crossed arms, will often provide clues about the intense conversation that is about to take place. Pay attention to the breathing pattern. A restricted breathing pattern or sighing is an indication that the patient is upset.

Another warning sign is the doctor shopper. If a patient has seen multiple physicians for the same complaint, it is unlikely that all of the physicians were problematic. It is more likely that the patient is the source of the problem, and it is unlikely that you will be the knight in shining armor that diagnoses a difficult condition or cures the patient of his or her malady. It is those patients that you want to set reasonable expectations very early in the doctor-patient relationship. Patients with chronic medical problems lend themselves to having difficulty with physicians and their staff. Patients who make frequent office visits — more than would be expected for their medical condition — may be difficult to manage. You can also expect to be challenging any patient who is taking multiple medications, especially analgesics. Patients who insist on being prescribed an unnecessary drug are likely to present a challenge and be a management problem.

Finally, be wary of the patient who arrives with a briefcase full of articles and citations gleaned from the Internet. I suggest that you do not dismiss the patient's efforts as it only demonstrates the patient's interest in his or her medical condition. I recommend that you direct the patient to credible Web sites or refer the patient to your own Web site if you have information on the medical condition. I usually do not read all of the patient's articles but instead suggest that the patient review sites that I deem authoritative and credible. I then offer to discuss the information or the articles on the next visit. This way I don't discount the patient's efforts but rather lead him or her to information that will be useful and not confusing or misleading.

Also, I suggest that patients with chronic medical conditions be discouraged from entering blogs with other patients. It is has been my experience that blogging lends itself to confusion. Well-meaning patients who have the same diagnosis will give your patients advice that may not apply to their disease or condition. For that reason, I suggest that they avoid Internet blogging.

THE THREE-STEP RESPONSE TO MANAGING THE DIFFICULT PATIENT[7]

Step #1: Don't Interrupt

Allow the patient to complete his or her discussion without any interruption on the part of the physician. During the average patient encounter, the physician will often interrupt the patient after only 16 seconds.[8] A patient will have spent a lot of emotional energy to speak to the physician about his or her negative experience. Make every effort to remain focused and listen to the patient, and do not speak until the patient is finished with his or her dialog. After the patient has had an opportunity to vent his or her concern, validate the frustration with empathy. Rather than becoming defensive, consider saying, "I understand that you are upset at having to wait, and I apologize for the delay."

Step #2: Involve the Patient in the Solution

Ask how to provide a solution. You will be amazed at how many times the patient will give you the answer or provide suggestions for resolving the problem. Ways to involve the patient include asking the patient, "What do you think I should have done?" or "Do you have any suggestions of how to solve this problem?" By involving the patient you have clearly demonstrated that you are listening to the patient's concern and that you are committed to making the situation better. Involving the patient also demonstrates that you are interested in his or her goodwill and that you care about the patient's experience with you and your practice.

Step #3: Provide the Patient with an Opportunity to Discuss Concerns

We are not mind readers, and we don't know what additional concerns patients may have. For example, patients may be concerned that the situation not be repeated with either themselves or with other patients. This is of particular importance when there has been a complication or with errors of commission or omission. There are patients who are altruistic and have a concern about their fellow patients, and want reassurance that the situation will not be repeated.

I am reminded of a story of a patient who had a mammogram but the radiologist didn't check the film's quality after the study. The radiologist had to bring the patient back for an additional mammogram, and she was charged for the additional study. The radiology department did not manage this properly, and the patient left the primary care doctor who ordered the study and the hospital and referred herself to Mayo Clinic.[9] Again, asking about patients' concerns demonstrates your caring and compassion. After all, patients don't really care how much you know compared with knowing how much you care!

A FEW SUGGESTIONS

I believe it is important to have a discussion with a difficult patient in a private location where the discussion cannot be overheard by others in the office. I suggest that you escort the difficult patient from the exam room to another secure location in the office to have your discussion in private and without interruption. I recommend that you sit *next* to the patient — not across the desk from the patient. The reason is that you want to avoid any barriers, including physical ones, separating you and your patient. You also want to maintain good eye contact with the patient. This is not the time to be looking at the chart or a computer screen. Inform your staff that you will be talking to a patient and that you are not to be interrupted during this conversation.

After you have listened to the patient, it is helpful to ask the patient additional questions. This sends the message you are interested in finding a solution and that you are actively listening.

At the end of your discussion, thank the patient for bringing the issue to your attention. You may even consider sending the patient a note acknowledging your discussion and your plan of action. If you have to get back to the patient, specify a day and time that you will be calling. If you don't have a response or answer at that time, call the patient and let him or her know the status of your follow-up and when you might be in contact again. Follow-up is vital to the success of your managing the difficult patient.

SUMMARY

Managing the difficult patient is part and parcel of the practice of medicine. You are likely to have satisfied patients who have a positive experience with your practice. However, there are going to be a few that will try your communication and interpersonal skills. Resolving the issues of the difficult patient can be gratifying and as rewarding as solving a difficult diagnostic problem or successfully resolving a medical problem using your surgical skills. Finally, if you can handle the difficult patient, the others are so much easier to manage.

REFERENCES

1. An PG, Rabatin JS, Manwell LB, *et al.* for the MEMO Investigators. Burden of difficult encounters in primary care: data from the Minimizing Error, Maximizing Outcomes Study. Arch Intern Med. 2009;169:410-414.

2. Baum N, Henkel G. Marketing Your Clinical Practice, 3rd ed. Sudbury, MA: Jones and Bartlett; 2004:68.
3. Saxton J. Sorry Works! Disclosure, Apology and Relationships Prevent Medical Malpractice Claims. Bloomington, IN: AuthorHouse, 2007.
4. Jackson JL. Difficult patient encounters in the ambulatory clinic. *Arch Intern Med.* 1999;159:1069-1075.
5. Travaline JM, Ruchinskas R, D'Alonzo GE. Patient-physician communication: why and how. *J Am Osteopath Assoc.* 2555;105:13-18.
6. Kroenke K. Unburdening the difficult clinical encounter. Arch Intern Med. 2009;169:333-334
7. Adams J, Murray R. The general approach to the difficult patient. *Emerg Med Clin North Am.* 1998;16:689-700.
8. Groopman J. How Doctors Think. New York: Houghton Mifflin; 2007.
9. Berry L, Seltman K. Managemen*t Lessons from Mayo Clinic: Inside One of the Worlds Most Admired Service Organizations.* New York: McGraw-Hill; 2008.

CHAPTER 17

Lessons to Be Learned from Patients and Colleagues

Jeff J. Segal, MD, JD, and Neil H. Baum, MD

It wasn't too long ago that doctors were able to take a leisurely history and conduct a thorough physical examination. Today, doctors are spending less time with patients, and they are hurried and often make mistakes. We believe that some errors can be avoided by lessons learned from colleagues who have made similar errors and also from our patients themselves.

GIVE PATIENTS CREDIT

Give patients more credit than they typically receive. They won't abuse any privileges you bestow — such as giving them your cell phone number.

One of us (JJS) practiced as a neurosurgeon in a small Midwest community. The answering service performed only one task well — it transferred calls from patients to the doctor — but it failed to shine in other areas.

One day, the doctor called the answering service and explained he was planning to swim laps at a neighborhood pool. If the service need him for an emergency, it could page him (on a vintage alphanumeric beeper), and the lifeguard would go to the pool and ask the doctor to respond. The doctor instructed the lifeguard and handed him the beeper.

One lap into the swim, the doctor felt a tap on his shoulder. The lifeguard explained the beeper had gone off. The doctor called the service. It had received a call from the hospital for a laxative order. Didn't seem like an emergency to the doctor. He called in the order. A little disgusted, he returned to the pool. Five minutes later, the lifeguard again tapped the doctor's shoulder. The answering service had called again. This time it was a patient who needed reassurance. The patient had explicitly explained to the answering service that his call was not urgent.

The answering service could not make the distinction among an emergency, an urgency, or a routine matter. The doctor had to fire the service. In its place, he hired a programmer to create an automated phone tree. Once implemented, the caller heard the message, "If this is an emergency and you need a call back within five minutes, press 1 now or call 911. If you need a call back within 30 minutes, press 2 now. If this can wait until the next business day, press 3 now." The doctor now knew how urgent the call was — directly from the patient's perspective.

The biggest risk was that every patient would treat every call as an emergency and press "1." It never happened. The patients triaged their own calls with sophistication. Calls labeled as emergencies were indeed emergencies. Calls labeled as urgent matters were urgent matters.

Many doctors hesitate to give out their cell phone number to patients, fearing a barrage of inappropriate calls at all hours. Patients rarely abuse this privilege. They respect that the doctor trusts them to use the number when necessary. Sure, one or two worried patients might call inappropriately. But this is the exception and not the rule. The odds are in your favor. You can give most patients your cell number. You'll be perceived as a caring, empathetic doctor.

LOOK AT HOW YOU COMMUNICATE

How you communicate with patients is no less important than what you communicate.

An emergency department physician in a large group conducted an experiment. Typically, he would do a history and physical, then order lab tests and x-rays. When *all* the laboratory and x-ray results had returned, he would speak to the patient, give a diagnosis, and recommend a course of action.

He decided to try a different approach.

As individual lab and x-ray results returned, he would pop his head through the curtain and quickly explain what he had just learned. For example, "Ms. Smith, I just got your CBC back. It's normal. Should know what your electrolytes are in a few minutes. I'll check back soon." Then a few minutes later, "Ms. Smith, I just got your electrolytes back. They're normal. I should have your x-ray results back in a few minutes. I'll check back soon." And so on.

This emergency department physician learned two things. He did not spend one minute more, in aggregate, communicating with his patients. His interactions — popping his head through the curtain — were brief. And at the end of the patient encounter, when he put it all together, even that interaction was quick.

But when his patients were asked to estimate how much time the doctor spent with them, they answered with a number double that attributed to his colleagues. So popping his head through the curtain — brief bursts of communication — had the effect of significantly changing his patients' *perception.*

Today, patients complain that the doctor talks to them for only a few minutes. By changing *how* you deliver information, the patients' perception can be significantly changed without investing more aggregate time per patient encounter — a benefit without an extra cost.

DEPUTIZE YOUR PATIENTS

Deputize your patients to keep things from falling through the cracks.

Several years ago, a friend of one of us (JJS) complained of difficulty abducting his shoulder. His strength deteriorated, and he saw a spine surgeon. An MRI was ordered and performed. A few weeks later, someone asked about his shoulder. He said he hadn't heard from his surgeon and just assumed no news was good news. He learned that assumption was flawed and was urged to connect with his doctor immediately. He did and learned he had a C4-C5 herniated disc pressing on the nerve innervating his deltoid muscle. Fortunately, the patient's strength mostly recovered without any intervention. But he was lucky.

How do we reverse a patient's default assumption that no news is good news? Put a sign in your office that explicitly states that if a patient has not received a lab result in the relevant time frame, his or her visit is free. In the business world, this is not a new idea. A sign over many cash registers states that if you don't receive a receipt, your purchase is free. The store's owner is deputizing you, the customer, to "guard the register." You are being incentivized to make sure the clerk doesn't stuff a $20 bill into his or her pocket, embezzling day after day.

Back to the doctor's office. You want to alert patients that they should expect to hear from you. No news is just that — no news. Neither patient nor doctor hopes that the lab result falls through the cracks. But now patients are served notice to call if there has indeed been no news. Even with electronic reminders and patient portals, it's a good idea to implement such a backup system.

ASK FOR FEEDBACK

Ask your patients to post their feedback about your care online.

Do patients read online reviews about doctors? Yes. Do they use these reviews to select their doctor? Again, yes. Many patients are using the Internet to choose a doctor. Even more are using the Internet to validate referrals made by their doctor or friends and/or family.

It is impossible to make 100% of your patients happy. You will inevitably receive a negative review. One of us (JJS) is frequently called by doctors who complain that a patient has slammed them on the Internet. Invariably they learn their online reputation is defined by that one patient. Why? There are zero to a handful of other reviews to balance the negative comment — even when the average doctor sees 1000 to 3000 patients a year. In other words, the doctor is mostly invisible on the Internet, except for the rant of an unhappy patient.

The solution to pollution is dilution. The simplest way to avoid being defined by one patient is to encourage all of your patients to post their feedback online. And make it easy for them. You can provide links to the major review sites on your Web site, hand the patient a card with the relevant links, or contract with an organization that enables point-of-service uploadable reviews. For doctors who are talented, and those willing to act on feedback, their reputations will flourish as the good reviews accumulate. Then when the inevitable negative review materializes, it will be balanced by a sea of positive reviews. Interestingly, the public perceives mostly positive reviews with an occasional negative as more credible and authentic than 100% positive reviews. If all you have are positive reviews, right or wrong, the public perceives this as marketing material.

Don't be afraid to ask your patients to post feedback online about your care. If you are doing a good job, you will be rewarded by the feedback. It's like getting a bucket of thank you notes every day. And even negative comments will typically be couched in constructive language. Finally, since patients are using the Internet to vet their doctor, those with the most reviews will never be short of patients to treat.

BE HONEST

Be brutally honest with your patients when you make a mistake. Doctors are human. We make mistakes. Hopefully the number of mistakes we make is low, and ideally we learn from them.

A plastic surgeon performed the wrong procedure on his patient. He intended to perform a liposuction, but did an abdominoplasty (tummy tuck) instead. An abdominoplasty incurs greater risk and has a longer recovery period. The surgeon made a mistake. Here's how he handled that mistake.

When the patient awoke, the doctor explained what happened. He then apologized. He stated he would perform a root cause analysis to understand why the mistake happened so it would never happen again. That knowledge would not affect this patient, but patients want to know that something has been learned to prevent mishaps that could harm other patients down the road. The surgeon refunded the patient's money. Finally, because the recovery was going to take longer than anticipated, the surgeon did what he could to prevent any inconvenience to the patient. He made sure there was food in the refrigerator. He made sure the patient's children had a ride to school.

When the patient returned to have her sutures removed, she started to appreciate how the doctor had managed the process. And six months later, she became this doctor's greatest referral source.

When you've made a mistake, be honest with the patient, and do what you can to right the wrong. Patients will not be pleased that a mistake was made. But most of the time, they will appreciate how you handle the aftermath.

By the way, the patient with the abdominoplasty never sued the doctor — even though she would have been guaranteed a settlement.

LEARN TO APOLOGIZE

Be comfortable with the words "I'm sorry."

One of us (NHB) left a vaginal pack in a woman after a cystocele repair. The pack ordinarily would have been removed in the recovery room. The patient returned a week later for a follow-up examination complaining of an "odor down there!" Upon examination, he found the vaginal pack and removed it. The patient was told the truth and received an apology along with the explanation.

"I'm sorry" is one of the most commonly used phrases in any language. Most of us don't think twice about offering an apology when we unintentionally bump into a stranger on the sidewalk. However, when we have made a mistake, and nearly every one of us has during our medical career, the words seem to get stuck in our throats and just won't come out easily.

Begin by admitting to yourself what has happened to the patient. Next think about the ramifications of your actions or inactions leading to or causing the problem. Look at the situation from the patient's point of view and try to understand his or her feelings. This is easy to do if you trade places with the patient and imagine how *you* would feel if you were in that situation. It is also important to forgive yourself for any causal role you had in the incident. Finally, plan and prepare your apology. This may mean writing down what you intend to say, how you want to say it, and when you should say it.

First comes recognition. We must be able to read our own feelings as well as the feelings of the patient and his or her family. If you feel regret or remorse, it is a good indicator that an apology is in order. If the patient is interacting with you differently or is reluctant to talk, that might indicate there are unmet expectations or you are not meeting the patient's needs adequately.

Next is an expression of regret. By expressing regret you are demonstrating an empathetic response that lets the patient know you understand his or her situation and that you feel badly about it. Consider verbiage such as, "I am so sorry. I know this outcome is not what you expected. It is not what I expected either." Such an expression of empathy does not admit liability, but does allow healing of the relationship to begin.

Third is responsibility and an honest and forthright explanation of what happened, why it happened, how it will affect the patient's short- and long-term health status, and what steps are being done to protect others from the same untoward result. It is our responsibility to provide all of this information.

Finally, provide the remedy or what is being done to correct the problem that the patient is experiencing. Included in the remedy is the issue of cost and who will bear the expense of remedying the problem.

A middle-aged man waits for more than an hour in the exam room to see the doctor. The doctor enters and sees that the man is visibly upset and that his jugular veins are clearly distended over his shirt collar. The doctor apologizes and explains the reason for the delay, but the patient is not mollified. The doctor then tells the patient that there will be no charge for the visit on that day. Immediately the patient exhales and relaxes. Rather than having this patient leave the office and tell dozens of other potential patients about his negative experience in the doctor's office, he now leaves and tells others about the sensitivity and kindness of the physician. Doctors spend their whole lives creating and protecting their reputations. Our reputation is certainly worth more than the $75.00 office visit.

TREAT REFERRERS PROPERLY

When a primary care physician (PCP) sends a patient to you for an evaluation, it is of paramount importance to return the patient to the PCP and to send a referral note explaining your findings.

A PCP refers a patient to a specialist. The specialist cares for the patient in his or her domain of expertise. The patient then needs a referral to *another* doctor. If the specialist selects a colleague but fails to confer with the PCP, he or she risks upsetting and even offending the PCP. It is common courtesy to call the PCP and ask which other doctor he or she would like to have the patient see. By doing so, the specialist reminds the PCP that the PCP is the captain of the patient's healthcare ship.

RESPOND TO PATIENTS' CRITICISM

It is important to respond to constructive criticism on patient satisfaction surveys.

Doctors often distribute patient satisfaction surveys. However, few medical practices take action on negative responses or listen to constructive criticism. One gynecologist received a recommendation that he wait until the patient is dressed and sitting in a chair before speaking to her after an examination. Typically he'd start talking, standing over the exam table, while the patient was supine and covered with a paper drape. Certainly this was good advice, and the doctor was well advised to take action from the patient's survey.

LISTEN TO YOUR PATIENTS

Don't interrupt patients when they are providing aspects of their history. The average physician interrupts a patient after only 18 seconds. We recommend that patients be allowed to tell their chief complaint without interruption. This requires active listening on the part of the physician and is universally appreciated by patients. So listen up; your patients might just teach you something and certainly will help lead you to the diagnosis.

Bottom Line: Doctors are historically good students. We are always growing the body of knowledge that we use to care for patients and learning new procedures and treatment options. We also need to learn how to provide outstanding care; and we can learn from our colleagues who are willing to share their mistakes and how to avoid them, and we can learn from our patients as well.

CHAPTER 18

Caveats for Doctors Providing Care for Themselves, Family, Friends, and Colleagues

PAUL KEPPER, MS, AND NEIL BAUM, MD

Nearly 30 years ago one of us (NHB) took his baby daughter to a pediatrician for a Benadryl injection. The baby was going to a dentist, but NHB didn't want to be the one who gave the little girl the injection. NHB asked the pediatric colleague if the he would give her the injection, and he agreed but said he wanted to pull her chart. NHB said, "Why do you need her chart?" The pediatrician, who was older and certainly wiser than NHB, took NHB into his office, asked him to sit down, and informed him that doctors frequently experience adverse events when caring for family and friends. This is because they fail to treat them as real patients and frequently use shortcuts that often lead to complications. This was one of the most valuable lessons NHB learned early in his career.

Another story worth relating further emphasizes the risks of providing care for colleagues. An orthopedist was in the doctors' lounge and asked a urologic colleague about the orthopedist's elevated prostate-specific antigen (PSA) level. The colleague, who was not his urologist of record, told the orthopedist about considering a course of antibiotics and then repeating the PSA level after completing the antibiotics. The urologic colleague never heard from the orthopedist until several years later, when the orthopedist was diagnosed with metastatic prostate cancer and sued the urologist for negligence of care. The lawsuit dragged on through the courts, but eventually the urologist was exonerated after great expense and mental anguish.

So what is a doctor to do when caring for colleagues, family members, or friends? This chapter will review the guidelines doctors should use when caring for this unique population of patients.

GUIDELINES

It is very common for doctors to provide advice and sometimes treatment to family members and good friends. It is also an admonition from the time of Hippocrates that doctors should not treat themselves nor should they treat their families. So how do we reconcile this?

In 1847, the American Medical Association (AMA) published its first "Code of Medical Ethics," which stated, "Doctors treat each other and each others' family members for free"; whereas the code mentioned if we were to treat our own family members, "we would be apt to be timid and irresolute."

According to the sixth edition of *The American College of Physicians Ethics Manual*, published in 2012, "Physicians should usually not enter into the dual relationship of physician-family member or physician-friend for a variety of reasons. The patient may be at risk of receiving inferior care from the physician. Problems may include effects on clinical objectivity, inadequate history taking or physical examination, over-testing, inappropriate prescribing, incomplete counseling on sensitive issues, or failure to keep appropriate medical records. The needs of the patient may not fall within the physician's area of expertise. The physician's emotional proximity may result in difficulties for the patient and/or the physician."

Treatment of family, friends, and self is widespread among physicians. We don't know many physicians who haven't provided medical care, including writing prescriptions, for family and friends. The most commonly written prescriptions include those for antibiotics, antihistamines, and contraceptives. Doctors will even prescribe controlled substances, including pain medications, for their family and friends. However, once a physician has treated a family member or friend, it may be more difficult to deny care to that person in future situations. For example, one of us (NHB) has written prescriptions for antibiotics for a family member complaining of lower urinary tract symptoms. With each recurrence, the family member called and requested a refill. In his heart, NHB knew this was not good medicine and that he was skating on thin ice. But he was locked in, having provided medication for the first infection. We were told long ago that prescription without diagnosis is malpractice and should be avoided. Therefore, treating sinus infections, upper respiratory infections, or urinary tract infections without an examination and a minimum of lab tests is not in the best interest of the doctor or the family member or friend.

Treatment of self and nonpatients (defined as people treated outside a standard office relationship, usually without documentation) is common practice. Self-treatment has been reported ranging from 52% to 84% of physicians.[1-5] Treatment of nonpatients is even more widespread, with some studies reporting nearly 100% of physicians engaging in this practice.[1,2]

Most physicians are not aware that ethical guidelines on the treatment of nonpatients even exist.[1] Section E-8.19 of the Code of Medical Ethics (available online at www.ama-assn.

org/ama/pub/physician-resources/medical-ethics/code-medical-ethics/opinion819.page) states that "physicians generally should not treat themselves or members of their immediate families" because their professional objectivity may be compromised. Exceptions are allowed for "short-term, minor problems" or "in emergency or isolated settings." The *American College of Physicians Ethics Manual* (available online at www.acponline.org/ethics/ethicman.htm) similarly asserts that "physicians should avoid treating themselves, close friends or members of their own families." It goes on to comment that "physicians should be very cautious about assuming the care of closely associated employees."

Some state medical boards take these positions a step further. North Carolina requires that the "physician must prepare and keep a proper written record of that treatment," and the Medical Code of Virginia specifies that "records should be maintained of all written prescriptions or administration of any drugs" regardless of the recipient of the prescription.

In addition, some insurance providers, including Medicare and Blue Cross Blue Shield, deny payment for the care that physicians provide for immediate family members, even in an office setting.

Legal considerations and laws should also be taken into account when deciding whether to treat nonpatients. Once a physician begins treatment, a patient-physician relationship is established. From that point on, the physician is liable for the interaction and its consequences. The scope of federal law for written prescriptions is limited to controlled substances, stating that a prescriber must have a bona fide patient-physician relationship, including a written record of the encounter. At a minimum, state law follows federal statutes. However, some states (Massachusetts, for example) further require documenting a medical history and a physical examination before prescribing any medication.

So the best advice is don't treat nonpatients except in cases of minor problems or emergencies, document what you do, and stay away from prescribing controlled substances.

Of course, this leaves a lot of area open for physician interpretation of each situation. Factors that might affect your decision to treat yourself or nonpatients are:

- The type of relationship and emotional closeness between you and the patient;
- Your areas of expertise or training;
- The need for an intimate history or examination;
- The medication or treatment requested; and
- Convenience.

HOW I (NHB) DO IT

A common scenario is a nurse or colleague stopping me in the hall and asking for a prescription for a diagnosis that he or she has made himself or herself. My response is almost always, "Sure I will write it. Please come to the office during my lunch hour or at the end of the day to fill out the forms so my office can create a chart for you. I will then examine a urine specimen; and if indicated, will gladly write your prescription without charge." Now I come across as a good friend; I am practicing good medicine; and I have provided the colleague, family member, or friend with expedited medical care.

If a doctor decides to treat a friend or family member, then it is imperative that the physician should document what took place, even if the treatment was minor.

This approach also applies to caring for staff members who have medical problems. If it is in my area of expertise, I offer care if the staff member agrees to become a patient and shifts the role from employer-employee to doctor-patient. If, however, the person is uncomfortable with that, I make arrangements with another colleague who agrees to provide care for my staff, which I reciprocate by providing care for his or her staff. If it is out of my area of medical expertise, I will call a physician who can provide the staff member with care, and ask if he or she would agree to see my staff member as soon as possible. The physician friend usually offers to see the patient the same day.

EXCEPTIONS

It is not always inappropriate to undertake self-treatment or treatment of immediate family members. In emergency situations or isolated settings where no other qualified physician is available, physicians should not hesitate to treat themselves or family members. In addition, while physicians should not serve as a primary or regular care provider for immediate family members, acceptable, routine care situations allow treatment of short-term, minor problems. Except in emergencies, it is not appropriate for physicians to write prescriptions for controlled substances for themselves or immediate family members.[6]

Bottom Line: For the most part, doctors should not provide medical care for themselves, family members, close friends, or colleagues. If a physician does treat such a person, then the care should be carefully documented and a copy of the record given to the individual who received treatment.

REFERENCES

1. Chambers R, Belcher J. Self-reported care over the past 10 years: a survey of general practitioners. *Br J Gen Pract.* 1992;42:153-156.
2. Christie JD, Rosen IM, Bellini LM, *et al.* Prescription drug use and self-prescription among resident physicians. *JAMA.* 1998;280:1253-1255.
3. Hughes PH, Brandenburg N, Baldwin DC Jr, *et al.* Prevalence of substance use among US physicians. *JAMA.* 1992;267:2333-2339.
4. Wachtel TJ, Wilcox VL, Moulton AW, Tammaro D, Stein MD. Physicians' utilization of health care. *J Gen Intern Med.* 1995;10:261-265.
5. Westfall JM, McCabe J, Nicholas RA. Personal use of drug samples by physicians and office staff. *JAMA.* 1997;278:141-143.
6. Aboff BM, Collier VU, Farber NJ, Ehrenthal DB. Residents' prescription writing for nonpatients. *JAMA.* 2002;288:381-385.

CHAPTER 19

Recalculating Route: How to Pivot When Problems Arise

Neil Baum, MD

If you travel with a GPS, it's likely you've had this happen. Your GPS is programmed to get you to your destination in a safe and reliable way until you miss a turn or an exit on the freeway. You go straight instead of turning where the system wants you to turn, and in an irritated voice, the GPS responds with "recalculating route."

It's amazing how human the equipment sounds when you've gone against its recommendation. Maybe that happens in your medical practice, too. Your hospital does something like start hiring physicians that will compete with your practice, or an insurance company wants to renegotiate your contract and reduce your reimbursement. You find that you may be forced to "recalculate your route."

It's possible, however, that there is a good reason for taking a new path instead of the familiar trail. Maybe you've been going the distance in your medical practice and using the same route or skills that you learned decades ago in medical school or in your residency or fellowship training. Maybe it's time to change the direction or simply to recalculate your route.

THE INTERNET

Probably nothing has changed the course and direction of modern medicine more than the Internet. The Internet has leveled the playing field between doctors and patients. Just a few decades ago, physicians had all of the information, and patients merely accepted everything that the doctor told them. That was the day of coming to the doctor with a chief complaint, having an examination, and receiving a prescription, with the doctor patting the patient on the back and offering to see him or her again in a few weeks.

Not today! The modern patient arrives in the office with a briefcase or folder full of material on his or her medical problem that the patient downloaded from the Internet. The patient has as much information as the doctor — or even more. Yes, much of it is inaccurate or not from credible sources, but, nonetheless, the patient has medical information. The doctor, therefore, must take into account the information that the patient has, sort out what is accurate and what is not, and then make recommendations and a plan of action that take into consideration the knowledge that the patient brings to the doctor–patient encounter. It is time to recalculate your route regarding the patient encounter: you can expect every patient is going to be Internet savvy, and you will no longer be the only one in the equation that has all of the information.

AFFORDABLE CARE ACT

In the past we enjoyed low volumes of patients and very acceptable reimbursements and profit margins. Not today! The passage of the Affordable Care Act means that between 20 and 40 million patients who were previously uninsured will be added to the healthcare system. Many of these previously uninsured patients will be older and sicker and require more time and medical resources. Compounding this situation is that there is no increase in the number of physicians being produced in our medical schools to care for this large number of patients that will be added to the healthcare system. As a result we will have to recalculate our route. We will have to become more efficient and be able to see more patients in the same amount of time, with the same staff, and yet preserve patient satisfaction.

FROM THE OPERATING ROOM TO THE OFFICE

Just a few years ago most procedures were conducted in the hospital, the operating room, or in outpatient surgery centers. Not today. More doctors are moving to an office-based practice where procedures once done in the hospital are now performed in the office setting. Thirty years ago, I performed five to six prostate operations a month in the hospital. Today, I perform a microwave procedure in the office under a local anesthetic. I estimate that in the near future 80% of all procedures will be done in the office or in one-day surgery centers, not in hospital operating rooms. It's time to recalculate your route if your route has been to make extensive use of the operating rooms in your hospital.

USE OF A SCRIBE

In the past, doctors would take the history of the present illness, the medical history, and the review of systems, followed by the physical examination and then institution of the treatment plan. For most physicians, the first encounter with a new patient can take 30 to 45 minutes. It is hardly a good use of the doctor's time to ask about previous surgical procedures, medications and over-the-counter supplements used, and how many cigarettes and alcoholic beverages are consumed each day. This can be done by someone else who is paid a much lower salary than the physician.

A scribe shadows a physician and takes notes either in the chart, or, better yet, on the computer, thus freeing the doctor to have more eye-to-eye contact with the patient and eliminating the need to have his or her face turned to the computer.

The scribe interacts with a new patient after the doctor introduces him- or herself to the patient. The scribe then takes the history of the present illness, and records the past medical history and the review of systems. While the scribe completes the evaluation of the new patient, the doctor can see several other patients or do a short procedure.

If you aren't using a scribe, it's time to recalculate your route and consider hiring someone else to gather this information from new patients. Remember, doctors should do what only doctors can do, and delegate all other activities.

ANCILLARY INCOME

Only a few decades ago, doctors received a fee for their services, which included seeing patients in the office and performing procedures in the hospital. There was no opportunity for any additional income. Today it is different. We now have an opportunity to earn additional income by owning diagnostic equipment such as CT scanners, having in-office laboratories, and owning outpatient surgery centers. This opens up revenue streams that can compensate for decreased reimbursements that nearly every practice faces. If you don't have any additional revenue streams beside the fees that your receive for the face-to-face care you provide, then recalculate your route.

USING NURSE PRACTITIONERS, MEDICAL ASSISTANTS, AND PHYSICIAN ASSISTANTS

Doctors for the most part are maxed out. They don't have enough time to see the patients they already have. As recently as 100 years ago, nurses were not allowed to even take a patient's blood pressure. Now physician assistants are assisting doctors and providing care for patients under a physician's supervision, making the doctor more efficient and more productive. If you are micromanaging your practice and doing everything yourself, then it's time to recalculate your route. It is time to delegate to nurse practitioners, medical assistants, and physician assistants. Again, what can easily be done by others should not be done by physicians.

OPEN SURGERY TO ROBOTIC SURGERY

Surgery has a long tradition of change and innovation. However, nothing has changed the course of modern surgery away from the traditional open surgical procedure more than the use of laparoscopy and then robotic surgery. Although the results of robotic surgery as compared with open surgery are controversial, the public and the media have touted the advantages of robotic surgery over traditional open surgery. If you are a surgeon and aren't offering robotic surgery to your patients, it may be time to recalculate your route.

HOUSE CALLS TO OFFICE AND BACK TO HOUSE CALLS

Seventy-five years ago, doctors routinely made house calls. Then there came a period when doctors believed that they needed more equipment than they could carry in their black bags and requested that the patients come to the office or meet them in the emergency department. Today the pendulum is swinging back to doctors once again making house calls. There is a budding industry of physicians who only conduct house calls and have reduced their overhead to their cell phone and their automobile. If you are in primary care, you may want to recalculate your route and offer house calls to your patients.

FEE-FOR-SERVICE TO CONCIERGE MEDICINE

Doctors have watched their reimbursements decrease and their incomes go south. (This might also be a reflection of poor investments and poor financial planning.) As a result, some established physicians with upscale patients who require more medical care are offering 24/7 access to the physician at an annual fee ranging from $1500 to $3000. This concept, concierge medicine, is catching on, and is attractive to physicians who don't want to be involved with the paperwork that has been inundating the medical profession in the past two decades. If you have patients who can afford the annual fee and you are willing to offer this kind of service, you may consider recalculating your route.

YELLOW PAGES TO SOCIAL MEDIA

I began practice 35 years ago, and the first thing I did after placing my name on the door of my office was to obtain a small Yellow Pages ad in the local phone book. These days, I doubt even five patients per year locate me via the Yellow Pages. But hundreds are able to find me through the use of Google and social media. If you still have more than your name, address, and phone number and perhaps your practice Web site in small print in the Yellow Pages, then it's time to recalculate your route.

PAPER TO ELECTRONIC MEDICAL RECORDS

For many years the standard of care was for physicians to make notes on paper for each patient and keep a file for each patient in a large filing cabinet. The computer changed all of that. We had to recalculate our paper route!

Bottom Line: Medicine is changing at a very rapid pace. It is difficult for physicians to keep up with all of these changes. However, the physician who doesn't make modifications and changes is going to find him- or herself without patients to care for. Therefore, it is necessary to take a look at our practices from 20,000 feet up. If we don't like what we see, then it just may be time to recalculate our route.

CHAPTER 20

Want a Successful Practice? Make Your Bed!

Neil Baum, MD

LESSONS FROM NAVAL ADMIRAL WILLIAM MCRAVEN, PRESIDENT OF THE UNIVERSITY OF TEXAS

Let me bare my soul; I'm an addict — not to drugs, but to graduation speeches. I have had the honor of giving two graduation speeches, but I have read, listened to, and watched several hundred speeches, especially college graduation speeches, because these are given by some of the best speakers who are invited to give the final motivational pitch before the graduates depart from their college or university. I clearly remember the graduation speaker — Walter Cronkite — who gave the commencement address to my class at Ohio State University in 1968 and how Mr. Cronkite convinced me that I could change the world with the skills I had learned in four years at Ohio State Medical School. Walter Cronkite's commencement address was the greatest speech I had ever heard until 2014, when I watched the graduation speech by Admiral William McRaven, who was a Navy Seal and, at the time, the president of the University of Texas. In this chapter, I take a few excerpts from that speech and suggest how they can apply to contemporary medicine.

1. Start your day with a simple task completed.

If you want to change the world...make your bed! McRaven's early training as a Navy Seal placed emphasis on a properly made bed. The sheets and blanket had to be so tight that the inspector or staff sergeant could bounce a half dollar off the bed and catch the half dollar in the air.

Why is this important? Whether you are a Navy Seal or a doctor, life is hard and often there is little that each of us can do to affect the outcome of our day. However, something as simple as making your bed can give you the lift you need to start your day and can provide you with the lift to end the day doing good for others and the world.

How does that apply to healthcare? I think it is a good idea to start each day with one small success. Making my bed didn't apply to me, because I would often awaken at 6:00 in the morning and my wife was still asleep, which precluded me from adjusting pillows, sheets, and blankets.

What was something else I could do that would provide me with a small success to start my day? Sometimes it was looking at my book of collected quotes on success and motivation and finding one that I would think about throughout the day. Other times it was three to five minutes of stretching exercises. This would limber me up and take away the snap, crackle, and pop when I got out of bed and headed to the bathroom. What I finally settled on was to take a vocabulary book and focus on just one word and its definition. I would use it in a sentence, I would add it to my calendar on my cell phone, and I would try to use the word in a sentence once or twice before leaving the house for the day. I considered this a way to start my day that would provide me with a taste of success that I hoped would lead to other small successes as the day went on.

2. You can't go it alone.

If you want to change the world...find someone(s) to help you paddle, even if it's upstream. McRaven faced many crises and obstacles, and he often relied on others to help him out of his difficulties. He believes it takes a team of good people that you can count on to get you to your destination in life.

It doesn't matter if you are an employed physician, in academic medicine, or in a small practice, you have to create a team and everyone has to pull their fair share of the load. You have to acknowledge everyone on the team and praise them for outstanding performance and pump them up or boost them when their performance is less than acceptable.

For example, I had eight employees, and there was a week when three of them were out — either on vacation or not well enough to come to work. The five remaining dug in and made sure that nothing fell through the cracks and that the majority of our patients were seen on time. On Friday afternoon, I called a team meeting and thanked them for their extra effort so that they knew I was grateful for all their hard work. To show my appreciation, I brought in a massage therapist and everyone got a 20-minute massage, which was my way of saying how much their hard work was valued.

Show your staff or team that you care about them. One of my employees was sick and needed to see a specialist. When she called the doctor's office, she was told that the next available appointment was in two weeks. I knew how sick she was and didn't feel it was acceptable for her to wait for two weeks. I spoke to the doctor and explained the situation, and he was able to see her at the end of his day. I sent the doctor a thank-you note and a small gift from myself and my employee. My employee was very appreciative of the effort that I extended on her behalf, and I think that it created a loyal bond between her and my practice.

3. Only the size of your heart matters.

If you want to change the world, measure a person by the size of their heart. The Seals had rigid criteria for who could be part of that elite organization. McRaven noted that it wasn't the candidate who was the strongest, the one who was the best shot, or the one who could hold their breath for the underwater swim the longest who made the best Seal. Instead, it was often what was in their heart that determined what kind of Seal they would make.

4. Life's not fair — drive on.

McRaven noted that great men and women are defined by how they deal with life's unfairness. Some of the examples he cited include Helen Keller, Nelson Mandela, Stephen Hawking, and Malala Yousafzai. His message is: don't complain, and stop having a pity party; stand tall, look to the future, and carry on.

You will have patients that you just can't seem to please. No matter what you do, it is not enough. You almost want to suggest that they go elsewhere for their medical care. But that's the easy way out. You can be sure that patient won't be touting your skills and your services if you dismiss him or her from your practice. Unless the patient is abusive of you or your staff or is asking you to do something that isn't ethical, then I believe, like Commander McRaven, that you have to step up to the plate and find a way to satisfy even the most difficult patient.

I remember a patient who had a prostate operation and was told that he could go back to work. I was completing his back-to-work form and when

I got to the date he could report back to duty, the patient asked me, "Dr. Baum, it's hunting season next week. Would you give me a few more days off?" Now I could have easily put in a date that granted him a few days in the woods hunting for deer or turkeys, but that would have been wrong, because he was completely capable of resuming his employment. I also could have told him no I wouldn't do it and not given him an explanation. However, I wanted him to know that I understood his request but wouldn't lie on his behalf. I explained that he was fortunate to have a job and if he wanted to go hunting, he should use his vacation days. He responded that he understood and would speak to his wife to figure out how he was going to manage his desire to go hunting.

Another example was a patient who requested that I send their records to another urologist. I was surprised, because I thought that my staff and I had done everything reasonable to help with his medical problems. I contacted the patient about his reason for his departure, and he gave a very vague response. I asked if it was something my staff or I had done, and he said it was not. I made a copy of his records, wrote a summary of his care to that point, and mailed the records to the patient. At the end of the letter to the patient, I wrote, "If there is anything else I or my office staff can do for you, please let me hear from you." It was nearly a year after the departing patient asked for his records that he made an appointment to return to the practice. I think by showing my concern for the patient, I left the door open for him to return to the practice. I hope my behavior showed him my heart.

5. Failure can make you stronger.

Admiral McRaven observed that true leaders learn from their failures; they use the lessons to motivate themselves, and not be afraid to try again or make the next tough decision.

6. You must dare greatly.

If you are in constant fear of failure, or hardship, or embarrassment, you will never achieve your greatest potential. Without daring greatly, you will never know what is truly possible in your life.

7. Stand up to the bullies.

Don't back down from the sharks. Bullies thrive on fear and intimidation, and, like sharks, they can sense fear in the water. If you don't find the courage to stand your ground, they will strike. There is great courage within all of us. Dig deep and you will find it in abundance.

An office nurse in my community was asked by her doctor to prepare testosterone pellets for a patient, but when she went to do that, the pellets were not in their sterile container. The nurse told the doctor, and the doctor wanted her to use them anyway. The nurse told the doctor that she wouldn't comply with his request and got his attention when she asked the doctor if he would insert nonsterile pellets into his father. I was so very proud of the nurse for standing up to the doctor — her employer — as she was thinking about the patient first.

That's the rule in our office: do what is in the best interest of the patient, and no questions will be asked.

8. Rise to the occasion.

Be your very best in the darkest moments. We will all face disappointment. That is the time, in that dark moment, you need to reach deep inside yourself and be your very best.

I will never forget the date I lost my first patient. It happened after a surgical procedure to remove a kidney stone from a patient with spina bifida. I was devastated and felt guilty that I caused his demise. The experience caused me to question my decision to become a doctor. I didn't know if I was capable of managing adversity, failure, and complications. I was experiencing mild depression and questioned my resolve in remaining in the profession. It was a professor who recognized my dilemma and took me out of the hospital for a cup of coffee. The professor explained that every doctor will encounter the loss of a patient at some time in his career... unless he or she is a radiologist or a pathologist. It comes with the profession. Not every patient will get better or be cured. We have to accept that we aren't god-like healers and that we will experience an occasional failure.

9. Give people hope.

This is the time to lift up those around you and give them hope that tomorrow will be a better day.

On August 31, 2005, Hurricane Katrina visited the Gulf Coast, including an almost direct hit on the city of New Orleans. The city was under mandatory evacuation. Thousands of citizens were left stranded at the Superdome and the Convention Center. People died of heat exhaustion in temperatures over 100 degrees with no water, and drowned when the levies of the Mississippi River were breached. Depression among the citizenry was rampant. Doctors and early responders were called upon to provide hope and to get started rebuilding the city and restoring law and order in the community. We have to do the same with our patients. Provide them with hope, but always tell them the truth. Patients expect the truth but they also want to have hope.

10. Never ever quit.

Don't ever, ever ring the bell. Seal training is the most daunting, punishing, and physically exhausting training experience. Seal trainees are told on the first day that if the pain is too great, the way out is to ring the bell three times. However, if you refuse to give up on your dreams and stand tall and strong against the odds, then life will be what you make of it, and you can make it great. Don't ring the bell.

Yes, American healthcare is in disarray. There is no short-term fix that can cure the system overnight. We have one of the greatest healthcare systems on the planet, even with all the problems that we have. Let's not ring the bell.

Bottom Line: I couldn't close this chapter any better than to quote Admiral McRaven: "These are just a few suggestions that may help you on your way to a better a world. And while these lessons were learned during my time in the military, I can assure you that it matters not whether you ever served a day in uniform. It matters not your gender, your ethnic or religious background, your orientation, or your social status. Our struggles in this world are similar, and the lessons to overcome those struggles and to move forward — changing ourselves and the world around us — will apply equally to all." So get started and make your bed!

CHAPTER 21

Barriers to Entry or Exit: Which Ones Are You Building?

Michael T. Harris, MD, and Neil H. Baum, MD

Think of your practice as if it were a castle. The goal is to get as many patients as possible into your castle. This also includes getting doctors to refer to your practice and/or insurance companies to include you on their panels. So regardless of your target market, by lowering the drawbridge for easier entry you are likely to attract more business to your medical practice. Continuing this metaphor, we want to raise the drawbridge to prevent people from exiting. If it is easy for patients to enter the castle, and they have a positive experience within the walls, and it is easier to continue to live there than to go elsewhere, then the castle is well-designed.

Therefore, it is important to think of barriers in both directions: barriers preventing access to your practice, which are to be minimized, and barriers to exit the practice, for which you should strive. This chapter will describe how to make your castle a fortress by removing barriers to entry and constructing barriers to exit the practice.

BARRIERS TO ENTRY

Before the Patient Arrives

Poor Initial Contact

Most doctors don't answer their own phones. So the first impression new patients and referring physicians get from your practice rests on the shoulders of your receptionist. If the phone is answered by a harried, stressed-out person whose first words are, "Doctor's office, please hold," all he or she may hear in return is "click." This is a true barrier to entry that may result in the caller hanging up and calling a competitor. This is easily remedied by scripting the greeting for all incoming calls. "Good morning, you've reached Medical Associates, my name is Elizabeth. How may I help you?"

Can't Get an Appointment for Weeks
What message do you send a potential patient who calls for an appointment and is told "nothing is available for three months?" If a woman with an acute onset of new symptoms (even ones the doctor or staff member thinks are minor) calls for an appointment, you can be sure she will be calling a competitor in a nanosecond if you don't plan to see her within the next 24 hours. You will have lost an opportunity for a new patient because you don't have a provision for seeing new patients with urgencies or emergencies. Leaving open slots for emergencies or utilizing scheduling templates available in most physician computer software will go a long way to help capture that new business.

No Web Site
If you are still depending on your *Yellow Pages* ad to let patients know where you are located and what your telephone number is, you are practicing in the era of leeches, ledger cards, and rotary phones! Patients are going to the Internet in large numbers and are looking there for health-related information. If you are not on the Web, you are missing out on a great opportunity to attract and interact with your existing patients as well as attract new patients.

Hospital with a Poor Reputation
Have you checked the reputation of the hospital where you admit your patients? The quality of the hospital can easily be checked on the Web site of the Centers for Medicare & Medicaid Services at www.hospitalcompare.hhs.gov. Now you can compare your hospital with other hospitals in the community with three clicks of a mouse. And all of your patients will check. If your hospital is deficient in quality measures, this is generating a barrier for entry not only for your hospital but also for your practice. (As an aside, you *must* participate in your hospital's quality improvement programs or you *will* suffer the consequences of diminished patient volume and lower income.)

Poor Online Ratings
Have you seen your scores on Healthgrades.com? Your patients have. You must monitor your own online profile to see what patients see when they Google you. In the very near future, doctors will be compensated based on

metrics that judge the quality of the services they provide to their patients. One measure of quality is patient satisfaction. You must start measuring your practice-based metrics so you will be in a position to favorably compare with your competitors — for patients and for dollars.

Getting There

Location of Office in a "Bad" Part of Town

In real estate, the key to sales success is location, location, and location. Location of your office is also important and can serve as a barrier to entry if the office is situated in a less than desirable area.

Bad Signage

How do patients arrive at your practice? Are there are well-marked signs on the building? Is it clear to patients entering the building how to locate your practice once inside the building? Are there directions on your Web site that describe how to find the practice? These are important questions that each doctor and practice has to answer because your patients are asking these questions on a regular basis.

Paying for Parking

Does your practice offer free parking? Are there ample parking facilities in close proximity to your practice? Practices that offer free or validated parking have a distinct advantage over practices that require patients to pay $15 to $20 (or even more, in some large cities) each time they visit your practice.

No Handicapped Access

Not only is it the law that you must provide handicapped access to your practice, but it is good for business as well. Take a look at your practice and see if it is accessible to wheelchairs, patients with motor impairment, patients who are visually impaired, and patients who have hearing problems.

Once the Patient Arrives

Lukewarm Greeting

The doctor is almost certainly not the first person that your patients meet when they walk in your door. In fact, it is likely that they have spoken with at least one or two people in your office more than once, and will now meet at least two people *before* ever setting eyes on the doctor. Make sure that patients are greeted as if they are old friends, and that the receptionist has been expecting them and is happy to see them. If your staff has done the right things on the phone, patients will actually be excited to "finally meet" your staff and become part of the practice.

Unpleasant Reception Area

It has been said that patients should not go to a doctor who has dead fish in his or her aquarium or dead plants in the pots! The same applies to the reading material in the reception area. Magazines that are more than a year old do not indicate a practice that is current, fresh, or going to be helpful. We suggest that you regularly purge your reception area and exam rooms of magazines and print materials that are more than three months old. A nice gesture if you see a patient reading a magazine that is a few months old is to offer to give it to him or her. It is an easy way to keep the old magazines out of the office.

It is also critical that your reception area looks and smells clean, and that the furniture and fixtures are in good repair. Your reception area should look more like a living room than an office.

Outdated Equipment

If your exam tables have plastic that is torn or rusted legs or stirrups, you are sending a terrible message to your patients. The same applies to your equipment. One of us (NHB) is a urologist, and it is considered standard state-of-the-art to have a flexible cystoscope. Having a rigid instrument certainly indicates that your practice is antiquated, and using equipment that is less than state-of-the-art may indicate that the doctor is not up to date with his or her clinical skills.

Dirty Restroom

What goes through your mind when you are on an airplane and pull down the tray on the back of the seat in front of you and find coffee stains and dried food from the previous passengers on the tray? You just might be concerned about how the airline conducts maintenance and repairs on the planes' engines. The same thoughts go through your patients' mind when they go into the restroom and find a full wastebasket, paper towels on the floor, spilled specimen cups, and no toilet paper. This is a reflection on your practice's hygiene and sends a message that may be a barrier to entry to your practice.

You Are in a Rush

Have you conducted patient satisfaction surveys? If so, what are patients saying about the doctors in the practice? Do the doctors appear to be always in a hurry? Do the doctors answer all of the patients' questions? Do the doctors stand during the entire patient encounter with their hand on the doorknob? If any of your patients answer yes to these questions, you are creating a barrier to entry. The patient may be there, but you will fail to "close the sale." And the patient will seek care elsewhere. Like any other skills, interpersonal skills can be learned.

BARRIERS TO PREVENT EXIT

Let's get back to our metaphor of the castle. Are you creating such an incredibly positive experience for patients that they would never think of leaving the practice? This is the kind of defense you want to have so that patients would never think of exiting the practice. Let's look at some examples.

Signs Clearly Marking the Practice

Make sure that the signs identifying your practice are clearly visible to any patient looking for your office. This includes the building, the directory inside the building, and next to the front door of the office.

Robust Web Site and Use of Social Media

If your Web site is more than an online version of your brochure and allows the patients an opportunity to interact with the doctor and the practice, you will have built a barrier to exit. Patients are expecting their doctor and practice to have an Internet presence. They are expecting to be able to obtain information on their medical problems with up-to-date educational material. They expect to be able to make an appointment online. They expect that they can have their prescriptions refilled with an online request. These electronic interactions are desirable, and some will soon be mandated by law, so now is the time to get started.

Email

These days, most patients have an email address and would like to communicate with their doctors using this technology. Patients are just as busy as physicians and are not interested in playing phone tag with their doctor. If they have simple questions, they would like to be able to have them answered without having to make an appointment. A doctor who encourages emails from his or her patients is building an exit barrier. This topic is complex, however, with significant privacy and malpractice implications, so be sure to check with your IT consultant and/or legal counsel before agreeing to email with patients.

Patient Record Access Portal

Patients want to have copies or access to their medical records. We live in a very mobile society, and patients do not always stay in one location. If they are away from their physicians, they want to be able to show their healthcare information to a new provider or an emergency department doctor, or just have the security of knowing that they own their data and records. The day is gone where patients have to beg for copies of their records or pay $1.50 per page to have them copied and mailed. Providing a patient portal makes your practice special and creates one more obstacle for the patient to leave your practice.

Same-Day or Next-Day Appointment

When patients have a medical complaint, in their opinion it is something that needs immediate attention. If you are able to accommodate emergencies and urgencies the same day a patient calls the office to request an appointment, you will have constructed a barrier to exit. This also applies to any new patient who calls the office for an appointment. You will endear yourself to this new patient, and he or she won't look for an excuse to leave your practice. Give patients easy access to your practice, and you will have devoted and loyal patients.

Welcoming Receptionist

The first introduction to your practice is the receptionist. The receptionist provides the *only* opportunity to create a positive first impression. If the receptionist is a happy person who likes his or her job and makes the patient excited and enthusiastic about coming to the practice, you will have a nice blockade for exiting the practice. If there is no glass partition or frosted window between the reception area and the back office, you will create a patients-first atmosphere in your practice.

Short Wait Times

Patients have a short fuse when it comes to waiting for their medical care.

Anything longer than 15 minutes is unacceptable today. The best way to get a handle on the wait times is to do a time and motion study, and record the time the patient was to be in the office, the time in reception area and the exam room, and the time that the patient waited to see the physician. If a patient's wait time is longer than 15 minutes, you will have demonstrated a lack of respect for his or her time, and you will have built a bridge rather than a barrier to exiting the practice.

Post-Discharge Phone Calls

Seldom do patients receive a call from the doctor or practice after they have had a procedure or after discharge from the hospital. Every patient who has a procedure or is leaving the hospital has a question(s) about their medications, their dressing, the dos and don'ts, and their follow-up appointment. The practice that calls the patient at home demonstrates the extra attention that its patients are receiving and is building a huge barrier to exit. And a side benefit to you is that this process dramatically reduces the volume of incoming phone calls from patients.

State-of-the-Art Technology

Patients who see that the practice has an electronic medical records system and uses electronic blood pressure cuffs and thermometers will assume that the clinical skills of the doctor are also in the 21st century.

Paid Parking

It is such a nice perk to offer to pay for patients' parking or offer a discount stamp for the parking lot in or near your office building. It's one more barrier to exit.

One-Stop Shopping

Patients who come to the office and are able to get their lab testing and imaging performed in the same place will be thankful for this service. It takes so much extra time to go to the off-site laboratory or imaging facility. You will really hit a home run with your patients if their workup can be conducted on their first visit. For example, a woman sees her doctor for a routine breast examination. If the doctor finds something on the examination and can immediately do an ultrasound and a biopsy during that same visit, he or she goes a long way toward alleviating the patient's anxiety by reducing the wait time for a diagnosis and treatment. This is even more the case if there is a pathologist in the same office who can immediately read the slides.

Insurance Assistance

Insurance forms can be very confusing. Offices with staff members that help patients with their paperwork and spend time explaining the insurance process have another arrow in their barrier-to-exit quiver.

Translators

We live in a multicultural and multilingual society. If you have patients that speak languages other than English and have an onsite translator, you will be able to endear yourself to these patients, and they will often send their friends and family members to your practice. This is especially true in communities with large immigrant populations. Spanish, Korean, and Russian communities are particularly close-knit, and are grateful for healthcare providers that speak their languages.

Unique Services

Have you looked at the services, procedures, or technologies that are offered by your competitors? Are you differentiating your practice from that of your competitors? If not, you are missing an opportunity to build an exit bridge. Take a look around and see what niches are out there. Remember there are riches in the niches!

Bottom Line: Barriers can be positive or negative. A negative barrier is an obstacle to enter the practice. Make every effort to identify and remove them. A positive barrier is a fence that prevents patients from leaving. Build and strengthen these barriers to exit. If you look at your practice as a castle and eliminate the negative barriers and fortify the positive ones, you will be on your way to having a very successful practice.

CHAPTER 22

An Incentive Plan That Enhances Productivity

John McDaniel, MHA, and Neil Baum, MD

If your practice is like most practices, you are likely to provide a bonus to your staff when the Christmas holiday arrives. Most practices provide a bonus regardless of the productivity of the practice, the gross or net income, or the number of new patients who enter the practice. Even if the practice is less productive, such as in 2020 with COVID-19 affecting the bottom line, practices will still offer a bonus to the staff. You check with your accountant or office manager to see what bonus you provided last year, and you increase the amount from 5% to 15%, depending on the profitability of the practice. Employees learn to expect the bonus and, employers cringe when they give out a bonus even though there has been no increase in productivity or profitability of the practice. This scenario is all too familiar to most of us. What is the solution? We can keep the *status quo* and begrudgingly continue with the December bonus as we have in the past. Another ineffective option is to stop the bonus program — in which case you know there will be blowback from the staff, and staff morale will certainly deteriorate. A third option is to use nonmonetary motivators, a choice that seldom placates the staff. The best approach is to implement a bonus plan based on incentives and productivity. The incentive bonus plan is truly a win for the employees and a win for the employer. As a further benefit, this plan ultimately improves patient satisfaction and leads to positive word-of-mouth marketing for your practice.

To summarize, there are three possible approaches to the bonus problem:

- Continue the *status quo*;
- Eliminate bonuses altogether; or
- Change the current method to combine both monetary as well as non-monetary rewards such as increased time off, gift cards, or discounted parking.

Continuing the *status quo* is, for most practices, not a reasonable solution. The problems continue, and, in fact, will continue to escalate each year. The practice's doctors feel resentful for offering a bonus if there has been no improvement in the bottom line, whereas the staff feel unappreciated when the practice is growing and improving and they don't enjoy the benefits of this enhanced productivity.

Eliminating bonuses would be easy, but this would create more controversy than continuing the current system. Ultimately, most physicians are committed to rewarding their employees in some fashion.

If the objective of an employee bonus is recognition, motivation, and employee retention, then nonmonetary *plus* monetary rewards can be very effective.

The best approach is to turn a bonus plan into an incentive plan. Employees will work harder to achieve a bonus when they know that the bonus is tied into reaching goals and objectives than when the bonus is merely given to them for showing up day in and day out and doing only what is required in their job description or the employee manual. A better solution is to set quarterly goals for the practice and give quarterly monetary rewards for reaching those goals. This is best accomplished by notifying employees about changes in the bonus structure and asking for their involvement and participation in setting goals.

IMPLEMENTING AN INCENTIVE PLAN

Start by sending an email or memo to the staff explaining the change in the bonus structure, describing the monetary parts of the plan and inviting input. This letter should not be sent right after Thanksgiving; wait until after the first of the year. Most of your staff can be expected to react to the communication positively and began talking about goals and suggestions. The next step is to hold a staff meeting on the rewards topic to resolve any misunderstandings.

An example would be to establish a monetary incentive such as one week's pay distributed as a yearly amount — for example, one-fourth of the total bonus distributed each quarter. With input from employees, you can develop your own quarterly performance goals, such as the following:

- Quarter 1: A dollar amount for collections.

- Quarter 2: Collecting copays at the time of each visit, thus reducing your billing expenses. The second quarter could also review denials and reward the staff for decreasing denials, because this is income owed to the practice that is being held by payers.
- Quarter 3: Number of surgeries performed or reimbursement for profitable office procedures; and
- Quarter 4: Successful attainment of the first three goals.

Other considerations for goals might include total patients seen each quarter; the number of new patients seen in each quarter; new referrals each quarter (especially in specialist practices); or reduction in accounts receivables. At least in the beginning, select one or two metrics to monitor for the bonus plan. If you take on too many goals, the program can become cumbersome and unwieldy.

At the end of each quarter, managers or team leaders report the results to the staff. If the goals have been achieved, the practice issues bonus checks at the beginning of the next quarter for the previous quarter. I suggest that you give the last quarter bonus right after Thanksgiving so that your staff can use the money for their holiday spending. I do not recommend creating goals that are not quantifiable, such as positive comments from the doctor's online reputation review site or results of patient surveys. These metrics are difficult to measure and can be manipulated by the staff.

RESULTS OF THE INCENTIVE BONUS PLAN

This kind of incentive plan changes the long-standing habit of automatically giving annual holiday bonuses. The employees are involved from the very beginning and have a "buy-in," because it is their program and they have agreed to the goals and the objectives. You can expect your staff to make acceptable suggestions and discuss new goals among themselves in preparation for future quarters.

It is imperative to warn the employees of the inappropriateness of discussing bonus amounts with fellow employees. You will find that you can eliminate much disgruntlement by standardizing the bonus amount and tying it to each person's compensation level.

You will find that most physicians will be satisfied with the results of reaching new practice goals. Just setting goals focuses employees' attention on critical areas of the practice or individual performance of job duties. Although goals change each quarter, employees continue to respond to previous quarters' goals.

GETTING STARTED

A practice that decides to implement a bonus or incentive plan needs to:

- Plan carefully;
- Communicate the plan clearly to every employee;
- Ensure measurable objectives; and
- Involve staff in the planning process.

Although these requirements may seem easy and obvious, they can be a challenge to accomplish and will take some time and effort to implement. The new system requires positive attitudes from the employees, and commitment on the part of the physicians to reward staff plays a key role.

Careful crafting of the bonus program at the beginning may avoid the need to change it in the future. It is better to implement a plan in slow, carefully developed steps, considering the future growth of the practice.

Clear communication with employees is essential. They need to understand how the plan works, when it becomes effective, and what period of time it covers. Use of email is adequate for brief, back-and-forth messages, but if a significant concern arises, a group meeting is the most effective way to communicate and reach a plan that is acceptable to everyone.

Setting objectives may be difficult. It is important to develop goals that involve every employee. You may consider separate goals for each department. Don't forget the need to measure progress toward goals objectively — in hard numbers. Choose objective goals that can be quantitated; subjective goals present measurement problems and can spark disagreements over whether or not they were accomplished.

You can anticipate great value in involving employees in the planning process for the bonus/incentive plan. This can be accomplished either informally or formally through committees and staff meetings. Any plan is more likely to succeed when employees have input into the process.

A sample bonus plan might work like this: In 2018, the practice collected $1 million. In 2019, the practice collected $1.1 million, for a $100,000 increase in productivity. Your incentive plan agrees to share 10% of any increase in productivity ($10,000) with staff. So in a practice with five employees, each would receive $2000.

Bottom Line: For most practices, the greatest overhead expense is nonphysician staff salaries. You certainly don't want to improve your own bottom line at the expense of your staff. However, if production increases and profitability is also increased, you will want to pass part of this windfall to your staff. An incentive or bonus plan is one of the best ways to accomplish both objectives. And satisfied staff members are much more likely to satisfy patients and speak well of your practice to outsiders.

CHAPTER 23

Practice Management Advice from Dr. Seuss, Theodore Geisel

David Luechauer, PhD, and Neil Baum, MD

David Luechauer, PhD, and William Locander, PhD, Dean of the College of Business at Loyola University New Orleans, have published a series of articles targeted at CEOs and chief marketing officers in *Marketing Management*, the publication of the American Marketing Association. A host of clients, from hospitals and airlines to professional sports teams and educational institutions, have used Luechauer and Locander's articles to explore the many ways applying Dr. Seuss can lead to everything from leadership development and teambuilding to operational efficiency and effectiveness on the shop room floor. In this chapter, we show how the words of Dr. Seuss can serve as lessons for members of the healthcare profession.

"You're in pretty good shape for the shape you are in."—*You're Only Old Once!*

Most people do not realize that many of Dr. Seuss's books were written with adult themes in mind or that they often explored serious issues, ranging from racism (*The Sneetches,* 1961) to war (*The Butter Battle Book,* 1984). Dr. Seuss wrote *You're Only Old Once!* in 1986, shortly after he had suffered through a series of illnesses during which he spent a considerable amount of time in doctors' waiting rooms. To pass the time, he began sketching images of hospital machines and scenes of medical procedures. In the book, Dr. Seuss talked about his visit to "the Golden Years Clinic on Century Square for spleen readjustment and muffler repair."

Our patients will laugh with familiar horror at the poking and prodding and testing in that book, where Dr. Seuss looked at what it's like to get older. Dr.

Seuss said, "I am fed up with a social life consisting entirely of doctors." The book follows an elderly man on a visit to the Golden Years Clinic, where he endures long waits and bizarre medical tests. *You're Only Old Once!* reached the top of the *New York Times* Best Sellers list and remained on the list for over 60 weeks. It remains one of the strongest indictments of the healthcare system ever written, and the message is as relevant today as it was in 1986. So what is Dr. Seuss's message to physicians?

Most practices have senior citizens who have unique needs and wants. This book encourages us to remember that we must acknowledge and honor those differences as we care for the aging American population. Aging brings significant physiologic alterations, including sensory changes, decreased manual dexterity, and progressive hearing loss. Practices that want to be attractive to senior citizens need to take these predictable changes into account and help their older patients adapt to them. The book also makes us remember that patients, no matter what their age, need and want to be treated like human beings, not as clones, cattle, numbers, or cadavers. We need to treat the person behind the ailment as well as the ailment itself.

"Think left and think right and think low and think high. Oh, the thinks you can think up if only you try"—*Oh the Thinks You Can Think*

Doctors need to add creativity and out-of-the-box thinking with our patients and with our colleagues. If we remained with the *status quo* and only practiced with what we learned in medical school and in our post-graduate training, we would be antiquated and a disappointment to our patients. We are not suggesting that every physician be an early adoptor — but definitely don't wait to be a member of the late majority or the laggards.[1]

For example, author Baum was trained at the Baylor College of Medicine in Houston, Texas, and arrived in New Orleans in 1978 with skills that enabled him to implant the first inflatable penile prosthesis in Louisiana. After the first few of these surgical procedures, the local urologic community was trying to denigrate the procedure and the surgeon. It was difficult to obtain privileges in several of the local hospitals, and the academic community maligned him to the local and state urologic community. It wasn't until a few patients agreed to do local seminars and a few TV appearances that dozens and soon hundreds of patients called to find out more about the operation and became patients in the practice.

This was an example of a marketing tactic known as *first-mover advantage* that more physician leaders need to consider. At its most basic level, it should serve as a reminder that we labor in a profession noted for constantly evolving and developing. We must all be aware that what we learned yesterday and practice today may be totally obsolete or even proven wrong tomorrow. Therefore, none of us can afford to rest on either our laurels or our credentials.

"I meant what I said, and I said what I meant. An elephant's faithful one hundred percent."—*Horton Hatches the Egg*

In the medical community, words like *faithfulness, honor, integrity, authenticity,* and *ethics* often are espoused, but a review of almost any study of either patient or employee satisfaction in the healthcare industry will reveal that they are not practiced as often as we would like to believe. In fact, our friends in the legal community often benefit from our lapses in these areas, and while many suits are frivolous, there is enough truth in enough suits to cast doubt or leave us vulnerable to those who want to catch us at less than our best.

Moreover, effective leaders protect their colleagues and employees. If a patient or another physician runs roughshod over an employee, the leader steps up and protects that employee. We take an oath to do no harm — and this applies to how we run our practices and treat our teams every bit as much as it pertains to how we treat our patients. This develops trust and loyalty within the practice, hospital, or organization.

Being faithful like Horton the elephant is not easy, especially when we are trying to be patient-focused. According to Locander and Luechauer,[2-7] faithfulness requires consistency of behavior. The leader — for example, the office manager — has to behave in a consistent fashion to all employees, not just a select few. For example, if a valued employee is repeatedly late for work, and no action is taken against the tardy employee, then the remaining employees will lose confidence in the leader and believe that the leader is showing favoritism to certain employees. There is no faster way to damage morale than to deviate from being consistent with everyone in the organization.

"You're on your own. And you know what you know. And YOU are the one who'll decide where to go . . . Step with care and great tact. And remember that life's a great balancing act."—*Oh, the Places You'll Go*

Speaking to this point, physicians and leaders face the challenge of balancing their personal and professional lives. This is a challenge that confronts every physician during his or her career.

Doctors are highly motivated to be effective in their professional lives, but maintaining a balance with their personal lives is a challenge for all of us. How you maintain this balance will ultimately determine not only your success but also your happiness. Perhaps the lesson we all must learn or relearn, is that "physician heal thyself" pertains to more than our physical well-being. We are accountable for modeling a way of life, mentally, physically, spiritually, and emotionally, that our patients can and would want to follow. A physician who saves a thousand lives but who has a dysfunctional personal life may not really be in the best position to dispense care.

Medicine is one of the noblest, if not *the* noblest, professions. It provides great satisfaction and gratification to those who practice it and those who receive our well-intended care. However, we are all challenged to remember that while we judge ourselves by our intentions, the world and our patients judge us by our actions. Actions speak so much louder than words. Therefore, we need to put balance into our careers. No one ever said medicine was easy or fun. But it can be both, and even more, if you have made an effort to balance your professional and personal lives. It can be done.[8]

"Why fit in when you were born to stand out?" (a Seussian sentiment, although he never uttered it in these exact words). We all know that copycats are a dime a dozen. The easiest thing in the world is to emulate or practice what others have done before you. Certainly, we cannot afford to perpetually reinvent the wheel or constantly discover fire. However, we can't stay stuck in the mud either. To this point, healthcare leaders should be bold, take risks, and move their practices, their hospitals, and the future of American healthcare forward. A well-known leadership maxim says that managers do things right, and leaders do the right things. That's the difference between fitting in and standing out.

"The more that you read, the more things you will know. The more that you learn, the more places you'll go."—*I Can Read With My Eyes Shut!*

We believe that leaders have a responsibility to get out in front and to truly lead. Leaders set the tone for the rest of the practice or the hospital through their actions. The best leaders typically are learners first. The great news is that you do not have to attend a conference or pay for an expensive workshop to get smarter. Technology allows leaders to leverage the wisdom of the world. As Dr. Seuss might say, "You can even become smarter in a box with a fox or on a train in the rain."

"With your head full of brains and your shoes full of feet, you're too smart to go down any not-so-good street."— *Oh, the Places You'll Go!*

The not-so-good street that many leaders end up on has to do with actions not matching words. A leader can have the best ideas and intentions yet go nowhere when the actions don't match up. A leader's actions must always be consistent and match his or her words. The leader must walk the talk. As physicians, we make choices and decisions on a daily basis. We will not be perfect or 100% accurate. However, we can and must be accountable for our choices and decisions. Moreover, when we do go down the not-so-good streets, we should treat them as opportunities to learn, not as opportunities for blame, denial, or whitewashing the truth.

"Be who you are and say what you feel, because those who mind don't matter, and those who matter don't mind." (These words are widely — and inaccurately — attributed to Dr. Seuss but actually came from Bernard Baruch, advisor to President Franklin Roosevelt.)[9]

If everyone is happy with the work you are doing, then you probably aren't leading much of anything, and your leadership skills will soon not be necessary. Leadership is about change and relentlessly seeking a better way. Medicine is about always trying to get better, to find a new treatment, a better drug, a less invasive diagnostic test, and ways to be more productive in the practice. It is quite common for many people in a practice to not be excited about change and a better way and to resist any changes in the *status quo*. Make sure you take inventory of those who mind and those who matter, and become an effective leader who gets everyone pulling for the changes that will make for better patient care, a happier staff, and, ultimately, a happier doctor.

"You have brains in your head. You have feet in your shoes. You can steer yourself any direction you choose."—*Oh, the Places You'll Go*

Do not be afraid to abandon an initiative that isn't working. Remember you can't get different results doing the same thing that doesn't work. Leaders often ignore signs that an initiative or project should change direction. Leaders can and should admit when a project has failed or an idea hasn't panned out. This type of transparency builds trust within an organization.

"Unless someone like you cares a whole awful lot, nothing is going to get better. It's not."—*The Lorax*

In mastering balance, we physicians cannot care about everyone and everything. However, it is incumbent upon each of us to care about something, to care a whole awful lot, and then do what we can to turn that caring into a reality. Whether it is providing low-cost and affordable service to a group of people who would otherwise be denied your care or finding a cure for the disease of your choice — we all have been given gifts, and it is up to us to use them wisely and well and not let them draw dust on the table. As the biblical injunction reminds us, from whom much is given, much is expected. We physicians have been given much, and giving back is more than just taking care of our patients. We can all practice Gandhi's timeless exhortation to "become the change we want to see in the world."

"From there to here, and here to there, funny things are everywhere."—*One Fish Two Fish Red Fish Blue Fish*

"If you never did, you should. These things are fun, and fun is good."—*One Fish Two Fish Red Fish Blue Fish*

Clearly, we don't all need to be Patch Adams. However, doctors need to add a little levity to their work and to their interactions with patients and their colleagues. Yes, we need to take our work seriously — but not necessarily ourselves. That does not mean we need to be a stand-up comedian or start out each patient encounter with a joke. But there's nothing in the Hippocratic oath that precludes the injection of a little humor as an elixir to help our patients feel better. For example, patients often ask one of us

(NHB) if certain supplements and herbs will cure their medical problem. The answer to that question might be something like, "As my wise old Jewish mother might say, 'It may not help, but it wouldn't hurt either.'" This is a humorous way to say, "You are wasting your money!" Remember "A merry heart doeth good like a medicine." (*Proverbs* 17:22).

Bottom Line: Let's hope that Dr. Seuss's wisdom is not offered only to children, because there is much value in healthcare leaders who are believed when they say ,"I meant what I said, and I said what I meant: A 'leader' is faithful, one hundred percent." What's our final suggestion? Pick up a copy and read *Oh, the Places You'll Go!* The words of Dr. Seuss will awaken and enlighten you — 98 and 3/4% guaranteed. *The Locander and Luechauer series first appeared in* Marketing Management, *a magazine produced for CEOs, chief medical officers, and other marketing professionals by the American Marketing Association. Reprints are available through www.ama.org.*

REFERENCES

1. Rogers EM. New product adoption and diffusion. *Journal of Consumer Research.* 1976;2:290-301.
2. Locander W, Luechauer D. Dr. Seuss's Sneetches. *Marketing Management.* 2008;17(1):44-47.
3. Locander W, Luechauer D. Trust & betrayal: Mayzie and Horton Leaders. *Marketing Management.* 2008;17(2):44-47.
4. Locander W, Luechauer D. Do you feel lucky? *Marketing Management.* 2008;17(3):55-58.
5. Locander W, Luechauer D. Leadership lessons from *The Butter Battle Book. Marketing Management.* 2008;17(4):43-45.
6. Locander W, Luechauer D. The places you'll go! *Marketing Management.* 2008;17(5):44-46.
7. Locander W, Luechauer D. Leadership lessons of Theodor Seuss Geisel. *Marketing Management.* 2008;17(6):43-46.
8. Baum N. Balancing your personal and professional lives. *Ochsner J.* 2008;8:160-162.
9. Baruch B. *Baruch: My Own Story.* Cutchogue, NY: Buccaneer Books, 1983.

BIBLIOGRAPHY

1. Dr. Seuss. *Oh, the Places You'll Go.* Random House, 1990.
2. Dr. Seuss. *The Butter Battle Book.* Random House, 1984.
3. Dr. Seuss. *Horton Hatches The Egg.* Random House, 1940.
4. Dr. Seuss. *I Can Read With My Eyes Shut.* Random House, 1978.
5. Dr. Seuss. *The Lorax.* Random House, 1971.
6. Dr. Seuss. *Oh, the Thinks You Can Think.* Random House, 1975.
7. Dr. Seuss. *One Fish Two Fish Red Fish Blue Fish.* Random House, 1960.
8. Dr. Seuss. *The Sneetches and Other Stories.* Random House, 1961.
9. Dr. Seuss. *You're Only Old Once.* Random House, 1986.

CHAPTER 24

Change Management: Managing Change in a Sea of Change

RON KING AND NEIL BAUM, MD

In the last decade, big changes in the healthcare profession have resulted in upheaval, stress and burnout, new types of reimbursement, and the implementation of technology with new ways of treating patients, such as telemedicine and genetic mapping.

Consider the book *Our Iceberg is Melting: Changing and Succeeding Under Any Conditions.*[1] The book tells the story of a colony of penguins living on an iceberg that is melting in Antarctica, making it necessary for the group to move to another, more stable iceberg. The other penguins will not listen to the penguin that has recognized that the iceberg is unstable and tries to alert the leaders and the wise elders of the colony about the perils of staying on their unstable iceberg. Most of the penguins are of the opinion that the iceberg that they have known for so long is fine and they don't need or want to change. The story is analogous to the common situation where people don't want to face up to difficult problems and are confronted with decisions that may require change.

However, when several of the penguins were presented evidence (data) that convinced them that their iceberg actually was melting, they rose to the occasion and:

1. Created a sense of urgency to deal with the difficult problem;
2. Put a group in charge of guiding the change;
3. Showed the possibility of a better future;
4. Communicated their vision to others;
5. Removed obstacles to action;
6. Persisted until the new way of life was firmly established; and, finally

7. Showed that stubborn, hard-to-die traditions would not save the colony from disaster if they stayed on the unstable iceberg.

So how does this apply to our medical practices that need to adopt to change in order to survive? Change does not take place easily in the healthcare arena. Healthcare workers and leaders often are comfortable with the *status quo* and often resist change. However, if we listen to our patients and pay attention to data regarding new methods of diagnosis and treatment, we will be in a position to challenge the *status quo*.

THE CHANGING FACE OF MEDICINE

Some examples of change that will have big effects on the healthcare profession in the very near future include telemedicine; precision medicine, and the changing role of the doctor–patient relationship in general.

Telemedicine

Telemedicine is slowly becoming accepted as a method of caring for patients without being eyeball-to-eyeball in the office or exam room. Today more than 15 million Americans have used remote medical care, thereby reducing healthcare costs by more than $6 billion.[2]

This new way of practicing medicine will consist of the virtual office visit. Doctors will be able to monitor chronic health conditions via computer. A Harvard study found that patients with hypertension who had "virtual" office visits over the Internet were able to control their blood pressure as well as people who had in-person office visits.[3] Patients in the virtual care group averaged about one fewer office visit than people in the other group over a period of six months, and they had fewer emergency department visits and hospitalizations overall. What does the future portend regarding change in healthcare? You can expect that in the future, virtual visits will become the norm rather than the exception. Virtual follow-up visits for other chronic diseases (e.g., congestive heart failure, diabetes, obesity, and benign enlargement of the prostate) also are on the horizon. In fact, many healthcare providers already use virtual care to follow 65 different kinds of chronic disease.[4]

Precision Medicine

Precision medicine uses 3D printing to create medications treating hypertension, high cholesterol, and heart disease. Ninety percent of prescribed medications are available as generic drugs and can be combined cost-effectively so patients take fewer individual medications. Imagine a patient with hypertension, diabetes, obesity, cardiac arrhythmia, and high cholesterol levels. This patient has a smartwatch or a smartphone that can record daily weight, glucose levels, blood pressure, and cholesterol levels. This information is sent electronically to a physician who makes adjustments in the medication and then transmits the information to a 3D printer in the patient's home that "prints" a pill that is precisely designed for that patient's condition at that time.

The new methods of data collection will soon affect the management of patients with certain cancers. Data — in particular, data stored in an electronic health record (EHR) — make personalized medicine possible. The EHR will contain clinical data such as diagnostic testing results, genetic test results, and pathology reports. The record also may include information about the patient's individual values, preferences, and lifestyle. The challenge is to ensure that the EHR not only contains all critical patient information, but also is organized so that clinicians can use it to provide optimal treatment for the patient.

For example, consider a 70-year-old patient who has newly diagnosed metastatic, non–small cell lung cancer. He has had a test to find out whether his tumor has one or more mutations that make it sensitive to a specific drug that has been suggested by his doctor. With the accumulation of voluminous amounts of data, it is necessary that the data be organized and comprehensive and that the data can be easily accessed. The data also must be interoperable among various medical systems to make the data useful.

The Changing Role of the Doctor–Patient Relationship

Seventy-five years ago, caring and compassion were major "treatments" doctors could offer. Over time, advances in medical science have provided new options that have often inadvertently distanced physicians from their patients.

Just a few decades ago, doctors had all the knowledge and information on health. Today, thanks to the Internet, patients can be just as informed as their doctors, because they have access to the same information that doctors have. As a result, patients want to be more involved in their healthcare decisions, and that means doctors must use innovative technology, informed patient engagement strategies, and different organizational structures to drive better patient experiences. These factors can result in disruptive, rapid change that results in alterations of the doctor–patient relationship. At the same time, because of the constraints of time and increased requirement for doctors to complete an abundance of paperwork, today doctors face a healthcare environment in which patients and their families often are excluded from important discussions about how to navigate the overwhelming array of diagnostic and treatment options available to them.

In 1988, the concept of *patient-centered care* brought attention of the need for clinicians, staff, and healthcare systems to shift their focus away from diseases and back to the patient and family.[5] The term was meant to stress the importance of better understanding the patient's experience of illness and of addressing the patient's needs within an increasingly complex and fragmented healthcare delivery system.

Now there is an approach called *shared decision-making*, a much needed change in the way doctors speak to patients so that they work together as a team or a unit to come to a decision regarding the care the patient will receive. The process by which the optimal decision may be reached is called *shared decision-making* and involves both the doctor and the patient. In shared decision-making, both parties share information: the clinician offers options and describes their risks and benefits, and the patient expresses his or her preferences and values. Each participant is thus armed with a better understanding of the relevant factors and shares responsibility in the decision about how to proceed. This is a welcome change that has improved the relationship between doctors and their patients. The change did not come easily to the healthcare profession; many doctors wanted to hold on to the attitude that they knew the best way to treat a patient and that the patient's attitude or acceptance of the treatment was of minimal importance.

According to a Cochrane review of 86 trials published through 2009, the use of patient decision aids for a range of preference-sensitive decisions led to increased knowledge, more accurate risk perceptions, a greater number of decisions consistent with patients' values, a reduced level of internal decisional conflict for patients, and fewer patients remaining passive or undecided.[6]

HOW CHANGE HAPPENS

Lessons from the penguins begin with creating a sense of urgency. Let's look at Alzheimer disease, which, as of 2018, affects 5.7 million Americans, a number that is expected to increase to 14 million by 2050.[7] This disease must be diagnosed early, before permanent changes occur, and then treatment solutions must be found that can reverse the tau and amyloid entanglements within the brain. Alzheimer disease has reached a level of urgency, and there must be motivation and resources to control this "melting iceberg" in American healthcare.

After alerting the masses of the problem, it will be necessary to put a team together to solve the problem. Consider the opioid crisis, which takes the lives of nearly 30,000 people every year. Powerful groups that have the clout to inform large numbers of people about the opioid crisis include organized medicine, Congress, and Department of Health and Human Services. Our message is that it is necessary to make sure there is a powerful group guiding the change — one with leadership skills, credibility, communications ability, authority, analytical skills, and a sense of urgency.

The change process begins with understanding, expecting, and accepting that change in healthcare is inevitable. Doctors have to know that the skills they learned in medical school and their training programs soon become obsolete. Rather than resisting or avoiding what doctors interpret as looming disruptions, it is important to proactively engage and embrace change. Whether it be an organizational shift, a change in business models being adopted, a change in reimbursements, recognizing changes in compliance, or an improvement in technology, it is important to seek to understand the goals and expected outcomes of such change. Otherwise, we just may be existing on a melting iceberg. The penguins will tell you that is an untenable situation, and change must take place in order to survive.

The next requirement for implementing change after a team has been selected is for a strategy and vision to be put in place. Once the plan is put into action, it is necessary to share with the rest of the doctors in the group as well as the staff the results, even if there are only short-term and incrementally small improvements. Measuring and monitoring outcomes of the change process are essential for recognizing whether or not the change process has fulfilled its purpose or been effective. The new ideas slowly will take hold and become strong enough to replace old traditions. It's not easy, especially in medicine, but it can be and must be done, because the healthcare iceberg already is cracking.

Bottom Line: The iceberg and penguin story teaches an important lesson. When doctors, administrators, ancillary healthcare workers, and employees are all on the same page with regard to change, it is amazing what can happen, despite adverse conditions. Ask yourself whether you are living on a melting iceberg or an iceberg that could melt. Melting icebergs come disguised in many forms: paper charts giving way to EHR; moving from volume of care delivered to value of care patients receive; distance learning; new methods of physician reimbursement; using new technology to be part of the caring process; and use of physician assistants and nurse practitioners to provide initial care for patients. Holding on to the *status quo* by using antiquated and irrelevant services that are decreasing quality or not providing improvement in outcomes, or a business strategy that makes increasingly less sense, suggests that you are on a melting iceberg and you need to take a lesson from the penguins.

REFERENCES

1. Kotter J. *Our Iceberg is Melting. Changing and Succeeding Under Any Conditions.* New York: Portfolio/Penguin; 2005.
2. Sprinkle T. Remote medical care is future of medicine. The American Society of Mechanical Engineers. https://www.asme.org/engineering-topics/articles/technology-and-society/remote-health-care-future-medicine.
3. Virtual visits and high blood pressure. Harvard Health Publishing. https://www.health.harvard.edu/staying-healthy/virtual-visits-and-high-blood-pressure.
4. McGrail KM, Ahuja MA, Leaver CA. Virtual visits and patient-centered care: results of a patient survey and observational study. *J Med Internet Res.* 2017;19(5):e177.
5. Gerteis M, Edgman-Levitan S, Daley J, Delbanco T. *Through the Patient's Eyes.* San Francisco: Jossey-Bass, 1993.
6. Stacey D, Bennett CL, Barry MJ, *et al.* Decision aids for people facing health treatment or screening decisions. *Cochrane Database Syst Rev.* 2011;10:CD001431-CD001431.
7. Alzheimer's Disease Facts and Figures. Alzheimer's Association. https://www.alz.org/alzheimers-dementia/facts-figures.

CHAPTER 25

Taking Telemedicine to the Next Level

SAJEESH KUMAR, PHD; JOHN WHITE II, MD, FAAFP; AND NEIL BAUM, MD

Telemedicine has reached critical mass: 48% of all physicians are actively using telemedicine to communicate with their patients.[1] The use of telemedicine has increased significantly since March 2020 when CMS waived requirements that limited telemedicine to distant site communication between patients and physicians and permitted it to include all patients who have Medicare and Medicaid. In addition, CMS has agreed to compensate physicians for virtual visits at the same rate as person-to-person visits.

It is now possible for physicians to provide safe and effective care without the necessity of examining the patient. We estimate that nearly 60% of primary care physicians' patients can be managed using telemedicine (Neil Baum, unpublished survey). However, with limited physical interaction with the patient, this will require both professional regulation and protection against the potential for liability and litigation.

Physicians and other allied healthcare providers may feel compelled to increase their presence online for reasons of efficiency, increased demand from patients for virtual visits, and ability to compete with other physicians who offer telemedicine services.

BRIEF HISTORY OF TELEMEDICINE

The forerunner of telemedicine actually was used in ancient times. The history of telemedicine closely parallels the history of communication and information technologies. The key technical feature of telemedicine is being able to communicate medical data over a distance. The history of remote medicine actually begins around 500 BCE, when ancient Greeks and Romans used long-distance communication for both military and medical purposes using fires, smoke signals, light reflection, drums, and pigeons. Native American tribes also used smoke signals to relay medical calamities and health events.

Telemedicine technically has been around ever since the invention of the telephone. The first article about telemedicine in a medical journal was published in *The Lancet* on November 29, 1879. It discussed how the "new" telephone could be used by doctors to reduce unnecessary office or home visits.[2]

Modern telemedicine was jump-started with the inventions of the electrical telegraph and the telephone. During the U.S. Civil War, the telegraph was used for ordering medical supplies as well as communicating deaths and injuries on the battlefield.[3] With the telephone, the era of the connected world arrived. Major city hospitals and doctor's offices installed telephones. Within a few years, many city residents also had telephones in their homes. Now physicians could talk over the telephone to their patients and give medical advice directly. Unfortunately, until recently, there was no business model for compensation for telemedicine for doctors who communicated with their patients over the phone. Doctors gave advice, diagnosed medical conditions, and prescribed medications using their cognitive skills but received no compensation for this level of communication. Also, the doctor was held legally responsible for the decisions that were communicated to their patients over the telephone.

With rapid rise of the use telemedicine in many areas of medical practice, the urologist, for example, will be able to increase their communication with their sexual medicine patients and be compensated appropriately.

Some of the earliest uses of telemedicine came in the 1960s and the 1970s, providing access to healthcare in rural areas and for medical emergencies in urban areas. The rise of the Internet in the 1990s provided support for practically all information and technology needed for telemedicine.[4]

Telemedicine has fully embraced the Internet as a communication tool. Many private practices and healthcare systems are in the process of allowing patients the choice of seeing their medical provider either through telemedicine or in person. Kaiser Permanente has reported that in 2017 more visits were conducted via telemedicine than face to face.[5]

BIRTH OF MODERN TELEMEDICINE

The recent development of telemedicine has been facilitated on two fronts: (1) advances in electronic methods of communication; and (2) the pioneering efforts of a few organizations and individuals. The former generally represented the interests of high-tech ventures, such as the manned space-flight program of the National Aeronautics and Space Administration (NASA).

A major step in the development of telemedicine was the introduction of television. By the late 1950s, developments in closed-circuit television and video communications were being used by medical personnel, who began to employ them in clinical situations. As early as 1964, a two-way closed-circuit television system was set up between Nebraska Psychiatric Institute in Omaha and the state mental hospital in Norfolk, 112 miles away.[6] The system permitted interactive consultations between specialists and primary care physicians, and facilitated education and training at the distant site. Another early example of television linking doctors and patients was at Massachusetts General Hospital/Logan International Airport Medical Station, which was established in 1967.[7] This facility used a two-way audiovisual microwave circuit and permitted healthcare to be provided to passengers and airport employees 24 hours a day by nurses, supplemented by physician expertise using an audiovisual link. More recently, the wide availability of videoconferencing has led to major growth in telemedicine. This has been made possible because of improvements in digital communications and introduction of low-cost computing, with many of the videoconferencing systems now based on personal computers and even on smartphones.

The recent developments of cellular phones, tablets, personal computers, and satellite communications have made mobile telemedicine possible. Early examples of such programs were the Alaska ATS-6 Satellite Biomedical Demonstration, in effect from 1971 to 1975, which assessed the viability of improving village health care in Alaska using satellite-mediated video consultation.[8]

THE VALUE OF A TELEMEDICINE CERTIFICATE

This is an exciting time to be in healthcare. The landscape is changing dramatically, and the rules and regulations are changing almost daily. Physicians and other healthcare providers must embrace new technology to assist in taking care of patients. The COVID-19 pandemic quickly brought telemedicine to the point where doctors and patients embraced the technology. This is due in no small part to CMS waiving HIPAA restrictions and allowing reimbursements that were equivalent to those for in-person visits to the doctor's office.

Is There a Way to Provide Care to Patients Without Accidental Exposure to COVID-19?

Telemedicine seems to offer an answer regarding the safety of office staff and providers. The World Health Organization defines telemedicine (also called *telehealth*) as the "the delivery of health care services, where the distance between the provider and the patient is a critical factor . . . for the exchange of valid information for diagnosis, treatment and prevention of disease and injuries."[9] Basically, telemedicine is using technology to evaluate and treat patients who are at a location separate from the physician.

Before the COVID-19 pandemic, telemedicine was more of a niche practice. Most insurances, including Medicare and Medicaid, made it difficult to facilitate telemedicine visits between a patient and their doctor, and most of these physician interactions were uncompensated. With the onset of the pandemic, it was quickly realized that allowing physicians to provide care via telemedicine might help "flatten the curve."[10]

Physicians can interact with patients using telemedicine in several ways. Some are synchronous, whereas others are asynchronous. Synchronous platforms are live, audiovisual communication directly with the patient. Examples of this include Zoom, Hale Health, Google Hangouts, Dox.me, and Doximity. Asynchronous platforms do not take place in real time. Examples include email and patient portal interactions.

Why Should Healthcare Professionals be Trained and Certified in Telemedicine?

Patients have quickly adapted to this new technology. Patients desire, and expect, quick access to their physician. Many patients have multiple, complex medical conditions; for them, getting out of the house, to the office, and then back home is a tremendous burden. They nervously sit in a waiting room, waiting to hear their names called, while surrounded by coughs, sneezes, runny noses, and stomach bugs. If they can receive adequate, effective and professional care in their homes, much of their fear and worry can be attenuated. Perhaps their long-term outcomes will improve as well.

As physicians, we are used to regularly updating our skills with reading, attending live or virtual conferences, and direct "hands on" training. In truth, by taking a good history, we can get most of the information we need to direct a patient's care. And, although there are limitations, you can perform a physical exam through the use of telemedicine. Using audio-only communication (like routine phone calls) we can listen to the patient's speech patterns to tell if they are in distress (e.g., extremely dyspneic, unable to speak more than a few words at a time); depressed (e.g., slow, unemotional or suicidal talk); or manic (e.g., pressured speech, grandiosity, rapid change in topics); and whether they have proper insight into their disease process. It is possible to use audiovisual communication to perform a very thorough exam. For example, you can watch the patient get up from a chair and walk across the room, look at their rash, see if they have pitting edema, move a painful extremity, and watch many of their cranial nerves function as they smile, laugh, raise their eyebrows, and so on. In fact, as technology improves, it is becoming easier to use interactive, connected, medical equipment such as stethoscopes, ophthalmoscopes, otoscopes, and ECG monitoring to actually see and hear the patient's lungs, oropharynx, tympanic membranes, and heart rate and rhythm.

Along with knowing what can be done via telemedicine, it is just as important to learn what cannot be done through telemedicine. If there is a poor connection, a physician may not be able to see the rash. Inadequate cell phone reception can make it difficult for the doctor and the patient to hear each other. And some problems, such as chest pain or abdominal pain, still need a trained, in-person physical exam. Furthermore, we must not forget that healthcare providers are more than just technicians. No matter how good an internet connection you have, you may not be able to console the grieving parent or spouse with a gentle touch of the hand; people still need a shoulder to cry on in times of distress.

By obtaining professional certification in telemedicine, we can show patients that we are staying abreast of the latest developments in healthcare. A formal certification in telemedicine is more than a diploma on the wall. Certification is a symbol of our sacred promise: *Primum non nocer*e, or first, do no harm.

Telemedicine and tele-education in health science is gradually spreading across the country. Advancement in telecommunication, information science, and technology provides an opportunity to exchange knowledge and skill across geographically dispersed organizations by networking academic medical centers of excellence with medical colleges and institutes to practice distance learning using information and communication technology–based tools. These may be as basic as commonly used Web-based tools, such as blogs, discussion boards, online multimedia, and mobile technologies, or as advanced as virtual reality, simulation, and telepresence-based collaborative learning environments.

Various modules of telemedicine education are being offered at the University of Tennessee regarding the use of telemedicine for patient care and also as a tool for remote care physicians to use to develop their skills. The distance medical education modules that have been adopted include virtual clinical grand rounds, lectures, tele-CME, teleconsultations, telepathology, teleradiology, tele-followup, and telementoring. This distant education program has immensely benefited the postgraduate students and physicians in enhancing their knowledge and keeping them abreast with recent advances in patient care and research in various specialties.

THE FUTURE OF TELEMEDICINE

Remote patient monitoring is going to be an important piece of the telemedicine puzzle in the near future. Remote patient monitoring involves using digital technology to collect medical data from a patient in one location and electronically transmitting that data to a healthcare team in a different location.[11] The healthcare team, consisting of physicians, nurses and other medical professionals, can remotely monitor a patient's pulse rate, oxygen saturation levels, and blood pressure using digital technology. These patients otherwise might have had to remain hospitalized for their COVID infection or other medical issue; instead, they can spend more time comfortably recovering at their own home.

In addition to remote patient monitoring tech, other tools are being developed and used in telemedicine. Ultrasound machines have gone from room-sized devices to digital wands that can wirelessly connect to a smartphone, tablet, or computer. Everything from echocardiograms to focused assessment with sonography for trauma (FAST) scans can be taken with these devices. The images can then be sent to a cardiologist or radiologist at a remote location to be read in mere minutes. Companies like ButterflyNetwork, SonoSite, and Clarius are designing and building smaller and smaller ultrasound devices that can take advantage of telemedicine.

The future of telemedicine involves the evolution of simpler, widespread devices that physicians have been using for decades. Digital stethoscopes, otoscopes, and ophthalmoscopes are becoming ubiquitous. With some brief training, someone could potentially place a stethoscope to their spouse's chest to let a remote physician hear heart and lung sounds. Similarly, a provider at a great distance from the patient may be able to actually "see" a patient's tympanic membrane or tonsils, which leads to an accurate diagnosis without having the necessity to touch or examine the patient.

Chronic disease management represents an untapped market for telemedicine. Patients with chronic conditions often require frequent visits to the doctor. Telemedicine can target these patient populations, which has the potential to decrease the number of emergency room visits and hospital admissions, improve outcomes, and, ultimately, decrease costs.

The future of telemedicine also will include the model of the "hospital at home," where patients who meet the criteria for hospitalization but are otherwise stable are treated at home for diseases such as chronic obstructive pulmonary disease, pneumonia, and heart failure. Studies have shown that the hospital-at-home model, when used appropriately, is more cost-effective than hospitalization.[12]

We estimate there will be an increase in telemedicine for mental health conditions, because in most cases the healthcare provider does not need to examine or touch the patient.

One of the obstacles is the need to expand the use of broadband Internet connectivity to all Americans. In order for telemedicine to become universal, everyone needs to have access to high-speed Internet service. Perhaps broadband Internet may become a public utility, just like electricity, which will make the technology available to everyone, including those in rural areas.

CONCLUSION

Considering the limited healthcare resources available in remote and rural regions, telemedicine has the potential to make optimal use of the few available resources. Universities are now demonstrating the effectiveness of telemedicine training in the fields of patient care, training, education, and skill development. There are limitations in deployment and sustaining such initiatives, however, because they need commitment and the support of all the stakeholders. Now a certification for application and use of telemedicine is available for those who wish to take their interest in telemedicine to the next level.

REFERENCES

1. Drees J. Nearly half of physicians seeing patients through telemedicine. Becker's Hospital Review. April 22, 2020. https://www.beckershospitalreview.com/telehealth/nearly-half-of-physicians-seeing-patients-through-telemedicine.html.
2. Aronson S. The Lancet on the telephone 1876-1975. *Medical History.* 1977;21(1):69-87.
3. Bashshur R, Shannon GW. *History of Telemedicine: Evolution, Context, and Transformation.* New Rochelle, NY: Mary Ann Liebert; 2009.
4. Preston J, Brown FW, Hartley B. Using telemedicine to improve health care in distant areas. *Psychiatric Services.* 1992;43(1):25-32.
5. Landi H. Kaiser Permanente's Bernard Tyson makes case for technology in the wake of viral telemedicine story. www.fiercehealthcare.com/hospitals-health-systems/kaiser-permanente-ceo-bernard-tyson-technology-investments-roi-social. *Fierce Healthcare.* March 25, 2019.
6. Wittson CL, Benschoter R. Two-way television: helping the medical center reach out. *Am J Psychiatry.* 1972;129:624-627.
7. Craig J, Petterson V. Introduction to the practice of telemedicine. *J Telemed Telecare.* 2005;11(1):3-9.
8. Foote DR. Satellite communication for rural health care in Alaska. *Journal of Communication.* 1977;27:173-182
9. WHO. A health telematics policy in support of WHO's Health-For-All strategy for global health development: report of the WHO group consultation on health telematics. Geneva,11–16 December, 1997. Geneva, World Health Organization, 1998. https://apps.who.int/iris/bitstream/handle/10665/63857/WHO_DGO_98.1.pdf?sequence=1&isAllowed=y
10. Schwamm LH. Can Telehealth Help Flatten the Curve of COVID-19?*Harvard Health Blog.* May 15, 2020. www.health.harvard.edu/blog/can-telehealth-help-flatten-the-curve-of-covid-19-2020032419288.
11. About Telehealth. Remote Patient Monitoring.CCHPCA.org, 2020. www.cchpca.org/about/about-telehealth/remote-patient-monitoring-rpm.
12. Cryer L, Shannon SB, Van Amsterdam M, Leff B. Costs for "hospital at home" patients were 19 percent lower, with equal or better outcomes compared to similar inpatients. *Health Affairs.* 2012;31:1237-1243.

CHAPTER 26

Patient Profiling Using Psychographics: Demographics vs. Psychographics and Why Culture Matters Most

Neil Baum, MD

PSYCHOGRAPHICS VERSUS DEMOGRAPHICS

Demographic information includes the basics: age, gender, race, address, insurance information, phone number, email address, and occupation. Although demographics are still valuable and can be used as a starting point, they don't shed light on the attitudes and the mindset of your ideal patients. The demographics are merely the dry facts.

Practices are used to thinking only in terms of demographics, because dividing a market up by age, gender, ethnicity, and other broad variables can help to understand the differences and commonalities among patients. The thinking was "our target audience is 45- to 65-year-old women" or "we are launching a marketing campaign aimed at urban Latinos." Today, that thinking can be limiting your marketing efforts. Demographics only segments the patients that you are interested in attracting, but it isn't specific enough to be maximally effective.

Psychographics, on the other hand, focuses on the interests, attitudes, and emotions of a segment of potential patients — exactly the things practices need to understand to best promote their services to a particular segment of the population that the practice wishes to attract. To reach these ideal patients, you must know what or who they value most, where they get their medical education and medical information, and what content appeals to them.

Psychographics are like demographics on steroids. Psychographic information might include your patients' habits, hobbies, health-related experiences, and values. Demographics explain "who" your patient is; psychographics explain "why" they become part of your practice.

Psychographic segmentation divides the market into groups based on social class, lifestyle, and personality characteristics. It is based on the assumption that the types of products and brands and individual purchases will reflect that person's characteristics and patterns of living.

You can only reach your target audience effectively when you understand both their demographics and their psychographics. The combination of both sets of data starts to form your patient persona — a detailed picture of the patients you would like to care for in the future.

EXAMPLE OF PSYCHOGRAPHICS AND DEMOGRAPHICS IN A PRIMARY CARE SETTING

Let's look at a 45-year-old woman with multiple medical conditions. Her demographic information might include the following:

- Female;
- Aged 45;
- Address, telephone number, email address, and insurance information;
- Married, with children;
- Dealing with issues of weight gain, diabetes, lack of energy or hormonal imbalance; and
- Household income $100K+.

Her psychographic information might include the following:

- Concerned with health and appearance;
- Wants a healthy lifestyle, but doesn't have much time;
- Enjoys going online in the evenings, big fan of Pinterest;
- Tends to favor quality over economy;
- Finds fulfillment in her career and family; and
- Values time with a small group of friends.

Looking at the two data sets, it's easy to see why you need both psychographic and demographic information. By using demographics alone, you have only a vague picture of your patient — you understand her challenges, but not where to find her and what really moves her to action. Psychographics gives you so much more understanding of the patient!

If you collect demographic information alone, you will have only a very hazy picture of this patient. Demographics provide you with information on how to find her and whether she has insurance to cover her healthcare costs. However, it is through psychographic information that you understand her challenges, and what really moves her to action. It is the combination of psychographics and demographics that gives you much more insight into your patients.

OBTAINING PSYCHOGRAPHIC INFORMATION

There are two effective methods for obtaining psychographic data: (1) interviewing your current patients; and (2) investigating your website traffic or analytics.

Interviewing Existing Patients

Start by thinking of your best patients. Next time you talk, ask them for a few more details about themselves. You can ask what they did over the weekend, if they have seen any good movies lately, found any great holiday deals, made any New Year's resolutions, and so on. Because we are physicians, we have the luxury of probing a patient's clinical, social, occupational, recreational, and emotional history.

Depending on your relationship with the patients, you can tell them exactly why you're asking and be more direct. In more than 40 years of practice, I've never had a patient fail to answer these questions or be upset about being asked for more information than their clinical history.

Want a larger sampling? Send out a patient survey and be honest — tell them you want to better understand what they care about. Most people are more than happy to share. This survey can easily be created on surveymonkey.com. The website is free, and it is easy to create a useful psychographic survey. You probably have collected email addresses as part of your demographic queries, and you can easily send out your survey to your existing patients.

Psychographic segmentation starts with development of a questionnaire that uses attitudinal, values- and belief-based statements, to which patients react. Consider providing a range of responses — for example, from "Strongly Agree" to "Strongly Disagree." Once survey responses are gathered, a factor analysis using statistical clustering is used to identify response patterns that indicate natural clusters based on similar answers.

Once all survey data are analyzed, consistent groups — psychographic segments — are defined. Additional social media monitoring and analytics (discussed in the next section) can provide added insights based on trends in consumer interests and attitudes. Of course, the very nature of answering a survey requires respondents to consider their thoughts and choose an answer. When survey questions are focused on a specific topic, such as hours of operation or use of ancillary services, as with attitudinal segmentation, the results may be skewed because many respondents rationalize their answers based on societal norms or, in the case of healthcare, published facts.

Psychographic segmentation, on the other hand, may include completely unrelated and discontinuous questions about personal values or beliefs, so respondents are less likely to rationalize. However, the research team must make the effort to draw connections between psychographic insights and the topic of focus to make these insights actionable, which may require additional research.

After using quantitative marketing research to identify psychographic segments, conducting qualitative research (e.g., focus groups and one-on-one interviews) with members of each psychographic segment can help interpret the quantitative data from the perspective of each segment.

Investigating Website Analytics

If you prefer a more behind-the-scenes kind of investigation, there's no better way than using website analytics. The Internet has made capturing psychographic data much easier and relevant to both patients and practices alike. The Internet also makes it easier to find like-minded patients, even if they're from a different community or even a different country.

One of the best is Google Analytics, which also is free. Look at your existing website and see what the landing pages are where patients will start to look at your content. You can also see the bounce rate or how quickly the viewer left your site without looking at the content. Using analytics, you can determine what has moved patients to click, call, or schedule an appointment in the past.

USING PSYCHOGRAPHICS IN YOUR MARKETING

Getting the psychographic data is important, but really applying it to your practice is how you make it effective.

We've gathered some hypothetical data using the techniques outlined in the previous section, so now let's apply our data to our marketing strategy!

Once you understand what is important to the target patient, you'll know where to find her and how to motivate her. You'll know how to give her what she wants — that offering deep discounts isn't going to motivate her.

When developing and executing campaigns, content, messaging, and so on remember this: communication resonates with people that share the same psychographics (passion points, interests, and beliefs), not demographics. Getting the psychographic data is important, but how do you apply the data to your marketing and make it effective?

Let's continue with the example of the 45-year-old female with diabetes and obesity. Once you understand what is important to her, you'll know where to find her on the Internet and how to motivate her. You'll know how to give her what she wants — that offering free WiFi in the reception area isn't going to motivate her to be part of your practice. Instead, she wants to hear that your nutritional counseling service has worked for others in your practice with similar medical problems and how it will give her better health without a huge time commitment. So make sure you highlight customer comments to that effect.

When you know that she's spending her free time on Pinterest, you can stop spending money on Facebook or newspaper and magazine ads. Instead, use her love of Pinterest and share time-saving household and nutrition tips and give her ideas for fun things to do with family and friends.

Watch what gets repinned and analyze what that tells you about her. Did she love the one about the smiley-face veggie platters for an after-school snack? Give her more ways to help keep her kids eating well. If the "girl's night out" inspirational quote went over big, give her more ways to have fun with her friends.

When you know that career and family are important to her, you'll want to create content on your website or your blog that highlights the impact that good health has on job performance and also help with her self-esteem and confidence both at the job and when off the clock.

Knowing more about her hobbies and interests will help you when you need to choose a prize for your next contest, what to blog about, and what sorts of images to use in your next ad.

Using psychographics allows you to do smarter keyword targeting and move your website to the top of Google using search engine optimization. For example, targeting one message about your weight loss program for teenagers to parents who are searching for "childhood obesity" and another message to parents who are searching for "nutrition for teenagers" is likely to be one of the options that parents will discover if they are searching the Internet for solutions for their children's obesity. Once you know the key differences in what your patients care about, you can target Facebook ads to parents who've liked specific pages or identified particular interests; you can figure out the hashtags that different psychographic groups use on Twitter and target differently to those groups.

As with other forms of market segmentation, psychographic segmentation enables practices to identify patient groups based on shared characteristics. One key distinction is that psychographic segmentation focuses on what motivates individual patients — which can be more informative when developing marketing plans, wellness initiatives, or disease management programs.

When used in conjunction with demographic or socioeconomic data, psychographics enables practices to gain a clearer picture of both internal and external factors that influence patients' behaviors. These insights can also be helpful for hospitals and other healthcare organizations to understand patients' decision-making processes better and to improve the relevance of communication — whether designed to boost brand awareness and loyalty or increase patient engagement with the practice.

Bottom Line: It is critical for practices to invest in and understand the psychographics of a patient population rather than concentrating only on age, gender, location, and so on. The use of psychographics will help you develop not only the messages and marketing campaigns but also the services that your practice offers and that specific patients want and need.

CHAPTER 27

Doctors and Magicians: What We Can Learn from Wizards

NEIL H. BAUM, MD, AND ROGER DOOLEY

One of my (NHB) hobbies is magic, and I have found that there are principles in performing magic that apply to physicians' interaction with patients. These principles are not meant to fool or deceive patients but have the purpose of enhancing communication with patients. After reading this chapter, hopefully doctors will think about adopting a few of the techniques that are used by magicians.

Here are seven ways that magicians make use of mental processes that can be used by doctors as they interact with patients to better engage patients and hold their attention, which will hopefully enhance patient compliance and improve outcomes.

1. PATIENTS FOCUS ON ONLY ONE THING

The success of magicians shows that we can pay attention to only one thing at a time. Many illusions are based on the magician showing you something with one hand while doing something you don't notice with his other hand. We may try to multitask in our daily lives, but the reality is that we are able to focus on only one task at a time. Multitasking is another way of saying, "We have more things to do than time allotted, so can you keep up?" Multitasking implies that multiple tasks are occurring at the same time, as if it would be effective to work on reviewing lab reports while simultaneously returning patient phone calls. The problem with the idea of multitasking is that our brain is not set up to switch tasks that way. According to an article published in *Neuron* by neuroscientists Paul Dux and colleagues, the brain's prefrontal cortex is unable to process two tasks at the same time, which contributes to our inability to effectively multitask.[1]

Neuroscientists compare our attention focus to shining a spotlight on something — we see what is lit, and lose focus on everything else. The term "tunnel vision" is particularly apt to describe how people focus on one small area at a time.

Doctors need to be sure they have their target's attention where they want it. If the patient is distracted by something external, or worse, by something else the doctor is doing, such as looking in the chart or at the computer, the key points of the discussion between the doctor and the patient will be missed. For example, if the doctor is interrupted by a phone call or a knock at the door by a nurse wanting to ask the doctor a question, this will cause both the patient and the doctor to lose focus, and the ability of the doctor and the patient to get back on track becomes compromised. Therefore, it is recommended that you leave multitasking to the telephone operators, and instead give your undivided attention to your patients when you are eyeball to eyeball with them.

If you are dealing with a difficult patient, this is a time that you must focus on the patient and make every effort to listen with all of your attention. If you are speaking to a patient with a problem, that is not a time to be signing lab work or going through your mail.

2. MOTION ATTRACTS OUR ATTENTION

Ever wonder why doves are such popular props with magicians? The explosive burst of white, flapping wings as the birds fly off is guaranteed to draw every eyeball in the audience. The ability of the birds to hijack the viewers' attention gives the performer a huge window of opportunity to start the next stage of his or her illusion.

Our brains are wired to respond to motion. In prehistoric times, movement might be a threat like the saber tooth tiger at the cave entrance, or perhaps a deer caught in the thicket that represents the next meal. Whether you are presenting to a group or speaking to a single patient, use motion to grab the attention of your audience, and use the motion to focus attention where you want it.

Perhaps you are trying to explain to a patient how the bladder and urethra work to provide the patient with a greater understanding of urinary incontinence. You can blow up a balloon, which represents the bladder. The stem of the balloon is symbolic of the urethra. Your patient will understand the process of bladder physiology from the minute the balloon is inflated until the balloon collapses.

If you are in primary care or are a nutritionist, you can use models of foods to avoid such as a saltshaker, a plastic model of French fries, and a plastic package of butter. Using these visuals helps a patient clearly see what foods should be avoided to prevent heart disease.

3. BIG MOTIONS BEAT LITTLE MOTIONS

If you were watching a magician standing on the stage and he made a small, quick move to his pocket, you would certainly notice it. Magicians know that, and prevent you from seeing their small moves by distracting you with a big move, such as pulling a colorful scarf out using a sweeping gesture with their other hand. They know the audience will tune out the small move in favor of paying attention to the big one.

Particularly if you are dealing with an audience that may be distracted, such as an evening program at a restaurant where alcohol is being served, you want to capture the attention of your colleagues. Using a laser pointer on your slides is a small motion that is less likely to capture the audience's attention than raising your arm and holding up your index finger as you state, "The first point I want to mention is. . . .." Make the same gesture as you want to call attention to the second and third points, and you can be sure that you your audience will be watching and focusing on your large movements and voice.

If you are speaking to a patient and you want to emphasize three recommendations for good health, raise your hand and show your index finger as you mention the first point, show your middle finger as you state the second point, etc.

4. THE UNEXPECTED ATTRACTS US

When watching a magician, the audience is always trying to pay close attention to spot any "shady" moves. It's rare to spot a skilled magician's tricks, though, not just because of the distraction techniques described above but also because the magician is disguising some moves as expected or normal actions. For example, if he scratches his ear, adjusts the cuff on his shirt, or makes another innocuous move we are familiar with, our brains tune it out as expected and uninteresting. That move may well mask a transfer of a prop or some other step in preparation for a magical appearance. On the other hand, if he placed his palm on top of his head or raised his left arm for no apparent reason, we'd all be watching with much greater attention or scrutiny.

Much as our brains focus on motion, they also focus on novelty. Surprising your patient with an unexpected gesture, a novel sound, or unfamiliar image will get the patient to look at and analyze what he or she is seeing. That's true even with text. "New!" is one of the most attention-getting words in public relations and marketing. For example, if you bring out a sample medication or handout and tell the patient you have a new treatment option that might be effective for his or her condition, this will likely resonate with your patient.

Offering a patient samples or a voucher for a month of free medication is something not expected by the patient. If you are sponsoring a free healthcare screening, giving the patient a flyer with the date, time, and location of the screening will be far better than merely mentioning the screening.

5. MIRROR NEURONS ENGAGE US

One reason we don't notice when a magician scratches his nose but slyly palms a coin that was hidden in his mouth at the same time is that we can easily relate what it feels like to scratch our nose. When the magician is performing that action, if we notice at all, our mirror neurons are lighting up as if duplicating that action ourselves. Magicians exploit this phenomenon with "decoy actions" — appearing to take a drink, for example, but really passing an item from the mouth to the hand holding the glass in the process. Our brains aid the deception by playing along with the decoy activity and not see the transfer from mouth to hand.

Even though physicians will never try to disguise sneaky actions, there is a lesson here. When people see someone performing a familiar action, either in person or by video, their brains will engage as their mirror neurons kick in. Magicians know how familiar physical actions engage our brain, and you should too.

You want to avoid actions that will signal the patient that something negative is happening. Make every effort to avoid yawning in front of a patient as this signals to the patient that you are bored with the discussion. You also want to avoid putting a hand on the doorknob when you are still speaking to the patient. This signals that you are mentally done with the conversation and are eager to leave. Bring closure to the patient interaction by asking the patient if he or she has any additional questions. After you have answered all of the questions, use your hand palm-up to invite the patient to the door and let the patient exit first while you follow. This demonstrates that the patient has brought closure to the doctor-patient interaction and shows respect to the patient by allowing the patient to exit first.

6. CUT THE CHATTER

If you've ever been to a magic show, either on a stage or close-up, you know that the magician often keeps talking. In the vernacular of a magician, this is called patter. Good magicians will talk about what they are doing, why it is difficult, or how dangerous the trick is, while their hands are busy with the trick. Their purpose, of course, is not to give you real information about their technique but rather to distract you. In essence, the magician's patter is another stream of information for your brain to process, and the overload makes it less likely that you will spot what deception is taking place. You can see this phenomenon in action in other media, like commercials, and you will observe that the voiceover doesn't conflict with important information on the screen.

Physicians, practicing in this era when doctors spend less time with patients and often interrupt the patient within 16 seconds of doctor-patient encounter,[2] are seldom known for having a stream of chatter. But excessive verbiage may distract your patient from hearing your treatment recommendations. Have you ever encountered a pharmaceutical representative who wouldn't stop talking while you were examining a promotion piece? It's hard to look at a detailed piece while the sales rep is spouting his or her sales pitch. The same applies to physicians communicating with patients. We need to think about not only what to say but when to say it and when not to engage in speech.

If you are showing the patient a trend in his or her weight, blood test results, or an x-ray, point out the pertinent data or findings, and then pause your discussion to allow the patient to comprehend or digest the information.

7. DEATH BY POWERPOINT

Even PowerPoint mavens can learn from magicians' patter. Lengthy text bullets in a slide are a perfect example of distraction that costs you and allows your audience to glaze over like deer in the headlights. Trying to read the text while making the same point verbally results in little to no comprehension and with loss of recall because the brain is too distracted to do a good job with either task. Remember it is difficult to multitask when trying to incorporate new information or new data.

Bottom Line: Magic has likely been around in some form at least as long as marketing and public relations, and physicians would do well to learn from prestidigitators and use some of their techniques in interaction with their patients. *Some of the content in this chapter is based on information from* Sleights of Mind: What the Neuroscience of Magic Reveals about Our Everyday Deceptions, *by Stephen L. Macknik. Susana Martinez-Conde, and Sandra Blakeslee (Henry Holt & Co., 2010).*

REFERENCES

1. Dux PE, Tombu MN, Harrison S, Rogers BP, Tong F, Marois R. Training improves multitasking performance by increasing the speed of information processing in human prefrontal cortex. *Neuron*. 2009;63:127-138.
2. Groopman J. *How Doctors Think*. Boston, MA: Houghton Mifflin Company; 2007.

CHAPTER 28

Doctors' Mental Health: If We Wait, It May Be Too Late

Brittney C. Bauer, PhD, and Neil Baum, MD

Losing spatial awareness and freezing up in the middle of an athletic skill (known as the "twisties" in gymnastics) is a limbic system response to perceived trauma that can be triggered by a number of mental, emotional, or physical stressors. Essentially, an individual's subconscious urges override the brain's typical cognitive processes and trigger an automatic "fight or flight" survival response. Unfortunately, the primitive brain response does not take into account that freezing up or aborting the skill is actually more dangerous — it just perceives a threat and attempts to avoid it. Typically, at some point after repeated exposure and conditioning, the brain stops recognizing the action as a threat and the "twisties" go away. However, it is a healing process like that of any physical illness, and it takes time and often therapy or rehabilitation to recover fully.

Simone Biles brought awareness to this issue and the link between mental and physical well-being when she withdrew from several events during the Summer Olympics in 2021. Biles told the public that she needed to remove herself from competition out of concern for her mental state and the impact that was having on her physical safety: "I have to focus on my mental health and not jeopardize my health and well-being."[1] This kind of honesty and candor from an elite athlete who is renowned for her unsurpassed mental and physical strength helps to destigmatize discussions around anxiety and depression. Biles received an abundance of support from the majority of the public, with only a few people criticizing her for withdrawing. Biles is not the only famous athlete who has been affected by mental stress. The tennis player Naomi Osaka withdrew from the French Open in May of 2021, stating that the mandatory post-match press conferences were harmful to her mental health.[2] Further, legendary swimmer Michael Phelps has been very candid about his struggles with anxiety and depression throughout his illustrious career, and now serves as a mental health advocate.[3]

It is thanks to the efforts of these mental health activists to fight the stigma surrounding mental health that people will be able to talk openly about their well-being. So how does Simone Biles' experience relate to the healthcare professions? We are all aware of the increasing rate of anxiety, stress, and burnout among physicians, which affects more than 50% of doctors in some specialties.[4] Unfortunately, most physicians can recall a mentor, colleague, or trainee who struggled with mental health, many of whom were lost from suicide. Rates of suicide among physicians have been estimated to be 40% higher than those in the general population in men and a shocking 130% higher in women compared with their non-physician peers. We need to face the reality that becoming and working as a physician is a high-risk endeavor, which includes not only exposure to infectious diseases, but also an increased risk of stress and mental disorders.

Rather than offering treatment only after we identify physicians who are experiencing stress, burnout, depression, and are at an increased risk of suicide, we need to begin with the prevention of these mental disorders. This improves the lives of healthcare providers, and also will prevent medical errors and decrease the number of physicians leaving clinical medicine due to burnout. Just as elite athletes are expected to "suck it up" and often are encouraged to perform despite physical pain and injuries, doctors also are members of a high-pressure profession and are expected to endure sleep deprivation, work even when ill, and hide their feelings from colleagues or employers. This is an untenable position and is not in the best interest of doctors or their patients.

PREVENTIVE METHODS FOR IMPROVING DOCTORS' MENTAL HEALTH

Having a luncheon to celebrate Doctors' Week or sending doctors cheerful emails thanking them for their dedication and compassion are not going to solve the problem. Although well-meaning, these approaches do little to lessen the massive problems of physician burnout and suicide. In the past, physicians with a mental illness who sought help have been stigmatized. We have made strides in helping doctors with drug or alcohol abuse who seek help and rehabilitation; however, physicians seeking other types of mental health treatment still face many obstacles, including the need to take time away from caring for their patients, shame, and fear of retribution. Additionally, medicine's culture of minimizing stress as part of the physician's badge of courage, rather than support and cooperation, leads to the epidemic of burnout. What if we had a paradigm shift in the profession and permitted doctors to speak safely of the challenges they experience during day-to-day activities in a safe and confidential environment, without fear of retribution?

As a preliminary step in this direction, the Mayo Clinic has introduced a coaching program for physicians. This program investigates the use of professional coaching — focused on goal setting, work choices, professional relationships, and influencing change at work — to reduce burnout.[5] Theirs is the first report specifically exploring the effects of coaching on physician burnout. The study included 88 practicing physicians, who began by filling out several self-assessment questionnaires addressing burnout, quality of life, resilience, and job satisfaction. The doctors then completed six sessions with a professional coach who had experience working with doctors. After just six sessions (3.5 hours total), the physicians filled out the same questionnaires to chart their progress. The doctors reported less burnout and a higher quality of life after coaching. The researchers also administered the same self-assessment questionnaires to a control group of physicians who were not coached. These physicians reported more emotional exhaustion and lower quality of life when left unaddressed. These encouraging findings are even more noteworthy when considering that the time spent on professional coaching to improve physician well-being was less than the time required to renew a doctor's CPR certification!

The Mayo Clinic study demonstrates that trained coaches (none of whom were medical doctors) can help resolve mental health problems. This provides a unique opportunity to train coaches from a variety of backgrounds to help enhance physician well-being. For example, an innovative program called the Confess Project (www.theconfessproject.com) is a nationwide initiative that trains barbers to be mental health advocates. If the Confess Project is effective in their mission, then we might consider other commonly used service providers (e.g., hairstylists, manicurists, masseuses) as mental health advocates as well.

Revisiting our earlier analogy, what did Biles do to help improve her mental state and return to the balance beam for event finals on the last day of Olympic competition? She removed herself from competition for a few critical days and gave herself a much-needed break from the high-pressure situation by practicing in a secluded training center out of public attention. While there, she focused on her most basic and fundamental skills to relieve stress and renew her mindset, trained on soft mats and foam pits to make sure that she could safely attempt to work again, performed fewer skills to give her body a physical break, and reorganized her routine to temporarily remove the more complicated and dangerous activities. In fact, for many athletes this kind of recovery strategy is a planned and structured component of their regular training program that enables them to perform at high levels during critical periods, and then recover during off-seasons to rest the mind and body in preparation for the future.

Unfortunately, doctors do not have on-season versus off-season responsibilities. Doctors are always on-season. Nonetheless, some of these recovery strategies could still be used as a proactive means of preventing physician stress and burnout. For example, doctors could periodically rotate through low-pressure clinic or laboratory settings that are largely out of public attention. While there, they could focus on only their most basic and fundamental skills to relieve mental stress, treat patients in a low-risk environment where they feel safe and relaxed, work fewer hours to give their body a physical break, and reorganized their routine to temporarily remove the more taxing and hazardous activities. Although this might not be possible for long periods of time, with a little organizational creativity it should be possible to routinely schedule "off-season" workdays every few weeks. Coordinating these proactive recovery periods will take effort, but this additional medical practice management task is surely worth the reward of helping physicians stay mentally healthy.

Bottom Line: Doctors, like professional athletes, are at risk for high stress, anxiety, burnout, depression, injury, and suicide. Perhaps we can begin with physician coaching to lower the risk of future mental health issues. We cannot wait until a doctor shows visible signs of mental illness or substance abuse to intervene. The solution is not to encourage doctors to keep pushing forward, neglecting their mental health, and feeling ashamed of drowning in stress and burnout. It is important to recognize that doctors need support as they are in a high-pressure and high-risk career. There should be no penalty for either doctors or athletes who seek help for mental health issues.

REFERENCES

1. Ramsay G, Sinnott J, Wright R. 'I have to focus on my mental health,' says Simone Biles after withdrawing from gold medal event. CNN.com. July 29, 2021. www.cnn.com/2021/07/27/sport/simone-biles-tokyo-2020-olympics/index.html.
2. Futterman M. Naomi Osaka quits the French Open after news conference dispute. *The New York Times.* May 31, 2021. www.nytimes.com/2021/05/31/sports/tennis/naomi-osaka-quits-french-open-depression.html.
3. Drehs W. Michael Phelps: "this is the most overwhelmed I've ever felt." *ESPN.com.* May 18, 2020. www.espn.com/olympics/story/_/id/29186389/michael-phelps-most-overwhelmed-ever-felt.
4. Shanafelt TD, Dyrbye LN, West CP. Addressing physician burnout: the way forward. *JAMA.* 2017;317: 901-902.
5. Nellis R. Professional coaching alleviates burnout symptoms in physicians. *Mayo Clinic.* August 5, 2019. https://newsnetwork.mayoclinic.org/discussion/professional-coaching-alleviates-burnout-symptoms-in-physicians/.

CHAPTER 29

Doctor Get Your A.C.T. Together: Access, Transparency, Compassion

Neil Baum, MD

Attention to access to care, compassion, and transparency (A.C.T.) will result in significant changes in medical practice in the near future and will allow us to continue providing quality medical care to our patients even with the many, rapid transformations taking place.

ACCESS TO HEALTHCARE

Access to healthcare means that a person can see the right medical doctor at the right time and in the right place for a fee paid by payers or a reasonable fee paid by the patient. Patient access to healthcare sets the baseline for all patient encounters with the healthcare industry. When a patient cannot access his or her clinician, it is impossible for that patient to receive medical care, and both patient outcomes and patient satisfaction scores will plummet. Lack of adequate access is a potential healthcare crisis for millions of people in the United States.

Easy and seamless access to the doctor and the practice builds patients' relationships with providers and is likely to achieve improved patient outcomes. There is an impending physician shortage, which means the situation of access to medical care will only become worse. Patients may face availability issues as older physicians retire at an early age, potentially shrinking the workforce. Provider dissatisfaction also is contributing to this shrinkage of the workforce. In a survey from the Physicians Foundation, 53% of providers reported low job satisfaction and 62% expressed a negative view of the future of the medical profession.[1]

Other solutions to the impending physician shortage include adding to the clinical workforce by expanding the number of available graduate medical education residency slots, expanding medical school loan-forgiveness programs, and removing barriers to immigration so that skilled, foreign-trained physicians are able to practice in the United States.

Access to healthcare involves two major and several minor components. The first and most frequently discussed is the patient's ability to pay. The second is the availability of healthcare personnel and facilities close to where people live. Other issues to be considered are that the practice must be accessible by transportation, should be culturally acceptable to the patients, and must be capable of providing appropriate care in a timely manner and in a language spoken by those who need assistance.

Telemedicine

Healthcare organizations have been using telemedicine to close care gaps caused by the long distances that many patients must travel to have access to in-person healthcare. Direct-to-consumer telemedicine allows patients to use their own computers or smartphones to conduct a video call with a provider. Many smaller facilities in rural areas also use telemedicine to connect with experts in urban areas. Telemedicine has the potential to keep patients from having to travel great distances to receive intensive or specialized care.

Telemedicine is not only for patients in rural areas. It can help expand access to care for two groups of patients: those in rural areas who live far away from a clinic or hospital; and those who have full schedules and may not be able to see a doctor during the practice's normal office hours.

Telemedicine also is changing how schools deliver healthcare services for both students and staff. Today's school districts do not have the funding to put a nurse in every school, and those nurses who do work in schools often are overwhelmed by a variety of issues, from complex emotional and behavioral health cases to children with one or more chronic conditions. School-based telemedicine uses telecommunications, including interactive video conferencing and store-and-forward transmissions, to deliver a variety of healthcare services to students attending that school. The current model of caring for schoolchildren often results in a disruption in learning — a child must be picked up by a parent or caregiver and then spend a half a day or more at the doctor's office, missing classroom learning.[2]

Telemedicine and remote patient monitoring will become an essential, cost-effective, and reliable means to expand capacity in a healthcare system marked by significant and persistent specialty shortages and geographic disparities between patients and providers. Diagnostic codes and a payment model must be developed for teleconferencing and telemedicine.

Access to care will improve if there is an improvement in the efficiency of the practice. There is a necessity to reduce government and insurance industry compliance and decrease the time- consuming regulatory burdens, such as prior authorization, that detract from patient care and increase costs.

Scheduling

Several simple fixes can improve access to providers. Practices that can extend their office hours or stagger appointments in such a way that patients can access their clinicians at convenient times provide greater patient access. Offices that conduct appointments only during traditional work hours (i.e., 9 AM to 5 PM) may not be accessible for those who must be at work during those times. Children who are in school may be unable to see pediatricians who are available only during school hours. Many healthcare organizations offer patients a typical set of office hours for patient visits, but for the working adult or parent, a clinic that is open between 8 AM and 6 PM is not always useful. Patients need convenient office hours that allow them to visit the doctor without interrupting their work or school schedules. An easy solution that can be accomplished with existing staff and no requirement for additional technology is to increase office hours. Access will improve if practices can start at 7 AM or also have early evening and weekend hours.

Access can be enhanced by improving the scheduling process. When patients do need to access in-person care, they often face find that it is difficult to schedule an appointment. When they contact a provider's call center or front desk to make an appointment, patients may encounter busy signals, may be placed on hold for a prolonged time, may have to struggle with technological issues such as being disconnected or finding their way through a phone tree, or may have trouble finding a time that meets both the patient's and the physician's schedule.[6]

Hospitals and medical practices can consider online appointment scheduling software, which allows patients to view and select appointments with their preferred providers. Online appointment scheduling improves convenience for patients and also allows them to see the right kind of doctor for their medical problems. For example, when a patient with a knee injury books an appointment, he can make sure he sees an orthopedist who specializes in knees rather than one who specializes in shoulders.

Making sure patients can make appointments with the right doctor, which can help improve their access to healthcare, ultimately drives more patients to the practice or to the hospital.

Transportation

About 3.5 million patients go without care because they cannot access transportation to their providers. Transportation is a critical social determinant of health that has recently gained nationwide attention.[3] According to an article published in the *Journal of the American Medical Association*, ridesharing services such as Lyft and Uber can improve that healthcare disparity and cut down on the $2.7 million the federal government spends each year on nonemergency medical transportation services.[4]

Uber and Lyft have plans to improve access to care arising from medical transportation issues. Both companies will help providers and patients connect with rides to medical appointments.[5]

COMPASSION

Doctors continue to be challenged to demonstrate compassion for their patients. This is very difficult to do in a 10- to 15-minute appointment accompanied by the requirement to enter data into the EHR. Multiple studies have documented that it is not unusual for a doctor to interrupt a patient only 11 seconds after the doctor initiates the discussion in the examination room.[7]

The healthcare industry, particularly physicians, is getting a bad rap about providing care and compassion compared to doctors of the past. Patients would like to return the days of TV doctors Marcus Welby, MD, or Dr. Kildare, who were quintessential examples of compassion. Today's physician depends on technology, medications, surgeries, CT scans, radiation therapies, biopsies, and blood tests, and that compassion — the "touchy-feely" part of medicine — appears to have become an afterthought. It is not rare to hear from patients that they had a medical appointment and that the doctor did not touch them or even perform a physical exam.

The Medicinal Value of Tactful Touching

From the time of Hippocrates, tactful touching has been a part of the healer's armamentarium. The Bible, both Old and New Testaments, contains numerous stories about the healing powers of tactful touching. Harry Harlow, a professor at the University of Wisconsin, performed a famous experiment that showed that primates deprived of touch did not grow and develop normally. It was Professor Harlow's opinion that essential needs like food, water, and shelter are not enough for survival. Primates, humans included, need to touch and be touched in order to survive and thrive.[8]

Another study conducted in English orphanages during World War II showed that even if infants received adequate food, they failed to thrive unless they were held and cuddled on a frequent basis. Touching does not provide calories; however, it provides a vital and necessary role in sustaining life. Neonatal mortality decreased and growth and development improved when laywomen were brought in to hold and to cuddle the babies for several hours a day.[9]

The number of Americans seeking alternative healthcare providers has been increasing for several years.[10] Patients are seeking healthcare from complementary providers such as chiropractors, acupuncturists, massage therapists, and physical therapists. These complementary providers make ample use of touching in their approach to patients.

Doctors no longer seem to touch their patients during most office visits. It is much easier to order a CT scan or an MRI than to touch or physically examine the patient. All of us remember those amazing physicians in medical school who were able to make a correct diagnosis based on the physical exam alone and were not dependent on technology and imaging. Most physicians have forgotten how to use those physical examination skills.

Another concern is that doctors are under pressure to see more patients and as a result, there is less time to tactfully touch our patients. Tactful touching creates a positive connection between doctor and patient. Sensitivity training coaches may warn against touching our patients, but I know the medicinal value of touching and will continue to use tactful, appropriate touching.

Compassion Is Good Medicine

There is scientific evidence that compassion is good medicine. Trzeciak and Mazzarelli[11] provide overwhelming evidence for the healing power of compassion in their book *Compassionomics: The Revolutionary Scientific Evidence That Caring Makes a Difference.*

Kindness brings longer, healthier lives — not only for patients, the book argues, but also for healthcare professionals. When a physician is compassionate, patients heal better and more quickly, and the doctors are happier and less subject to burnout.

Studies have shown that warm, supportive interactions with patients from either doctors or nurses right before the patient goes in for surgery result in patients being calmer at the start of surgery and a decrease in the need for opiate medication following surgery. Patients also spent less time in the hospital.[12]

Technology

With the advent of artificial intelligence, we soon may not be required to take a history of the present illness, record the past medical history, or perform the review of systems. With a few clicks and within a few seconds a diagnosis with a rank of probabilities will appear on our computer screen and will recommend what studies to be ordered and what treatment might be appropriate.

Many of us fear the phrase, "The algorithm will see you now!" Medical algorithms, however, are a valuable but currently underutilized resource in healthcare. Their use at the point of care can significantly improve the quality and cost-effectiveness of medical care.

Just as airplane pilots use checklists to safeguard against mistakes and rely on formulas to plot the right speed and trajectory to take off and to get the plane safely to its destination, medical providers can also use algorithms and checklists as a guide. Medical errors are believed to be responsible for more than 100,000 deaths a year.[13] The use of algorithms may well help lower this number and may guide a doctor quickly to the diagnosis. However, an algorithm never will be able to provide compassion, caring, and empathy. If we take the time to talk to our patients, to be good listeners, and to look at patients instead of computers, there will always be a need for doctors.

TRANSPARENCY

No one would consider staying at a hotel, buying an airline ticket, or buying an automobile without knowing the price of the service or product. Guess what? Patients also want to know the cost of their medical care before they visit the doctor or have the study or the procedure. We are in an era of rising copays, rising deductibles, and more patients having greater financial responsibility for their medical care.

There is a negative impact from not having cost transparency. According to a report from InstaMed, 74% of providers saw an increase in financial responsibility in 2015. High out-of-pocket costs can be prohibitive, causing some patients to skip recommended care.[14]

According to a poll of over 1500 patients, 25% are avoiding medical care due to its high cost.[15]

Another issue regarding price and transparency is patients' lack of understanding and confidence in the bills they receive from hospitals and medical practices. A review of patients' confidence in the accuracy of their medical bills demonstrated that just 33% of consumers felt very confident that bills from their hospital or provider are accurate. That feeling seems to have some validity: 47% of respondents also reported a billing or payment issue during their most recent healthcare experience. Such mistakes are among the ways a hospital or health system could jeopardize patient loyalty. In fact, 42% of patients say incorrect or confusing bills would cause them to seek care from a different provider.[16]

The goal of pricing transparency is that, as people have higher deductible plans, they must have the ability to select the best doctor or facility at the best price.

When, for example, patients are given the option to select an MRI provider based on cost, they select a more cost-effective option and reduce the cost by an average of $220 per person. There is proof and evidence that you can lower costs by having people use pricing transparency tools.[17]

Finally, as part of the discussion on transparency, offer your patients various ways to pay their portion of the charges. This means not only accepting, cash, checks, credit cards, and PayPal, either in person or online, but also being able to offer reasonable payment plans. Your staff should understand the practice's financial policy and apply it consistently to all patients who ask to establish a payment plan. That means being prepared to set up automatic monthly payments for large balances before they become a collection issue.

Bottom Line: The contemporary physician is going to have to adapt and change, which will probably mean learning to embrace technology. But that doesn't mean we have to forget the basics and why we became doctors in the first place. As long as we focus on the patient and provide access to care, remain compassionate, and have price transparency, we will be successful, have happy patients and a happy staff, and just may be home for dinner!

REFERENCES

1. Heath S. Patient engagement. Could low provider morale affect patient healthcare access? PatinetEngagement.com. https://patientengagementhit.com/news/could-low-provider-morale-affect-patient-healthcare-access.
2. Factors behind the adoption of school-based telehealth. mHealth Intelligence. November 21, 2016. https://mhealthintelligence.com/features/factors-behind-the-adoption-of-school-based-telehealth.
3. Health Research & Educational Trust. Social Determinants of Health Series: Transportation and the Role of Hospitals. American Hospital Association. www.aha.org/transportation.
4. Powers WP, Rinefort S, Sachin H. Nonemergency medical transportation — delivering care in the era of Lyft and Uber. *JAMA*. 2016;316:921-922.
5. Recapping HIMSS 18 patient engagement technology news. Patient Engagement HIT. https://patientengagementhit.com/news/recapping-himss18-patient-engagement-technology-breakthroughs.
6. Heath S. Effective patient engagement strategies using health IT. EHRIntelligence. https://ehrintelligence.com/news/effective-patient-engagement-strategies-using-health-it.
7. Singh ON, Phillips KA, Rodriguez-Gutierrez R. Eliciting the patient's agenda — secondary analysis of recorded clinical encounters. *J Gen Intern Med*. 2019;34:36-40.
8. Tavris CA. Teaching contentious classics. Association for Psychological Science. September 30, 2014. www.psychologicalscience.org/observer/teaching-contentious-classics.
9. de Roiste A, Bushnell IWR. Tactile stimulation: short and long-term benefits for preterm infants. *British Journal of Developmental Psychology*. 1996;41:41-53.
10. Tindle HA, Davis RB, Phillips RS, Eisenberg DM. Trends in use of complementary and alternative medicine by US adults: 1997-2002. *Alternative Therapies in Health and Medicine*. 2005;11(1):42.
11. Trzeciak S, Mazzarelli A. *Compassionomics: The Revolutionary Scientific Evidence That Caring Makes a Difference*. Pensacola, FL: Studer Group; 2019.
12. Egbert LD, Battit G, Turndorf H, Beecher HK. The value of the preoperative visit by an anesthetist. A study of doctor-patient rapport. *JAMA*. 1963;185:553-555.
13. Abbasi J. Headline-grabbing study brings attention back to medical errors. *JAMA*. 2016; 316:698-700.

14. LaPointe J. Providers see increased patient financial responsibility. Revcycle Intelligence. https://revcycleintelligence.com/news/74-of-providers-see-increased-patient-financial-responsibility.
15. Heath S. Healthcare costs dampen patient engagement despite satisfaction. Patient Engagement. May 19, 2016. https://patientengagementhit.com/news/healthcare-costs-dampen-patient-engagement-despite-satisfaction.
16. Pecci AW. Want to drive patients away? Stick with outdated billing practices. *Health Leaders.* November 14, 2019.
17. Gruessner V. Cost transparency, "consumer-driven healthcare" impacts payers. Healthpayer Intelligence. February 4, 2016. https://healthpayerintelligence.com/news/cost-transparency-consumer-driven-healthcare-impacts-payers.

CHAPTER 30

Is There a Moral Issue When Doctors Prescribe Placebos?

Neil Baum, MD, and David F. Mobley, MD

A placebo is an inactive treatment, sometimes called a "sugar pill." A placebo may be given in a pill, capsule, liquid, or tablet form, or it may be an injection or a medical treatment or device. Whatever the form, placebos often look exactly the same as the real medical treatment that is being studied, with the only difference being that the placebo does not contain the active medication or treatment or procedure.

The human body has an uncanny ability to heal itself. History has demonstrated that a little nudge from a shaman, witchdoctor, or a "real" doctor with the initials MD after his or her name initiates the healing process.

By definition, placebo interventions do not have any direct pharmacologic or therapeutic effects on the body. However, all treatments are delivered in a context that includes social implications, physical cues, verbal suggestions, and treatment history.

An example of the importance of context is the following story. Virtuoso violinist Joshua Bell, who is one of the best concert violin players in the world, wearing a baseball cap and sunglasses, played for 45 minutes, on a violin worth $3.5 million, at a Washington, DC subway station during rush hour. Over a thousand people passed by Bell; however, only seven people stopped to listen to him play, and only one person recognized him. Just a few nights before his performance in the subway station, he had played at the Kennedy Center and the cost of the tickets was $100. This is no surprise; the social context in which a behavior occurs affects how it is interpreted. The same applies to the use of a placebo and who is prescribing the "drug" and under what circumstances and in what context the placebo is recommended. Joshua Bell played incognito in the Metro station as part of a social experiment about perception, taste, and the priorities of people. The experiment can be extrapolated to demonstrate the importance of the context in which an event or even a placebo is used for treating a medical problem or condition.

Two elements are involved in the context of using placebos.[1] The first element is the external context. In this context, the success of a placebo comes from verbal suggestions, such as stating in a positive fashion, "This is going to make you feel better"; the context of the place where the placebo is given, such as in a doctor's office; and, finally, social cues, including eye contact, body language, voice cues, and, of course, the doctor wearing a white coat and perhaps even having a stethoscope draped around his\her neck.

The second element is the internal context. This context consists of memories, emotions, expectancies, and appraisals of the meaning of the context for future survival and well-being. An example of the internal context of the patient's outcome expectations might include the use of self-talk such as, "I'm sure this 'medication' will make my pain go away."

All of these features, in both internal and external contexts, combine to make up the treatment context and are the "active ingredients" of placebo effects.

HOW DO PLACEBOS WORK?

We often ask, "How is it possible that a pill or medication that contains no active therapeutic ingredient, or even sham surgery, can result in improvement in the patient's condition?" Numerous studies have investigated the mechanism of action of placebos.

One study published in 2016[2] may have identified what goes on in the brain during a placebo effect. Researchers used functional magnetic resonance imaging to scan the brains of people with chronic knee pain. Then all the patients were given a placebo and had another brain scan. The researchers noticed that those patients who felt pain relief had greater activity in the middle frontal gyrus brain region, which makes up about one-third of the frontal lobe.

Although placebo interventions do not have any direct therapeutic or physiologic effects on the body, all treatments are delivered in a context that includes social and physical cues. These clues might include as the healthcare provider wearing a white coat and verbal suggestions that the "drug" will be effective and relieve their symptoms and complaints. A substantial part of the therapeutic benefit patients receive when undergoing medical treatment is caused by their brain's response to the treatment when it interprets the context in which the placebo is presented. Studies have demonstrated that how the placebo is presented will affect the response.[3] For example, a white tablet is less effective than a blue or green tablet. A capsule appears to achieve a greater placebo effect than a tablet. A placebo given multiple times a day is more effective than one given just once a day. Also, an injection of harmless saline (saltwater) is more effective than a tablet or a capsule.

Whether treatment consists of an active drug or a placebo, the clinical setting that surrounds treatment includes multiple types of context information that are perceived and interpreted by the patient's brain. The external context includes treatment, place, and social cues, along with verbal suggestions such as, "This will be very likely to help relieve your symptoms."

Placebo responses have been demonstrated to be effective in multiple clinical disorders, including pain relief, Parkinson disease, overactive bladder, benign prostatic hypertrophy, and irritable bowel syndrome. Some cases of improvement may be related to the context in which the placebo is administered. A large part of the overall therapeutic response to drugs, surgery, psychotherapy, and other treatments may be due to the treatment context or the manner or atmosphere in which the placebo is administered. It is interesting to note that in some cases, individuals who show the largest drug effects to real pharmacologic medications also show the largest placebo effects, which is one indicator that some drugs and placebos may share mechanism of action within the central nervous system.[4]

Placebo treatments can also affect hormonal responses that are mediated through the hypothalamic–pituitary axis.

Placebos also have an impact on the immune system, particularly T lymphocyte proliferation and the release of interleukin-2 and interferon-γ from peripheral lymphocytes. Relatively little is known about the brain mechanisms underlying such effects on the immune system, although recent work suggests that they are mediated by noradrenergic sympathetic efferents,[5] which require the hypothalamus and pituitary gland for their expression.

On the neuroendocrine level, there appears to be a relationship between placebos and the release of dopamine. One landmark positron emission tomography study of dopamine activity found that placebo administration increased dopamine binding in patients with Parkinson disease, particularly in those patients who perceived an improvement in clinical status with placebo treatment.[6]

The take-home message is that the psychological context may have more pervasive effects on physiology than is generally recognized.

Although there is no single mechanism of action for the placebo effect, it is undeniable that in certain clinical settings the placebo does have a place in the armamentarium of healthcare providers.

THE ETHICS OF USING PLACEBOS

There are two different options for delivering a placebo. The first is a placebo-controlled study. Such a study consists of two groups. One of the groups receives the medication that is undergoing study, which contains the active ingredient. The patients in this arm of the study do not know whether they are receiving the drug or the placebo. The second group receives the placebo. They, likewise, are not told whether they are receiving the placebo or the active ingredient. In this kind of study, the investigators and those who analyze the data are not aware which patients have received the placebo and which have received the active drug. In a double-blind, placebo-controlled trial, the investigator do not know whether the subject has received the real drug or the placebo. (This is in contrast to a single-blind study, where the investigator may know whether the patient is receiving the placebo or the active medication, but the subject does not know.) Only after the study is completed and the data have been analyzed may the patient be informed whether he or she received the active drug or the placebo. Patients are informed both verbally and in a written consent prior to entering the study that some of them will receive the active drug and some will receive the placebo. Patients first are screened to determine whether they fit the criteria to enter the study, and they sign an informed consent document that informs them that they may or may not receive the active drug. We believe that this is ethical and that there is no violation of patient confidentiality or breach of the Hippocratic Oath if a patient receives placebos in the situation of a clinical trial comparing active drug to an inert pill, or a real procedure compared with a sham procedure. An example of a sham procedure is giving a patient who has a torn meniscus in his or her knee a general anesthetic, making a small incision on the knee, and closing that incision with Steri-Strips or sutures. This sham procedure is compared with the patient who undergoes a procedure in which an arthroscope is inserted through small incisions and the torn meniscus is repaired.[7]

One of the most obvious ethical issues regarding placebos is their use when no comparison with a pharmacologic medication is involved and the patient is not informed that he or she is receiving an inert drug or medication. According to the World Medical Association's Declaration of Helsinki, which addresses ethical issues surrounding the use of human subjects in research, placebo use is acceptable when there is no proven acceptable treatment for the condition under investigation. This organization has declared that placebos are acceptable when "for compelling and scientifically sound methodological reasons" it's necessary to determine the experimental treatment's efficacy or safety, and when patients who receive placebo "will not be subject to additional risks of serious or irreversible harm as a result of not receiving the best proven intervention."[8]

Historically, deception has been considered a major component of the use of placebos, and this remains one of the main ethical problems regarding their use. Traditionally, a full disclosure of potential side effects is considered the most ethical and appropriate course of action regarding all medications prescribed, including placebos. In some cases, however, it is important to disclose the most critical information about possible adverse events in order to avoid undue patient distress.

More research may be needed, including opinions from ethicists, philosophers, and medical practitioners, to better understand the role of deception regarding the use of placebos.

A key premise underlying medical ethics discussion is the notion that the placebo effect necessitates patient deception. Indeed, the American Medical Association guidelines imply that placebo treatment necessarily entails a form of deception. The ethical issue that must be considered is whether that deception is ever justified. Recently performed experiments with open-label, transparently prescribed placebos have begun to challenge the notion that deception is necessary in eliciting the placebo effect. If we focus on disclosures where the truth is revealed to patients in placebo studies, that raises the question of whether deception is unethical. Blease *et al.*[9] concluded that informing patients that they are receiving placebos fulfills current American Medical Association guidelines for placebo use, and proposed future research directions for harnessing the placebo effect ethically.

A recently passed law, Cures Act 2021, which will go into effect in 2021, entitles patients to their medical records. Transparency is going to be necessary regarding the patient's diagnosis, any medications that have been prescribed, and the discussions that have transpired between the doctor and the patient. Consequently, it will no longer be possible for a doctor to prescribe a placebo without disclosing that the use of an inert substance has been recommended to the patient.[10]

CURRENT ETHICAL GUIDELINES ON THE USE OF PLACEBOS

The following rules might serve the physician as guidelines for the justified use of placebo in clinical practice:

- The intentions of the physician must be benevolent: his or her only concern is the well-being of the patient. No economic, professional, or emotional interest should influence the decision. If the physician does what is in the best interest of the patient — and that may be the use of a placebo — there is no ethical breach on the part of the physician.
- The placebo, when offered, must be given in the spirit of relieving the patient's suffering, and not merely mollifying him, silencing him, or otherwise failing to address his distress. It is important always to keep the patient at the center of the ethical decision of using a placebo. The best advice for a physician is this: always to do what is in the best interest of the patient and you will be standing on firm ground.
- As soon as a placebo has been proven ineffective, it should be withdrawn immediately. In these circumstances, not only is the placebo useless, but it also undermines the subsequent effectiveness of other medications by undoing the patient's conditioned response and expectation of being helped.
- The placebo cannot be given in place of another medication that the physician reasonably expects to be more effective. Administration of placebo should be considered when a patient is refractory to standard treatment, suffers from its side effects, or is in a situation where standard treatment does not exist.

- The physician should not hesitate to respond honestly when asked about the nature and anticipated effects of the placebo treatment he is offering. The physician must reveal the use of a placebo if the patient asks.
- If the patient is helped by the placebo, discontinuing the placebo, in absence of a more effective treatment, would be unethical.

We have seen that in almost any clinical trial there is a positive response in the placebo arm, almost regardless of the condition being treated, and that the difference between placebo response and active drug response often is negligible. In a 12-week trial, this is often true. In a one-year trial, however, the placebo arm almost always reverts back to baseline symptoms or results. In other words, it is common for placebos to have an effect in the short term, but not for the long term.

Bottom Line: The placebo can be of service to physicians in many clinical situations. Therefore, it should not be denied its rightful place in medical treatment as long as ethical guidelines have been followed. *Acknowledgment: The authors wish to thank Dr. Drew Chastain, Professor of Philosophy at Loyola University in New Orleans, who was the inspiration for this topic.*

REFERENCES

1. Wager TD, Atlas LY. The neuroscience of placebo effects: connecting context, learning and health. *Nat Rev Neurosci.* 2015;16:403-418.
2. Tétreault P, Mansour A, Vachon-Presseau E, Schnitzer TJ, Apkarian AV, Baliki MN. Brain connectivity predicts placebo response across chronic pain clinical trials. *PLoS Biol.* 2016;14(10), e1002570.
3. Khan A, Bomminayuni EP, Bhat A, Faucett J, Brown WA. Are the colors and shapes of current psychotropics designed to maximize the placebo response? *Psychopharmacology.* 2010;211(1):113-122.
4. Benedetti F, Amanzio M, Baldi S, *et al.* The specific effects of prior opioid exposure on placebo analgesia and placebo respiratory depression. *Pain.* 1998;75:313-319.
5. Exton MS, Gierse C, Meier B, *et al.* Behaviorally conditioned immunosuppression in the rat is regulated via noradrenaline and β-adrenoceptors. *J. Neuroimmunol.* 2002;131:21-30.
6. De La Fuente-Fernandez R, Stoessl AJ. The placebo effect in Parkinson's disease. *Trends Neurosci.* 2002;25:302-306.
7. Katz JN, Brownlee SA, Jones MH. The role of arthroscopy in the management of knee osteoarthritis. *Best Pract Res Clin Rheumatol,* 2014;28(1):143-156.
8. WMA declaration of Helsinki-ethical principles for medical research involving human subjects. World Medical Association. www.wma.net/policies-post/wma-declaration-of-helsinki-ethical-principles-for-medical-research-involving-human-subjects/.

9. Blease C, Colloca L, Kaptchuk TJ. Are open_label placebos ethical? Informed consent and ethical equivocations. *Bioethics.* 2016;30:407-414.
10. Porter AS, O'Callaghan J, Englund KA, Lorenz RR, Kodish E. Problems with the problem list: challenges of transparency in an era of patient curation. *J Am Med Inform Assoc.* 2020;27:981-984.

CHAPTER 31

Lessons Learned from Lego Building Blocks

NEIL BAUM, MD

Healthcare continues to evolve, and we as a profession need to do so as well. One example of a well-known company that has gone through this process is the Danish company Lego. The first Lego brick was created in 1949, after which the company experienced rapid growth for decades. However, from 1992 through 2004, its dominance began to slip. Lego was on the verge of bankruptcy and almost went out of business. Along the way, the company lost touch with who cared about its product and what those customers — parents and children — wanted.

Through some hard lessons learned and some great strategic decision-making, Lego has refocused its offerings on the art and science of building, along with strategic licensing of leading brands. By asking, "Who cares?" or conducting customer surveys, Lego has been able to reverse its decline; and, in 2014, it became the biggest toy company in the world.

The popularity of Lego bricks results from the endless possibilities of what you can build. Their versatility is magnified when you realize how many ways you can connect them. You can arrange six eight-stud Lego bricks in an astounding 915,103,765 different ways. If you can dream it, the Lego Group believes you can build it.

I don't know of too many doctors who have not bought Lego for their children, played with Legos themselves, or at least stepped on a Lego brick in their child's bedroom. Since its inception, Lego has produced over 650 billion bricks and pieces. That's nearly 93 blocks for every man, woman, and child currently living on the planet. They've also manufactured *4 billion* Lego mini figures — one small Lego "person" for every 1.75 people on earth.[1]

Arguably more impressive is the company's unprecedented record of recent success. Ten years ago, Lego was struggling on every financial front and headed toward economic ruin; however, it turned the business around. In the past five years alone, the company has quadrupled revenue while growing net income by 9% and gobbling up market share. Maybe there's a lesson we can learn from Lego!

The following sections present five building blocks that Lego has learned on the road from near financial ruin to world-renowned success. I hope you can add a brick or two based on Lego's success in your medical practice.

BUILD CONNECTIVITY AND INTERDEPENDENCE

Fact: every Lego piece connects to every other Lego piece in one way or another. There is no silo of blue pieces that refuse to connect with the reds. Yellow pieces aren't busy trying to establish their own kingdom. Larger Lego pieces don't dominate or demand more attention. All Lego pieces work together toward a common purpose. This is a metaphor worth noting. Your practice, like Lego, has to interconnect with all the other pieces, i.e., patients, hospitals, providers, insurance companies, and your community.

Consider these questions about the connectivity and interdependence of your practice:

- How much time and energy is spent defending your silos (i.e., your turf, budgets, personnel, and other resources) as opposed to working together for a common purpose?
- Do your teams encourage connectivity and interdependence? For example, is your staff cross-trained?
- What do you do when divisive behaviors or conflicts arise? How does your practice handle difficult patients or staff squabbles?

The time for turf protection is over. What we need to do is focus on the patient. Quality is going to be defined as outcome divided by costs. But the outcomes are going to be from the patients' point of view, not necessarily from that of the doctor or the insurance company.

BUILD THE RIGHT TEAM

In his seminal work, *Good to Great*,[2] Jim Collins discusses the need to get the right people on the team. He argues that before an organization (practice) can be truly great, it must get the right people on (or off) the bus and ensure they are sitting in the right seats.

A decade ago, Lego was hemorrhaging money and floundering and soon to be relegated to the bin where Lincoln Logs and the Erector Set are now to be found. Much of Lego's remarkable turnaround is credited to getting the right people on the bus, starting with CEO Jørgen Vig Knudstorp. Knudstorp provided the clarity, decision-making, and accountability needed to take Lego through a very difficult period. He bit the bullet and made difficult decisions that were in the best interests of the customers and their parents.

Following Knudstorp's model, consider these questions about your staff:

- Would you re-hire, right now, each person in your practice if given the chance?
- Do you have the right people in the right places? Are the staff and the doctors' practicing at the top of their licenses?
- Is someone hindering performance? What should you do to get it right? Do you have one or more person who has a bad attitude that is infecting the rest of the staff?

BUILD A SIMPLE AND CLEAR PATH

At one point Lego lost sight of its direction. The company said "yes" to a lot of ideas — good, bad, or otherwise. As a result, Lego branched into areas ranging from toys to video games to theme parks. To correct the situation, Lego significantly reduced the number of stock keeping units offered, sold off the theme parks, and reconnected to its signature Lego brick with a few raised circles and a few recessed openings. . . . you Lego aficionados know what I mean!

Consider these questions about your team or practice's path:

- Does every employee know what matters most? What matters most is making sure that each patient has a positive experience with the practice at every interaction with the practice.
- Has saying "yes" to low-value efforts cost your practice money, energy, or commitment? Are you and your practice not following the 80/20 rule, or the law of the vital few, which states that for many events and activities, roughly 80% of the effects come from 20% of the causes? Are you focused on the 20% that is dragging the practice down and sapping your energy and productivity?

- What should you do today to ensure the practice is on the right path? For example, do you have regular staff meetings to correct any problems or deficiencies?

BUILD VALUE BASED ON THE CONCERNS OF THE CUSTOMER

Nothing is more frustrating to a Lego user than having a brick or bricks missing from the box or package of bricks. I have probably built several hundred Lego "sculptures" over the years, and I can count on one hand the number of times a brick or a piece has been missing from the plastic wrappers that contain all the pieces for the model. If the Lego store is contacted, it will find the missing piece and send it along with another toy and an apology note. Wouldn't it be nice if healthcare did the same thing and sent an apology note if someone in the practice made a mistake or an error? I know it is difficult for physicians to accept blame and say "I'm sorry," but there is no better way to cement a relationship between a doctor or practice and a patient than by showing empathy and apologizing for an error or oversight.[3]

Lego customers, a group that includes both adults and children, spend an incredible 5 billion hours every year playing with Lego products. I am certain that Lego users know more about Lego bricks and mini-figurines than some of the people who manufacture the product. Lego has found the use of focus groups to be a necessity. Watching children play with those brightly colored bricks led to Lego creating and launching the Lego Friends line in 2012. The Friends line doubled first-year sales projections and tripled overall corporate sales to girls in 2013. I recently met a five-year-old child who built a Lego Star Wars sculpture that included more than 1000 pieces by himself, using only the accompanying manual included with the product. (I hope he decides to become a doctor someday, because he will make a great addition to our profession!)

Consider these questions about your patients:

- When was the last time you observed your patients interacting with your practice? How often do patients try to communicate with you via email?
- Are you making assumptions about your patients based on outdated or inaccurate information? For example, are you continuing to obtain PSA results for prostate cancer screening in men over age 70?

- How might you better capture the needs and wants of your patients? Are you surveying your patients on a regular basis? Are you taking action on the patient surveys?

BUILD STRONG PARTNERSHIPS

Lego has found tremendous success through building and nurturing strong partnerships. The Lego Batman and Lego Star Wars products are just two examples. By partnering and producing these products, Lego has raised the company's visibility, increased sales, and encouraged fans of their partners to purchase and collect Lego products. You can do the same:

- Is your practice nurturing important partnerships with your hospital, your payers, and the community?
- Should some relationships be revisited or dissolved? Are you checking on your payers and making sure that they are paying in a timely fashion? Have you considered dropping poor payers?
- Do your partners elevate your practice's performance and stature? Are your partners pulling their fair share of call and overhead? If not, how are you addressing that problem?

WHAT ARE THE LESSONS FROM LEGO?

Lego's goodwill is based mainly on the outstanding product, not costly advertising campaigns. I don't know about you, but I have not seen a Lego ad in an in-flight magazine or on TV. The Lego brand allows it to charge a premium price and encourage repeat business. I pay top dollar for a Lego toy or model and never flinch at a $50 price for a box of its Harry Potter- or Star Wars-themed toys.

The lesson for entrepreneurs is just like the "field of dreams" . . . if you build a great product, they will come. As the product constantly improves, the value of the brand increases, creating a barrier to entry that keeps other competitors from wanting to enter the marketplace.

Indeed, the idea of overcoming obstacles and constraints can help your practice build on its established strengths. The Lego Group motto is, "Only the best is good enough," and the company name derives from the Danish words *Leg godt*, meaning "play well." The drive to innovate was deeply embedded in the corporate culture. In the early years, this idea helped the company develop its brand and instill pride in its employees. But after a time, it had come to be seen as a mandate to create new toys at any cost. Lego has emphasized that the company cannot be complacent and rest on its previous products. Lego's message to the healthcare industry is that medicine cannot remain stagnant but must continue to improve and offer better treatment and services to patients.

Bottom Line: Those colorful little bricks with the little elevations are an example of creativity, fun, enjoyment, and connection with our inner child. In that respect, one could argue that Lego bricks are an ideal analogy for the beauty of creativity. As anyone who has ever played with the ubiquitous bricks can attest, the best ideas sometimes come from thinking "inside the Lego box."

REFERENCES

1. Smith C. Business statistics\fun gadgets. LEGO facts, history, records and stats. DMR. January 28, 2019. https://expandedramblings.com/index.php/lego-stats-facts-and-records/.
2. Collins J. *Good to Great.* New York: HarperBusiness; 2011.
3. Baum NH. Apology: The power of "I'm sorry" in patient satisfaction (and avoiding litigation). PatientExperience.com. September 10, 2012. http://patientexperience.com/apology-power-im-sorry-patient-satisfaction/.

CHAPTER 32

Road to Retirement: Part I — Not Necessarily the Road Less Traveled

JOEL M. BLAU, CFP; RONALD J. PAPROCKI, JD, CFP, CHBC; AND NEIL BAUM, MD

Probably the greatest decision a doctor makes — after selecting a spouse and deciding where to practice — is the decision when and how to leave the practice of medicine. A few decades ago, doctors worked until the day they died. Many may have literally worked themselves to death. Doctors may be forced to retire because of their own health problems or because of a contractual arrangement mandating retirement at a given age. However, today many doctors are making the decision when to leave their practices, but most haven't given enough thought and prepared properly for the next phase of their lives. The following will address the basics of the retirement process, along with checklists of what needs to be done to leave a medical practice through the front door without encountering psychological, financial, or legal problems.

PSYCHOLOGICAL PREPARATION

Today more physicians are disappointed by the increasingly onerous atmosphere of medical practice and are thinking of retiring at earlier ages. For most physicians, contemplation of retirement generally is not pleasant. Retirement means leaving a profession that has occupied them intellectually and emotionally for a lifetime. Physicians are fearful that there will be a void of personal gratification and validation. Physicians are concerned that retirement will create a life with nothing important to do and that boredom and deteriorating health are all that will be in store for them.

Few studies have examined the factors affecting the well-being of physicians in retirement. One study of Canadian physicians found that few doctors had hobbies, friends, or even close family relationships that might fill the void caused by retirement.[1]

FINANCIAL CONSIDERATIONS

Retiring physicians often face unexpected expenses or find that their financial situation won't provide for the comfortable life they expected. This was all too common for many physicians with investments that all but disappeared during the economic downturn that began in 2008.

Physicians contemplating retirement within the next few years need to understand the future risks of the financial situation they may be facing. People are living longer, which means you may have to provide for a bigger cushion in retirement than you may have initially intended. In addition, uncertainty over future Social Security benefits as baby boomers continue to retire adds to the concerns. As a result, you could face a personal shortfall, especially if you incur unforeseen expenses from a medical condition or some other situation.

So what could/should you do? Even if retirement is imminent, you may be able to make up lost ground quickly or take other steps to protect yourself. Here are several ideas to consider:

- **Maximize retirement savings vehicles.** Just a few years of making contributions at or near the maximum level can significantly bolster your account. If you have any qualified retirement plans that you are not fully funding, determine if your cash flow will allow you to do so.
- **Work on the budget.** If a financial planning retirement needs analysis determines that you may have a potential shortfall, you might want to dial down your expectations. Make realistic estimates about the income you expect to have coming in and the expenses going out. Although you will likely be paying less for housing (see below) and other items such as life insurance, especially if your children are already adults, consider the impact of potential increases in some expenses such as travel expenditures.
- **Move to a smaller home or condo.** For most people, housing is the largest overall cost, representing on average more than one-third of overall spending. If your kids no longer live with you, but you're still living in the large home where you raised them, it may be time to downsize. In addition, you might want to move to a state with a different climate,

taking state income taxes into account. Of course, various other factors such as proximity to family and personal preferences will come into play.

- **Refinance your current home.** If you decide not to downsize, you should consider refinancing an existing mortgage if you are paying a rate higher than those currently available. At the beginning of 2013, mortgage rates had reached historic lows. Even though rates have increased slightly since then, you may save tens of thousands of dollars over time by refinancing. Keep in mind that your interest payments will generally continue to be tax-deductible.
- **Do not stop working altogether.** Just because you have reached retirement age does not mean you have to stop working completely. If needed, you could pursue part-time employment. For some individuals, working full-time a little longer is also a viable option.

RETIREMENT ACCOUNTS

Individual retirement accounts (IRAs) continue to make up the bulk of many physicians' retirement planning assets. They are hesitant to make any changes to these IRAs, including taking withdrawals or moving their account to another advisor, due to the perception that various taxes and penalties would be incurred. There are, however, several reasons why rolling over your IRA funds may make sense. You may be dissatisfied with the investment return from the IRA, or you may be interested in pursuing other investment opportunities. One reason might be the need for immediate cash. Loans against an IRA are not allowed, but many investors are unaware that if you withdraw funds from an IRA, but redeposit those funds back into an IRA within 60 days, there is no current income tax ramification. When all of the requirements are met, IRA rollovers are tax-free and exempt from the usual 10% penalty on early withdrawals before age 591/2.

However, it is important to keep in mind that there are several potential pitfalls with IRA-to-IRA rollovers:

- **Missing the 60-day rollover period:** The rollover must be completed within 60 calendar days from the date a distribution is made from the IRA. For years, the IRS has ruled the 60-day requirement could not be waived, even when the delay was not the taxpayer's fault. Recently, the IRS has indicated that it's more willing to grant an exception or waiver under extenuating circumstances, but it is still best to play it safe and stay within the 60-day rollover period.

- **Failure to roll over the same assets that were distributed:** To qualify for a tax-free rollover, the cash or other assets withdrawn from the IRA must be transferred within 60 days. You are not allowed to substitute other property. For example, in a recent Tax Court case, an individual withdrew cash from his IRA and used the money to invest in common stocks. He then transferred the stocks to a new IRA within the required 60-day rollover period. The Tax Court ruled that the transfer was taxable, since there was a change in the distributed assets.
- **Rolling over to the wrong IRA:** The tax-advantaged rollover is valid only if you make a timely rollover to an IRA that you personally own. If you mistakenly transfer the rollover funds to your spouse's IRA, or some other account, the transfer is fully taxable.
- **Initiating more than one rollover during the year:** You are allowed to roll over funds from one IRA to another IRA only once a year. The one-year period begins on the date you receive the distribution, not the date on which you roll over the funds into the IRA. The one-year rollover rule applies separately to each IRA that you own. One way to avoid this restriction is to utilize a "trustee-to-trustee" transfer of IRA assets from one IRA to another IRA.
- **Rolling over a "mandatory distribution":** The law requires you to begin minimum distributions from an IRA by April 1 of the year following the year in which you reach age 70½. You cannot avoid the minimum distribution rule by rolling over the distribution to another IRA. Mandatory distributions may be avoided if the retirement plan assets are not held within an IRA, but are kept within the plan, and you have not yet retired. This exception, however, is not available for distributions made within an IRA.
- **Rolling over IRA assets to a Roth IRA:** In general, the rollover from a regular IRA to a Roth IRA is completely taxable.

BENEFICIARY DESIGNATIONS

There is never a bad time to revisit the beneficiary designations you have made over the years. Unfortunately, once various beneficiary forms are completed, they are often forgotten about, emerging only after the death of the account owner. In many cases, executors find that no beneficiaries have been named at all, creating confusion, anger, and time delays in settling an estate. In other cases, the named beneficiaries may no longer be members of the family due to divorce or death.

One of the main reasons for this oversight is that many of the financial accounts requiring a beneficiary designation are established earlier in life. There may be a life insurance policy that was purchased when you were first married, an IRA that you opened prior to marriage, and other such accounts.

Having a sound financial plan dictates that you ensure there are designated beneficiaries for all your retirement plan accounts, life insurance policies, and other assets, and that they are the intended recipients based on your current familial arrangement. It is often not as cut-and-dried as it first seems. The following guidelines should help you avoid the most common mistakes:

- **Do not leave the beneficiary lines blank.** If you don't name specific beneficiaries for your accounts, or if you name your estate as the beneficiary, your heirs will likely end up in probate court. This can be both time-consuming and costly. If assets go to your estate, they are subject to the reach of creditors. A better option is to choose individual beneficiaries and list them on the forms.
- **Use trusts for beneficiaries who are minors.** In some states, minors face restrictions until they turn 18 or 21. If you designate a minor as a beneficiary, a court will appoint a guardian to manage the funds until the child reaches the age of majority. Alternatively, you might establish a trust to handle the funds and name the trust as the beneficiary. Thus, you maintain control now and provide asset protection for minors when you are gone.
- **Understand the key rules.** Beneficiary designations on retirement accounts and insurance contracts will override your will. If you want someone other than your spouse to inherit retirement account assets, your spouse must sign a written waiver. Without the waiver, a non-spouse beneficiary designation will be invalid upon your death.
- **Inform your beneficiaries.** Do not keep your beneficiary designations a secret. Also, let the people you have designated as beneficiaries know where to find important documents and contact information for your professional advisers. On the other end, make sure your advisers have the vital contact information.

- **Double-check names and numbers.** Make sure they are spelled correctly and that figures are accurate. This is particularly important when listing Social Security numbers as well as telephone numbers and addresses.
- **Use percentages instead of dollar amounts.** For example, suppose you have an IRA worth $100,000, and you designate a nephew as beneficiary of $75,000 of that amount. If the IRA drops in value to $75,000 or below at your death, your nephew gets the entire amount — any remainder beneficiaries receive nothing. Perhaps a better way to meet your objectives is to give your nephew 75% of the overall account value.
- **Name contingent beneficiaries**. If your primary beneficiary has died and you have not updated your accounts with a new primary, the assets would go to your contingent (or "secondary") beneficiaries. If a contingent beneficiary was never named, the assets are transferred to your estate (see above). Avoid potential problems by indicating contingent beneficiaries in appropriate places.

Finally, don't stuff all the paperwork in a desk or drawer somewhere and forget about it. Make the proper beneficiary designation adjustments when warranted and review these periodically with your advisor to ensure that they remain up-to-date and make financial sense.

SOCIAL SECURITY

It is estimated that over the next few years more than 70 million baby boomers will reach age 62 and become eligible for Social Security benefits. Many are undecided between collecting Social Security benefits early or waiting until the normal retirement age of 66. Historically, many of those eligible have collected at age 62 because of financial necessity, health and longevity concerns, or a desire to collect as much as possible from the system amidst fears of its eventual insolvency.

Retiring early means more payments from the government, but a smaller check each month for the remainder of your life. Unfortunately, there is no "one size fits all" answer to when you should start receiving Social Security benefits. The sliding scale used to calculate benefits, which pays a smaller monthly check if you retire "early" and more if you wait longer, depends on the year in which you were born. Your lifetime payout depends on how long you live. First, visit Social Security's Web site (www.ssa.gov/planners/calculators.html) and find out when you're entitled to full benefits.[2] If you were born from 1943 to 1954, you can start collecting benefits at age 62 but you'll only get 75% of what you'd receive if you wait until you're 66. If you wait until 67, you get 108% of your monthly benefit. At age 70, you'll collect 132% of the benefit amount, which is the maximum you can get by delaying or deferring benefits.

Why should you wait to take Social Security until age 66? If you plan to work and will earn in excess of the annual limit before you reach full retirement age, you may lean toward waiting until you are 66. Social Security benefits are reduced if you collect benefits before full retirement age and earn more than the annual limit. You may also consider working until you are 66 if you are single, have little in savings, or have a longer life expectancy. If your spouse is still working and has earned income, which may cause a larger portion of your Social Security benefits to be taxed, you may want to hold off until your income and tax rate are lower. If your spouse's benefit is smaller than yours or your spouse is much younger than you, keep in mind that your combined life expectancy will be longer than either of your single life expectancies. This means that if you take social security at age 62, and your spouse's benefit is based on your benefit, it will mean a significantly reduced benefit for your surviving spouse's lifetime.

For others, it makes sense to start receiving Social Security benefits at age 62 for the peace of mind of having the money in hand, rather than waiting an extra three to five years, even if it means a reduced benefit and fewer total dollars received over your lifetime. For those who will not have earned income in excess of the annual earnings limit between age 62 and full retirement age, it may make sense to collect at 62. Collecting at 62 also may look better than 66 if you have health issues or a shorter-than-average life expectancy. Finally, if your spouse's benefit is larger than your own, you may choose an early retirement.

Ultimately, since you don't know how long you'll live, your decision will likely have less to do with maximizing your total Social Security payout and more to do with your overall personal retirement plan and your financial objectives for retirement. This decision can be made with greater certainty and predictability for your situation with the assistance of a financial advisor.

Bottom Line: If you follow the advice we have provided and start planning for retirement early, you will find that the golden years really are available to all when you pass the stethoscope to your younger partners. Remember, with careful financial planning the best is yet to come!

REFERENCES

1. Grauer H, Campbell NM. The aging physician and retirement. *Can J Psychiatr.* 1983;28:552-554.
2. Social Security. Retirement estimator. www.ssa.gov/planners/calculators.html. Accessed March 25, 2015.

Road to Retirement: Part II — Advice on Advisors

ADVISORS

The relationship with your financial advisor is a true partnership, where both parties are working toward a common goal — your financial stability and financial independence. A financial advisor may help manage your investments, perform portfolio evaluations, and serve as an educator to ensure you have a greater understanding of the investment environment. In addition to registered investment advisors, there are a number of other financial-based professionals who may be in a position to assist you with many financial planning areas. The following list of professionals, as well as their industry-focused professional designations and educational requirements, should serve as a guide in your search for advice:

- *Accredited Asset Management Specialist (AAMS):* This is a 12-module, self-study course. Modules cover asset management, investment policy, risk, return, performance, asset allocation, investment strategies, tax issues, retirement planning, insurance products, estate planning, ethics, and legal and regulatory issues.
- *Accredited Tax Advisor (ATA):* This self-study program includes six courses and is a graduate-level course. Prerequisites are a bachelor's degree, professional experience, a description of goals, and tax planning experience.
- *Accredited Tax Preparer (ATP):* This course provides basic background on tax preparation issues for individuals and sole proprietorships.

- *Chartered Financial Analyst (CFA):* This is an intensive three-year program, with three six-hour exams. Prerequisites for the designation include a bachelor's degree or comparable work experience, and three years of investment management experience.
- *Certified Financial Planner (CFP):* The Certified Financial Planner Board of Standards is a regulatory organization for financial planners. It awards the CFP designation to individuals who meet its requirements. The curriculum covers insurance, income taxation, retirement planning, investments and estate planning. In addition to self-study programs, classroom instruction programs are offered at colleges and universities across the country.
- *Certified Investment Management Analyst (CIMA):* Prerequisites are three years of investment management consulting experience, an interview, and a preliminary exam. The program covers due diligence, asset allocation, risk management, and other investment management consulting concepts.
- *Certified Investment Management Consultant (CIMC):* CIMC certification is a two-level, self-study course that covers investment management consulting. It also addresses asset allocation, formalizing investment policy, and active versus passive investment performance evaluation.
- *Certified Specialist in Tax-Sheltered Accounts (CSTSA):* The CSTSA self-study program is for advisers who work with 403(b) plans.
- *Chartered Life Underwriter (CLU):* The CLU self-study curriculum includes 10 courses — eight required and two electives. Prerequisites are three years of business experience and client service in the financial field.
- *Chartered Financial Consultant (CHFC):* The CHFC self-study program includes 10 courses — nine required and one elective. Prerequisites are three years business experience and client service in the financial field.
- *Chartered Mutual Fund Counselor (CMFC):* This nine-module, self-study course is a primer on mutual funds.
- *Chartered Retirement Planning Counselor (CRPC):* The CRPC program is an 11-module, self-study program for advisers who provide retirement planning for individuals.
- *Chartered Retirement Plans Specialist (CRPS):* The CRPS program is targeted at advisers who work with qualified and nonqualified retirement plans.
- *Master of Science/Financial Planning Concentration:* This graduate-level program focuses on financial planning, wealth management, tax

planning, retirement planning, and estate planning. Participants must have a bachelor's degree to enroll and must complete 12 courses for 36 credits.

As is the case with all professional designations, having one does not necessarily mean a person is good at what he or she does. Word of mouth, through referrals made by friends and colleagues, is an excellent way to meet potential advisors. Even though they may come highly recommended, it is always a good idea to interview a number of advisors to determine compatibility. Only in this manner will you be able to determine who you are most comfortable partnering with in guiding you toward, reaching, and ultimately maintaining true financial independence and long-term security.

RETIREMENT INVESTING

The need for retirement planning does not end with the onset of retirement. A new retiree's focus should shift from building wealth to managing and preserving it. One major challenge is making the investment portfolio supply cash flow for the duration of life — and through various economic and market conditions.

Factors that drive a portfolio's longevity include asset mix, spending level, and the investment time frame. Certain aspects of these factors are within an investor's control while others are not.

Asset Mix

Asset mix refers to the ratio of stocks to bonds in a portfolio. This determines risk exposure and expected performance, and is one of the most important decisions investors of all ages make when constructing an investment portfolio. Historically, stocks have outperformed bonds and outpaced inflation over time. Consequently, the larger the equity allocation, the greater a portfolio's expected return — and risk.

Keep in mind that risk and return go together. A higher allocation to equities increases the risk of experiencing periods of poor returns during retirement. But if you can handle the risk, having more equity exposure in a portfolio enhances its return potential. Growth can bring higher cash flow, inflation protection, and portfolio endurance over time. While it is logical that investors should have an equity component in their portfolios, the actual weighting should be dependent on one's time frame, risk tolerance, and spending flexibility.

Spending Level

Portfolio withdrawal typically is described in terms of either a specified dollar amount (e.g., $100,000 per year) or a percentage of annual portfolio value (e.g., 5% of assets each year):

- **Specified dollar amount:** Withdrawing a fixed amount each year and adjusting it for inflation can provide a stable income stream and preserve your living standard over time. But the portfolio may survive only if future withdrawals represent a small proportion of the portfolio's value.
- **Percent of annual portfolio value:** Withdrawing a fixed percentage of assets based on annual asset value makes it unlikely that you will deplete retirement assets because a sudden drop in market value would be accompanied by a proportional decline in spending. But this method can produce wide swings in your living standard when investment returns are volatile.

Retirees who need relatively consistent cash flow may want to combine these two methods.

Investment Time Frame

Investment time horizon may be the hardest to estimate, especially if it is the same as your lifespan. In this case, you can only guess how long your portfolio must support spending. If you plan to bequeath assets, your investment timeframe may extend beyond your lifetime. This may influence your risk and spending decisions as well.

Timeframe forces a tradeoff between the short and long term. Retirees with a longer investment time horizon might choose a higher exposure to equities. But they may have to offset this risk by being more flexible about spending over time. Elderly retirees and others with a short time horizon may choose a less risky allocation or a higher payout rate, although they can experience rising spending levels, too. In any case, retirees should think carefully about equity exposure and avoid taking more risk than they can afford.

Planning involves assumptions about the future — assumptions that may not pan out. Although you cannot avoid making assumptions, you can ask whether they are realistic and consider how your lifestyle might change if future economic and financial conditions are much different than projected.

Although you cannot fully control these and other factors involved in portfolio endurance during retirement, having more wealth can improve the odds of having a less stressful financial life. A more substantial nest egg might enable you to take fewer risks, enjoy a higher sustainable spending rate, or extend the productive life of your portfolio.

INVESTMENT WEB SITES

Thanks to modern technology, it is easier than ever for physicians to take control of their financial situation. Whether you are researching investment options or performing financial planning retirement projections, online resources abound.

For investors, perhaps the most difficult task is keeping track of various investment portfolios. While it's obviously important to know what you own, it is equally important to know how well, or not well, specific investments and the overall portfolio are doing, on both a dollar and a percentage basis, over varying time periods. Morningstar's portfolio tracker (www.morningstar.com) is a great tool to use to keep a close eye on your investments. You can enter your holdings on a screen or import the data from Quicken, Yahoo, and even many online brokerage statements. Heavy on analytics, it provides overviews and performance charts, and allows you to view a visual map and analysis using several factors, including a breakdown of holdings by asset allocation percentages. Similar tracking can also be accomplished through the MSN Money Web site (http://www.msn.com/en-us/money/personalfinance).

One of the best overall financial sites is Yahoo Finance (www.finance.yahoo.com). Yahoo's text-based interface makes navigating through the site simple as well as fast. The opening page provides up-to-the-minute market data, prices on individual stocks, and bond market commentary. From this site, you can also access respected outlets such as Briefing.com, *Financial Times,* and *Business Week.* Of particular interest is the stock research link, which takes you on a journey of exceptional research tools covering stocks, bonds, mutual funds, and options. International news also is available, as well as financial-based chat rooms.

Economic data, and the expectation of new data being released, certainly are major factors affecting stock market movement. Moody's Analytics economy website (www.economy.com) provides access to raw data and general economic news, both domestic and worldwide, and helpful commentary to interpret it all.

For a general financial education, spend some time with the solid tutorials on market basics with The Motley Fool (www.fool.com). Ease is the key on this site, as all of the educational information and tools are easily accessible from the website's "Fool's School." Another option for general market and retirement planning education is the CNN Money website (www.money.cnn.com). This site takes advantage of the long-time involvement of many experts with varied interests and specialties. It serves as a valuable reference for both investment novices as well as the more seasoned physician investor.

Given that there are more mutual funds to choose from than common stocks, there is an abundance of sites dedicated to evaluating both load and no-load mutual funds. The leader in the field of mutual fund research is Morningstar (www.morningstar.com). Via its Web site, visitors can obtain a one-page summary of almost any mutual fund. Included are analyst reports and the Morningstar ratings.

While most sites provide a variety of financial news, one of the best sites dedicated to U.S. and global events is the *Wall Street Journal* (www.wsj.com). Links on the home page will take you to news by region as well as topic.

For those who are students of technical analysis, the site to visit is Bigcharts (www.bigcharts.com), where you can easily chart individual securities and mutual funds.

There are, of course, many other sites investors may find valuable. For one of the most comprehensive glossaries of financial terms, go to www.investorwords.com. For a nice overall investment site, take a look at www.investorguide.com. For economics-based articles, both Bloomberg Business (www.bloomberg.com) and Barron's (www.barrons.com) offer an online alternative to their written publications.

Bottom Line: Doctors are advised to prepare for retirement long before they remove the shingle from the door. Having success in retirement means having the proper advisors to prepare the pathway to this important stage in a physician's life.

Road to Retirement: Part III — Other Options for Retiring Physicians

With retirement not turning out the way they hoped, some physicians who had long ago hung up their stethoscopes are now returning to the workforce. Just a few years away from practice, however, can create obstacles to re-entry. The good news is that the demand for physicians is high, and some programs actually assist retired physicians back into work. We'll go over just a few of the many positions doctors can consider when coming out of retirement

RE-ENTRY

One of the obstacles you'll need to consider in physician re-entry is that practices and hospitals might not be able to bear the costs of liability insurance of a physician who hasn't been active for a long time.

Returning to the physician's life may seem most attractive to a retired doctor, especially if finances are prompting the move back into the workforce. And you'd think it would be an easy transition coming back. After all, because of his or her ample experience, a retired doctor would need no training — or so it would seem.

In the United States, if you let your license expire and have been inactive for an extended period of time (which, in many states, is only one or two years), re-entry could require new training. This may involve continuing education and passing the Special Purpose Examination (SPEX). This makes sense: if it's been several years since he or she last practiced, a doctor might need to brush up on his or her knowledge and skills.

In addition to that, experts in medicine emphasize that technology in the field is continuing to change at an accelerated pace. Doctors may need to prove that they're literate in those technologies and can work with electronic medical records.

Several re-entry programs around the country help get a doctor up to speed. Some states provide the service, while others might require the doctor to pay for it. This is an important matter to look into, as the costs of a re-entry program, which can be upward of $20,000, can be difficult for a retiree.

LOCUM TENENS

Because many retired physicians aren't eager to return to the same schedules, demands, and restrictions of their old job, one popular option is to become a locum tenens doctor. From the Latin for "to hold the place of," locum tenens doctors are those who substitute for others on an as-needed basis. You can get such a job through a staffing agency that will place you with the right healthcare facilities. You could be with one facility for anywhere from a day to a week to a month.

Flexibility is one of the major advantages of this type of job. For instance, part-time locum tenens work is easier to find and often suits the life of a retiree. You'll have some freedom to build your own schedule. Some things to consider, however, are that it might require traveling and working off-hours. Before joining a staffing agency, check to see whether it pays for travel and accommodations.

Of course, this option will also require an active license, and, depending on where you practice and if you've been inactive for awhile, it may entail the re-entry process we discussed. In fact, depending on the travel required, going into locum tenens work might even necessitate getting licensed in multiple states.

HEALTHCARE ADMINISTRATION

Retired physicians are often very familiar with all of the elements that make a healthcare facility run smoothly, which is why some look into healthcare administration.

The job of healthcare administrators is to manage the facility and oversee staff. They are often responsible for developing the rules and regulations of the facility, as well as managing finance, marketing, and human resources issues. Thomas Dolan, president and CEO of the American College of Healthcare Executives, says that knowing how medicine is delivered and having clinical experience helps in becoming an administrator (personal communication).

Of course, not all retired doctors will be up to the task of becoming an administrator. Although the healthcare experience will certainly help, it takes a different set of skills to manage a facility than to practice medicine. "The real challenge" for such a transition, says Dolan, "is for those doctors who are not trained in business." Today, many administrators hold specialized degrees in healthcare administration, nursing administration, or business administration. And, if you're interested in nursing home administration, this will require getting licensed.

The good news is that, according to the U.S. Department of Labor, the demand for healthcare administrators is on the rise.[1]

TELEMEDICINE

Doctors who want to spend their retired years at home but would still like to earn an income might consider telemedicine.

Although it may sound cutting edge, telemedicine is technically an old practice, inasmuch as it's medicine over a distance. It used to be done using a messenger or mail system (and eventually the telegraph and telephone), allowing doctors to correspond with patients. Now, with so many advances in telecommunications, telemedicine is easier and more effective than ever.

If you have computer literacy, a phone, and a reliable Internet connection, you might be able to find part-time or full-time work from home helping to treat patients via the Web. Services like AmeriDoc.com like to argue that most visits to the doctor can be handled over the phone. They say that virtual doctor consultations are an efficient alternative that can also alleviate demands on doctors' offices.

AmeriDoc states on its Web site that, as one of their telemedicine doctors, you can diagnose minor medical problems and even prescribe non-controlled medications (as opposed to controlled medications, which are more tightly regulated).[2]

CONSULTING

A great way to continue contributing your expertise to the healthcare community while maintaining a semi-retired lifestyle is to become a consultant.

Your consulting could go beyond medicine, as well. Some healthcare facilities take on medical consultants to help plan new facilities. They may take on consulting physicians to take the burden of this planning off their practicing physicians who need time to focus on patients. And you don't necessarily have to become a consultant for a healthcare facility. Because medical consultants are needed in so many fields, you have a lot of options.

For instance, companies that manufacture medical devices often require medical consultants for their advice on the product and liability issues. Law firms often seek medical consultants for expertise or testimony in cases, such as those that involve malpractice. Others take on consultants to verify the medical accuracy of their publications or advertisements. Also, consider government organizations such as the Social Security Administration, which need medical consultants to help evaluate disability claims.

WRITING AND EDITING

Do you enjoy keeping a journal? Do you ever notice egregious mistakes and misinformation about medicine floating around in popular publications? If you have decent writing skills or a sense of proper grammar, you might enjoy writing and editing.

It can be the perfect opportunity for retired physicians who simply prefer staying within the comfort of their home while making some extra money. The amount of medical information online has exploded, and more and more people like to look up their own symptoms on the Internet before even calling the doctor. Web sites that want to provide reliable information might offer freelance work for a retired physician to write online articles or examine other articles for accuracy. Of course, this type of work will require a certain amount of computer literacy.

With their new freedom, other retired physicians choose to flex their more creative writing muscles. Some choose to incorporate their expertise in writing medical suspense novels, for instance. If you can find a publisher for the kind of writing you'd be passionate about, this might be the ideal second career for you.

VOLUNTEERING

If personal fulfillment is the primary concern and finances are not an issue, a retired physician can find plenty of opportunities to become a community volunteer. Many physicians who don't need to return to work for financial reasons simply want to give back to the community and serve those who might not otherwise be able to afford proper healthcare.

You might be surprised, however, to learn how much some physicians enjoy volunteering in free clinics more than their paying job. Not only is it personally rewarding, but doctors say that it's refreshing to not have to deal with the administrative problems or red tape associated normally with their job. They don't have to be concerned about what an insurance company will pay for or what test to do first to ensure maximum insurance payment.[3] An additional bonus that volunteering offers for recently retired doctors is the ability to keep abreast of changes in the field. Unfortunately, however, one of the obstacles to retired physicians working in free clinics is that they may need malpractice insurance. If you don't have it, free clinics might turn you away.

Bottom Line: Peace, relaxation, leisure time: This is what most people hope for during retirement. Doctors, who typically make large salaries, are especially stereotyped as retiring early and spending the last third of their life on the golf course or traveling the world on cruise ships. For many, however, retired life doesn't turn out like that. Some find boredom and restlessness sink in all too quickly. Others encounter unexpected expenses or find that their financial situation won't provide for the comfortable life they expected. Hopefully this chapter will provide you with suggestions for life after retiring from a medical practice.

REFERENCES

1. Bureau of Labor Statistics. www.bls.gov/ooh/management/medical-and-health-services-managers.htm.
2. Ameridoc. http://ameridoc.com/services.html. Accessed August 3, 2015.
3. McGrath J. 10 jobs for retired doctors. How Stuff Works. http://money.howstuffworks.com/second-career-ideas/10-jobs-for-retired-doctors7.htm#page=6.

CHECKLIST FOR RETIREMENT

The following checklist will help retiring physicians start to sort through some of the issues that have to be considered for a successful transition from practice to retirement:

1. Notify your state medical society of your intent to retire.
2. Notify your patients of your plan to retire. You should give them ample time to find another physician. You may consider placing a notice in your local newspaper to inform the community of your retirement. (A sample patient letter is shown in Figure 1.) You should provide patients an opportunity to have their records transferred to another physician. (A sample transfer of records letter is shown in Figure 2.)
3. Notify your employees of your plan to retire. You may have loyal employees who will need to find new employment after you retire, and you need to give them ample time to seek new employment.
4. Arrange for storage of your medical records. Most states require you to retain all patient medical records for a minimum of seven years. If another doctor takes over your practice, he or she must agree to keep those records on your behalf. With the use of electronic medical records, this requirement will be much easier than paying for storage of paper files.
5. You will also be required to keep records pertaining to the business aspect of your practice.
6. You must notify your malpractice insurance carrier of your impending retirement. It is a good idea to purchase tail coverage (as opposed to occurrence-based coverage) to ensure that you and your practice will be covered in the event a malpractice claim is filed against you after you have retired.
7. Check your office lease and be certain that you can sublet and then be released by the landlord from further liability for rent and damages.
8. Plan the sale of your practice. If you are in a partnership with other physicians, you may have a buy/sell agreement in place that provides for the buyout of a retiring partner. If you are in solo practice, you may wish to hire a broker to sell your practice or take in an associate for a year or two prior to retirement with the intent that the associate will buy the practice upon your retirement.

9. Obtain final statements from supplies and vendors to be certain that all final payments have been made.
10. Change your mailing address and cancel journal subscriptions that you do not wish to continue to receive.

Disclaimer: None of us are licensed attorneys, accountants, or financial advisors, and you should consult with your advisors prior to acting on any information you read here.

Dear Patient:

SAMPLE LETTER TO PATIENTS TO ANNOUNCE RETIREMENT

After years of serving you and other patients, I have decided to retire from active medical practice. Accordingly, I will close my office permanently on <date of closing the practice>. Between now and then, I will be happy to forward a copy of your records to a physician of your choice. If you are unable to select a physician in the interim period, I will gladly send a copy of your records to you.

I am enclosing two copies of an authorization for the release of records. Please complete the authorization and return one copy to me; the other copy is for you. If you need help in selecting a new physician, you may call the referral service of our local medical society at <number of local or state medical society>.

I extend to you my best wishes for your health and happiness.

Sincerely,

<Your Name>

FIGURE 1. Sample patient letter.

Date:

To: *<Your own Name>*, MD

AUTHORIZATION TO TRANSFER RECORDS

I hereby authorize you to transfer or make available all of my medical records or reports relating to my care to the following physician: <name of physician patient wants records sent to> at <address of physician requested by the patient>.

I agree to pay reasonable clerical and copying costs for these records.

I acknowledge receipt of a copy of this authorization for my records.

<patient's signature>

<Your Name>

FIGURE 2. Sample transfer of records letter.

CHAPTER 33

Artificial Intelligence and ChatGPT: Physician Friend or Foe?

Neil Baum, MD, and David F. Mobley, MD

The past 500 years have seen a number of events that have changed the world. The invention of the printing press by Johannes Guttenberg in the 16th century might be considered the beginning of education for large masses of the population. Next, the steam engine appeared in 1712 and made transporting and moving goods and services more accessible and economical. In 1879, Thomas Edison invented the light bulb, which began to illuminate the world and dramatically improved the quality of all lives. This was followed by Henry Ford and the invention of the assembly line, making transportation within reach of the middle class. Then came the Internet in the 1960s, achieving widespread use in the early 1980s. This revolutionized nearly every area of business, medicine, industry, and our personal lives. In December 2022, OpenAI (OpenAI.com) released ChatGPT. This use of artificial intelligence (AI) will change the delivery of healthcare throughout the world. ChatGPT has applications that can be used for managing both clinical and nonclinical aspects of medical practices. This chapter presents a brief history of Chat GPT; discusses its potential medical applications, including obtaining a prior authorization; and considers the ethical and legal concerns of using AI in the healthcare profession.

A BRIEF HISTORY OF CHATGPT

ChatGPT was developed by OpenAI and was launched as a prototype on November 30, 2022. By mid-December 2022, the program had over one million users. OpenAI allows the public to use and experiment with the technology at no charge. Like Grammarly.com, free versions allow users to try the technology without charge. The company plans to monetize the program with upgrades, ChatGPT Plus, which currently costs $20 per month. OpenAI's market valuation in 2023 was $29 billion.[1]

APPLICATIONS AND POTENTIAL USES OF CHATGPT IN MEDICAL PRACTICES

An easy way to start the ChatGPT experience is by using it to assist with mundane tasks such as writing back-to-work certificates, medical exemptions from jury duty, and letters to insurance companies to pay for patients' expensive medications. Initially, ChatGPT functions as a high-level personal assistant to speed up bureaucratic tasks and increase time for patient interaction.

ChatGPT also could assist in more serious medical activities, such as triage algorithms to choose which patients can access kidney dialysis or intensive care beds, which is critical in settings where resources are limited. The technology could be used to enroll participants in clinical trials. The potential in the medical field is almost endless.

It is too early to know all the ethical implications of adopting ChatGPT in healthcare and research. The more this technology is used, the more precisely the implications will be understood. However, questions regarding potential risks and oversight of ChatGPT in medicine will inevitably be part of future conversations.

Here is an example of one way ChatGPT could be used to automate administrative tasks. Obtaining prior authorization is time-consuming, accounting for many frustrating hours of uncompensated physician time each week. Obtaining prior authorization is considered a veritable nightmare for most medical practices. ChatGPT can be used to streamline the process. What usually takes 30 to 60 minutes per prior authorization can be reduced to seconds. Here is an example that could be used in a medical practice:

A urologist wants to write a letter to the patient's insurance company requesting prior authorization for a multiparametric MRI (mpMRI) to aid in the diagnosis of prostate cancer. They open ChatGPT in openAI.com.

The physician or an appropriately trained assistant provides the patient's information but does not include the patient's name or any other identifying information, because they cannot be sure the site was encrypted or if they are at risk for a HIPAA violation. They give ChatGPT the following instruction:

> *Write a letter to United Health regarding patient John Doe (membership ID XXXXXXXX, Birthdate XX\XX\XXXX), who has an elevated PSA, 8.3 ng/mL, a free/total PSA ratio of 19% (normal is greater than 25%). I am requesting a multiparametric MRI and a prostate biopsy to complete his evaluation for prostate cancer. Please provide recent references regarding the appropriateness of this procedure. Signed Dr. X, MD.*

This letter was generated in less than 45 seconds, with another 60 seconds required for the nurse or the medical assistant to add the patient's name and identification number.

This was the letter created by ChatGPT:

> *Dear United Health,*
>
> *I am writing to request approval for a multiparametric MRI and prostate biopsy for patient John Doe, who holds a membership ID of XXXXXXXX and was born on XX/XX/XXXX.*
>
> *Upon examination, Mr. Doe's PSA levels were elevated at 8.3 ng/mL, with a free/total PSA ratio of 19% (normal is greater than 25%). Given these findings, I strongly recommend a multiparametric MRI and prostate biopsy to assess the condition of Mr. Doe's prostate gland and determine if further treatment is necessary.*
>
> *Could you please approve this study for Mr. Doe's benefit and make sure he receives the care he needs?*
>
> *I am including recent references that show how important it is to manage men with an elevated PSA level. These are references from peer-reviewed literature on the value of mpMRI in managing patients with elevated PSA levels. It is essential to remain up-to-date on the latest advancements and recommendations.*
>
> *Thank you for your attention to this matter. Please feel free to reach out to me with any questions or additional information.*
>
> *Sincerely,*
>
> *Dr. X, MD*

Recent references on mpMRI

Multiparametric magnetic resonance imaging (mpMRI) helps diagnose prostate cancer. Here are some references that can be useful:

1. *National Comprehensive Cancer Network (NCCN) guidelines for prostate cancer. The NCCN guidelines provide recommendations for the use of mpMRI in diagnosing and managing prostate cancer. The guidelines can be found at www.nccn.org/professionals/physician_gls/pdf/prostate.pdf.*
2. *European Association of Urology (EAU) guidelines for prostate cancer. The EAU guidelines also provide recommendations for the use of mpMRI in diagnosing and managing prostate cancer. The guidelines can be found at https://uroweb.org/guideline/prostate-cancer/.*
3. *American Urological Association (AUA) guidelines for prostate cancer. The AUA guidelines provide recommendations for using mpMRI in the initial diagnostic evaluation of men with suspected prostate cancer. The guidelines can be found at www.auanet.org/guidelines/prostate-cancer-diagnosis-and-treatment-clinically-localized.*
4. *Prostate Imaging-Reporting and Data System (PI-RADS). PI-RADS is a standardized reporting system developed by the American College of Radiology (ACR) to provide a consistent reporting method for prostate mpMRI findings. The latest version of PI-RADS can be found at www.acr.org/Clinical-Resources/Reporting-and-Data-Systems/PI-RADS.*
5. *European Society of Urogenital Radiology (ESUR) guidelines for prostate MRI. The ESUR guidelines provide recommendations for the use of mpMRI in the diagnosis and management of prostate cancer. The guidelines can be found at www.esur.org/guidelines/genitourinary-radiology/prostate-mri/.*

These references provide comprehensive information on using mpMRI for diagnosing prostate cancer, including indications, interpretation of findings, and recommendations for clinical practice.

This prior authorization was faxed to the insurance company, and approval was obtained in 24 hours. The permission could have taken days or weeks if a nurse or physician assistant made this request using the phone. This is just one example of ChatGPT's effectiveness in the medical office setting.

The world of possibilities of ChatGPT is almost endless. Other AI platforms are being developed, and as physicians, we will constantly be discovering new ways AI can assist and improve patient care. Algorithms for differential diagnosis in rare or obscure conditions will be developed. A physician confronted with a confounding clinical situation may be able to tell AI the symptoms and objective findings and rapidly receive help in preparing a differential diagnosis. Treatment algorithms likewise will be developed and rapidly available. The uses in clinical practice will be limited only by our imagination. Improvements in AI will be constantly occurring, improving the lives of clinicians and patients alike.

POTENTIAL ETHICAL, MORAL, PRIVACY, AND LEGAL CONSIDERATIONS WITH AI AND CHATGPT

In the world of education, professors and teachers are being inundated with student work that is, in fact, ChatGPT-generated work. Algorithms are being developed to uncover work submitted by students that is not their original work. There is a challenge among students who will be using ChatGPT to help them with research, to use the information generated appropriately as an aid rather than as the writer of papers.[2]

In the medical field, we must ensure we don't fall prey to "the easy way out." New technology, especially technology in its infancy with which we are only now developing familiarity, leaves openings and questions regarding moral, ethical, and perhaps legal issues yet to be uncovered. We are unaware of any lawsuits against medical practices regarding documents created with ChatGPT. Still, caution with these AI-developed documents is encouraged. For example, if a physician asked ChatGPT, "What is the best first-line treatment for......?" Relying on that recommendation without confirming its accuracy might result in improper patient care, with all the attendant liabilities. High-quality, accurate data is the cornerstone of how we practice medicine and provide evaluation and treatment options to our patients. Physicians now can benefit from ChatGPT to help obtain clinical information. It can be an aid in making medical decisions. Still, data from peer-reviewed published papers, along with data presented at medical conferences, will likely remain our best source of reliable medical decision-making material for the present time.

Incorporating this new technology in medical research, especially in reporting results of medical research, will be a huge boon. Still, it also could lead to incorrectly reporting data. This opens the possibility of misleading conclusions because of potentially unreliable results, with unwelcome consequences to authors and patients. Consent and confidentiality also are considered in using AI in medical research.

Keeping in mind that the "A" in AI stands for "artificial," it is essential for clinicians and staff generating ChatGPT that documents must be reviewed for accuracy. The same holds true for using AI for clinical decision-making. Ultimately, physicians are responsible for the use of information from their medical practice and for their patient's care. With this new technology, we will enjoy many time-saving and educational opportunities. Still, it remains up to us to ensure the validity of what we prepare and present.

Bottom Line: Artificial intelligence and ChatGPT have exploded into nearly every business and sector, including the healthcare profession. However, privacy and ethical concerns must be addressed to ensure data security and responsible AI use. Overall, ChatGPT promises to improve healthcare efficiency, accessibility, and medical breakthroughs. The ChatGPT train is leaving the station — all aboard!

REFERENCES

1. Varanasi L. ChatGPT creator OpenAI is in talks to sell shares in a tender offer that would double the startup's valuation to $29 billion. *Insider.* www.businessinsider.com/chatgpt-creator-openai-talks-for-tender-offer-at-29-billion-2023-1. Accessed January 18, 2023.
2. McDade A. Studies show ChatGPT cheating is on the rise among students — young and old — as teachers remain divided on bans. *Business Insider.* February 8, 2023. www.businessinsider.com/teachers-caught-students-cheating-chatgpt-survey-shows-2023-2

CHAPTER 34

Ten Reasons to be Glad You Are a Physician

Jon Hultman, DPM, MBA, and Neil Baum, MD

In this Chapter, we suggest that physicians take a good look at what our profession offers and reflect on why healthcare (i.e., medical practice) is such a desirable occupation. Although we often hear the comment, "If I had to do it over again, I wouldn't become a doctor," or "I wouldn't recommend being a doctor to one of my children," we think we should be grateful and thankful rather than griping and resentful. We list 10 reasons why doctors should be happy about their choice of profession.

1. Doctors are in a field where there is growing demand, a declining supply, and formidable barriers to entry. Every other industry would kill for this type of economic advantage. If you believe that the healthcare industry is tough, imagine working in an industry such as digital cameras or print newspapers. Can you imagine working in an industry or profession for which demand is declining, or where there is an over-supply of competitors who can provide the same services that you do at a much cheaper price or send it to India and China to produce at a fraction of the cost, or if almost anyone can quickly gain access to the field with minimal or no barriers to entry? The dynamics in our profession assure us that there will always be work and future employment.
2. We have instant status. If you have the letters MD after your name, you have credibility that is immediately accepted by your patients. For example, if a patient comes to a doctor he or she has never met before, the patient will willingly divulge the deepest secrets of his or her medical history, including menstrual history, bowel habits, and even sexual history. No other profession guarantees its young members such instant credibility. We should never take that for granted, should always uphold a high standard of confidentiality and ethical behavior, and should never take for granted our lofty status with our patients.

3. We are in the top 5% of wage earners in the United States. Many of our colleagues are complaining about their incomes. If we compare the average physician's salary with those for all other jobs, our salaries are at the top. Also, most of the others in that rare top 5% do not have the same upside potential that we do. Many successful physicians earn two to three times more than the average physician.
4. We are fortunate not to be compelled to retire at a certain age. Because the practice of medicine is not physically demanding, many physicians can work into their 80s if they so desire. A national survey conducted by Wells Fargo found that 25% of the respondents will need to work until at least age 80 before being able to retire comfortably.[1] Respondents in this survey were between 20 and 70 years of age, with incomes ranging from $25,000 to $99,000 (which is currently considered middle class). Their median savings goal for retirement was $350,000, but their current median savings were only $25,000, or 7% of their goal.[1] We hear similar complaints from doctors who say that they will never be able to retire, and many physicians believe that they will need a minimum of $2 million or more in order to comfortably retire. As severely as their retirement plans may have been hit by poorly performing investments, however, most doctors have already saved more than $25,000 toward retirement; and if they don't hit their goal of several million dollars, they will have the option of supplementing their income by continuing to practice part-time for as long as they choose to work.
5. Doctors, compared with many other professionals, have a wonderful lifestyle. The practice of medicine affords most men and women with the ability to spend time with their families, being able to take two to four weeks of vacation each year, and having an option of working 8- to 10-hour days. Except for the hours when physicians are on call, they have reasonable lifestyle choices. Many younger physicians today are opting to work fewer hours per week, even if it means a lower income. Doctors also have the ability to select a geographic location and the kind of practice they wish to have, a choice that is not as readily available to other professionals. Many career choices have geographic limitations as to where employees can live or are at risk for the possibility that they could suddenly be transferred anywhere at the whim of a superior, but physicians can work anywhere they choose. They

can determine where they would most like to live before embarking upon their careers.

6. There are more opportunities for physicians than for those in other professions, especially for those entering practice within seven years of graduation from training programs. Doctors can elect to work for themselves, join a large group practice, or be employed by a hospital or academic healthcare center. Although an employed physician must answer to a boss, starting salaries for employed physicians have increased, and these doctors function relatively independently when compared with other types of professionals who are employed by a large group, company, or organization.
7. Doctors can carve out the exact kind of practice that makes them most comfortable. If a doctor is interested in seeing only patients with certain diagnoses or in providing only a limited number of treatment options, he or she can easily do so. If a doctor wants to see certain kinds of patients (e.g., geriatric patients, pediatric patients), this can easily be done. If the doctor wishes to see patients who speak only another language beside English, this, too, can easily be achieved. If you want only patients who pay cash or want to have a concierge practice, where a limited number of patients pay an annual fee to have 24/7 access to your practice, then this is also within the realm of possibility.
8. For the most part, physicians are told almost on a daily basis how terrific they are. There isn't a day that goes by that most physicians don't receive a compliment or accolade about the care they provide. If ego satisfaction and gratification are your drivers, you have selected the right profession. One of us (NHB) has saved complimentary letters from patients and with those patients' permission has placed the original letters in a scrapbook that is in the reception area. After nearly 30 years in practice, he has 10 volumes of leather-bound books with all of the letters received from satisfied patients. They are the most looked-at books in the reception area. Also, collecting compliments has now become more important than ever, as they can be posted on your Web site and submitted to online reputation management programs to balance the occasional negative online report sent by a dissatisfied patient. Certainly if you have l0 or 20 positive responses, it will easily dilute the occasional negative note so that it does not significantly impact your online reputation rating.

9. The practice of medicine provides job security and a future of guaranteed employment. It is a sad commentary that so many graduating lawyers are unable to find a job practicing law. This is not the case with American medical doctors. Everyone who graduates from medical school and a training program can find a job. It may not be a perfect job but, nonetheless, it is a profession that is in demand and will certainly provide a future of job security.
10. Even though we face the challenge of declining reimbursements and higher overhead costs, a different career track wouldn't have eliminated these detractors. These same challenges exist in every industry and in every profession. These challenges in other industries have resulted in extinction, because competition has created ways to do the same things either better or less expensively. Companies, organizations, and practices have done so because they have found ways to be more efficient and more productive. Ultimately, they have done things better. Healthcare is one of the industries that have focused on creating greater efficiencies and lowering operating costs and becoming more efficient and more productive. This presents an opportunity for improving quality, preserving patient satisfaction, and, yes, improving the bottom line (i.e., increasing productivity).

Bottom Line: In spite of all the hardships and detractors associated with modern healthcare, we have much to be thankful for. Those working in other industries have their lists of complaints but they are often powerless to make changes, because they are neither owners nor partners in the business. If they are members of a large organization, many layers of bureaucracy must be penetrated in order to make changes. Doctors enjoy the opportunity to have significant control and the tools to implement change and to tweak our practices to improve the services that we provide our patients. If we put our problems and complaints with modern medicine on a scale and then weigh those issues and concerns against the benefits of being a doctor, we will find that the scale weighs heavily on the pluses, and we should be thankful that we are physicians.

REFERENCE

1. 80 is the new 65 for many middle class Americans when it comes to retirement, Wells Fargo retirement survey finds. Wells Fargo. November 16, 2011; https://www.wellsfargo.com/about/press/2011/20111116_80IsTheNew65/.

www.ingramcontent.com/pod-product-compliance
Lightning Source LLC
LaVergne TN
LVHW052310200926
848481LV00002B/516
* 9 7 8 1 9 6 0 7 6 2 3 7 5 *